Generative AI and Large Language Models

Concepts and Architectures

Generative AI and Large Language Models
Concepts and Architectures

Apurva Vashist
Associate Professor
Department of Computer Science
Guru Tegh Bahadur Fourth Centenary Engineering College
New Delhi

PHI Learning Private Limited
Delhi-110092
2026

In fond memory of ***Shri Asoke K. Ghosh*** *(October 1942 – February 2024), Founder Chairman and Managing Director of PHI Learning, whose vision endlessly inspires.*

The Legacy Continues. . . .

Published by Pushpita Ghosh, PHI Learning Private Limited, Rimjhim House, 111, Patparganj Industrial Estate, Delhi-110092 and Printed by Syndicate Binders, A-20, Hosiery Complex, Noida, Phase-II Extension, Noida-201305 (N.C.R. Delhi).

₹ 575.00

GENERATIVE AI AND LARGE LANGUAGE MODELS: Concepts and Architectures
Apurva Vashist

ISBN-978-93-7929-182-0 (Print Book)
ISBN-978-93-7929-425-8 (e-Book)

Contents

Preface

Generative Artificial Intelligence (Generative AI) has emerged as one of the most transformative advancements in the field of Artificial Intelligence. Unlike traditional AI systems that focus on analyzing and classifying data, generative AI enables machines to create new and meaningful content, including text, images, audio, video, and code. This shift marks a new era where AI acts not only as a tool for analysis but also as a creative and collaborative partner.

This book is designed to provide a clear, structured, and comprehensive introduction to the concepts and applications of Generative AI. It begins with fundamental ideas, including the definition, working mechanisms, and evolution of AI, and gradually progresses to advanced topics.

In addition to theoretical concepts, the book highlights real-world applications across domains such as healthcare, finance, education, cybersecurity, and media. It also addresses important challenges, including issues of accuracy, ethical concerns, privacy, and the responsible use of AI technologies. Written for undergraduate and postgraduate students, researchers, and professionals, this book aims to bridge the gap between theory and practice. It presents complex topics in a simple and systematic manner, making it suitable for both academic learning and practical understanding.

It is hoped that this book will encourage readers to explore the potential of Generative AI while promoting its responsible and ethical use in solving real-world problems.

Apurva Vashist

Acknowledgements

The successful completion of this book would not have been possible without the support and contribution of several individuals. I owe special thanks to the entire team of PHI Learning Private Limited.

I would like to express my sincere gratitude to Mr. Deepanshu Goyal for his dedication, continuous support, and valuable assistance in achieving this goal. His commitment and efforts have played an important role in the development of this work.

I am also thankful to my family, students, and well-wishers for their encouragement and support throughout this journey.

Apurva Vashist

CHAPTER 1

Introduction to Generative AI

It is possible that Generative AI would be one of the greatest digital transformations in the present day. Traditional AI is relying on the existing data which is analysed and classified, while generative AI, on the contrary, takes the new meaningful content, be it text, audio or even video, the new and the old can always be brought together in a conversation. The aim of the current chapter is to act like a bridge between the readers and the refreshing but at the same time challenging core concepts, by introducing them simply and scientifically, with the right foot in the door, and opening up further, into the whole world of generative AI.

The text begins with a definition of generative AI and a distinction between the two artificial intelligence strategies. Next, it looks for the historical journey of AI that ranges from rule-based systems of the early period to cutting-edge models of deep learning that have brought forth generative models. The reader is provided through a transparent and direct comparison between the two types of models, discriminative and generative, that is primarily concerned with the difference in their goals and operation.

The later chapters communicate a study of the varieties of the generative family tree, as well as the new ones coming from the industries of education, healthcare, media and research, for example, where generative AI already operates. At the same time, these new AI systems have numerous advantages, they also possess several challenges and limitations, thus the discussion is open to a critical examination. Finally, the text wraps up with a glimpse into the current generative AI field, where the most important players, tools, technologies, and trends that define this fast-changing area are already unfolding.

The primary goal of this first chapter is to provide a solid conceptual framework so that readers feel secure in their progression to the more complicated themes in the following chapters.

1.1 WHAT IS GENERATIVE AI?

Generative Artificial Intelligence (Generative AI) is a subdivision of AI that replicates human content creation by recognizing trends in existing data.

Generative AI outputs include text, images, audio, video, or code. The results are produced in such a manner that it is very often impossible to tell apart human-generated and machine-generated content.

Generative AI is based on deep learning and neural networks. The huge data volumes—both structured and unstructured—enable the models to grasp the data's underlying structure, relationships, and patterns. Afterwards, the models can generate new content that is akin to the existing one in terms of style and pattern.

A major difference in AI is between generative AI and discriminative AI. Discriminative AI systems sort or tag data, for instance, they can tell whether an email is spam or not or pinpoint the objects in a picture. Generative AI, in contrast, does not stop at classification but actually produces new data. As an illustration, by simply recognizing cat images, a generative model can concoct a completely new cat image that never existed as shown in Figure 1.1.

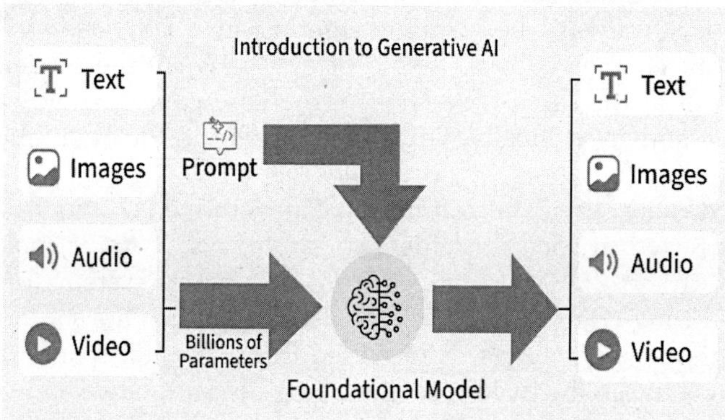

Figure 1.1: *Generative AI.*

1.1.1 Working Mechanism of Generative AI

Typically, generative AI systems proceed in two steps: training and inference. In the first step, the training phase, models learn from very large datasets with lots of different examples such as text, images, audio, or other types of data. Deep learning algorithms help the model to learn millions or even billions of parameters that represent the various relationships and structures in the data.

After the training is done, the model goes into the phase of inference where it can create new content according to user input or prompts. The output generated by the model is not a reproduction of the existing data but a new creation done in a proper way by mixing the learned patterns.

1.1.2 Generative AI across Different Media Types

Generative AI is a versatile tool that can work with different forms of data in various fields:

- **Text Generation:** The output of LLMs (Large Language Models) is very similar to what a human would write because they generate it by the coming word or token predicting the previous words or tokens in the sequence. This allows for the generation of various text types like essays, summaries, dialogues, and reports.
- **Image Generation:** The diffusion models can create high-quality images by the stepwise process of converting totally random noise into an informative visual representation gradually based on the textual or visual incentives.
- **Audio and Speech Generation:** Generative audio models are capable of producing very convincingly sounding human speech, music, or sound effects by first analysing and then recreating acoustic patterns in the audio datasets used for training.
- **Video Generation:** The most advanced multimodal systems today can produce short videos incorporating text, images, and time information to create moving visual content.

1.1.3 Intelligent Agents in Generative AI

The recent developments have resulted in the introduction of AI agents as a part of generative systems. The agents are designed to act as independent parts of the system with abilities such as reasoning, planning, and retrieving information, and even executing complicated tasks. The agents have large language models as the core of their reasoning and thus are able to interact with external tools, databases, and APIs to achieve the multi-step goal. This ability is a turning point for generative AI as it will not only be able to produce content but also make smart decisions.

1.1.4 Training and Adaptation of Generative Models

Generative AI models are mostly trained initially on vast general-purpose datasets using self-supervised learning techniques. The models that are pre-trained can then be fine-tuned to the specific domain or task. Fine-tuning helps organizations to tailor the models for particular usage like medical analyses, legal papers, or technical writing. Among the various tuning techniques, parameter-efficient fine-tuning methods allow such adaptation without necessitating the retraining of the whole model from scratch.

1.1.5 Retrieval-Augmented Generation (RAG)

One of the principal issues that the generative AI is faced with is the accuracy of the facts. To tackle this drawback, modern machines take up a method called Retrieval-Augmented Generation (RAG). RAG systems do not depend on a model's internal knowledge only but rather use external databases or documents to get the relevant information and take it into account in generating the response. This technique results in greater reliability, less hallucination, and enables models to be updated with new data. More deeply explained in Chapter 5.

1.1.6 Capabilities of Generative AI

Generative AI has capabilities that are not limited to the following list but include the following main points:

- Text can be created that is both coherent and relevant in context
- Realistic images as well as artworks can be produced
- Human speech and music imitating the human voice can be generated
- Software development would be easier as the AI would generate code for the programmer
- Creative tasks like designing and content creation would get more support from the machine.

The above-mentioned abilities position generative AI as a strong instrument in the sectors of education, healthcare, entertainment, research, and business automation, to name a few.

In summary, Generative AI represents a significant shift in the field of artificial intelligence—from systems that only analyze data to systems that can actively create new knowledge and content. Understanding its principles and mechanisms forms the foundation for exploring more advanced topics in the chapters that follow.

1.2 EVOLUTION OF AI AND DEEP LEARNING

The evolution of Artificial Intelligence has been a constant and almost imperceptible change from primitive rule-based software to very intelligent generative systems as shown in Figure 1.2. It is necessary to understand the whole story of this transformation if you want to have a grasp of the current situation with Generative AI.

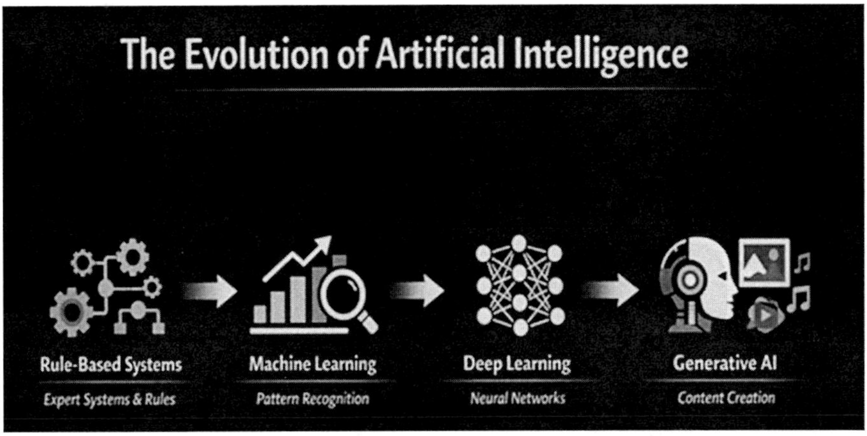

Figure 1.2: *Evolution of Artificial Intelligence.*

1.2.1 Initial Stage: Rule-based Systems

The very first AI applications were not actually "learning" systems in the modern sense of the term. They were based on a fixed set of rules and logical conditions developed by human experts. Such systems, called expert systems, were effective in scenarios with limited variables but, unfortunately, they could hardly cope with real-world situations where the problems were complex and unpredictable.

They did not have the ability to change over time and did not even learn from the experience.

This incapacity drove the research in a different direction towards the machines that would be able to learn from data rather than be restricted to the rules written by the human beings.

1.2.2 Rise of Machine Learning

The evolving AI; another major step in this regard was to The Machine Learning (ML) that was not simply a matter of programming but rather the data training of algorithms to recognize patterns automatically.

The machine learning made a point that:

- Computers could learn from demonstrations
- More data = better systems
- Experience = predictions

The next techniques that were brought into the limelight during this phase were decision trees, statistical models, and shallow neural networks. Machine learning was certainly a great boon for structured data problems like spam detection, recommendation systems, and fraud analysis.

On the other hand, conventional machine learning had a key drawback that it still required the manual feature engineering which was the laborious task of identifying and extracting the right pieces of information for the model by humans.

1.2.3 Transition to Deep Learning

Increase the volume of data and computing power, and a new method came into the picture: Deep Learning.

Deep learning was a revolutionary turn for AI as:

- Machines were able to understand characteristics through raw data by themselves.
- The capturing of complex patterns was done automatically.
- Non-structured data such as pictures, sound, and words were all accessible.

The technology that powered the deep learning revolution was deep neural networks, which are multi-layered neural networks. These networks were modelled after the human brain's architecture and were capable of learning through the layers of representation.

1.2.4 Breakthrough Architectures

The deep learning epoch unlocked new AI potential that came along with the different types of models built for the specific purpose:

- Convolutional Neural Networks (CNNs) were the ones that opened the door for machines to analyze and recognize images and all other visual inputs.
- RNNs and LSTMs were the ones who made it possible to process sequential data like communication and text.
- Transformers took NLP, and along with it, the whole language model industry was born.

The gradual progression of these techniques accepted AI as a domain that was not merely good at prediction but could also comprehend language, perform object recognition, produce translations, and even make content.

This changeover got rid of one of the most significant hurdles that machine learning faced—reliance on humans for feature design.

1.2.5 From Deep Learning to Generative AI

The most recent stage in AI evolution is Generative AI. While earlier AI systems focused on analyzing or classifying data, generative models learned to create new data.

Technologies such as:

- GANs (Generative Adversarial Networks)
- Diffusion Models
- Large Language Models (LLMs)

enabled machines to generate realistic images, write human-like text, compose music, and produce synthetic content.

This stage represents the shift from AI as an analytical tool to AI as a creative and collaborative technology.

1.2.6 Key Factors Driving Evolution

The quick development of AI was mainly due to a trio of major forces:

- **Big Data Availability:** Huge amounts of digital data made it possible to learn better.
- **More Computing Power:** GPUs and online servers made deep learning feasible for practically everyone.
- **Innovative Algorithms:** New network designs like transformers sped up the journey.

1.2.7 How We are Doing Now

Currently, AI has advanced from mere automation systems to models with the same reasoning, understanding, and human-like content generation capabilities as humans. Deep learning is now the principal technology of today's AI, and Generative AI is the most sophisticated demonstration of this.

The said evolutionary process—from traditional rule-based systems to machine learning, through deep learning to generative models—has been and continues to be the driving force behind the entire AI application spectrum as discussed in this book.

1.3 DISCRIMINATIVE VS GENERATIVE MODELS

Machine learning models can generally be classified into two primary groups: discriminative models and generative models. Knowing the distinction between these two methods is necessary for understanding the basic concept of Generative AI as shown in Figure 1.3.

1.3.1 Discriminative Models

Discriminative models are concerned with determining the decision boundary among various classes. The question they seek to respond to is:

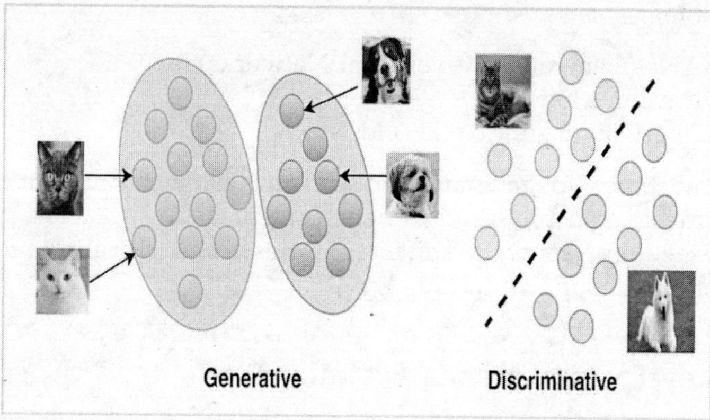

Figure 1.3: *Discriminative vs Generative Models.*

"Given an input X, what is the most likely output Y?"

Instead of trying to understand how the data is generated, these models directly learn the relationship between inputs and outputs. In simple terms, they try to model the conditional probability:

$$P(Y \mid X)$$

Discriminative models are widely used for tasks such as classification and prediction. Examples include:

- Logistic Regression
- Support Vector Machines
- Decision Trees
- Traditional Neural Networks

These models are highly effective when the objective is to classify or label data, but they cannot generate new data samples. Their purpose is analysis and prediction, not creation.

1.3.2 Generative Models

Generative models take a fundamentally different approach. Instead of only learning how to classify data, they aim to understand how the data itself is produced.

They attempt to model the underlying distribution of data by learning:

$$P(X, Y) \quad \text{or} \quad P(X \mid Y)$$

This enables generative models to:

- Create new data samples
- Simulate realistic content
- Handle missing or incomplete data
- Generate outputs similar to the training data

For example:

- A generative model trained on images of cats can create completely new cat images.
- A language model trained on text can generate new sentences and paragraphs.
- Popular generative modeling approaches include:
    - Generative Adversarial Networks (GANs)
    - Variational Autoencoders (VAEs)
    - Diffusion Models
    - Large Language Models (LLMs)

Key Conceptual Difference

The core difference can be summarized as:

- Discriminative Models → Learn to classify or predict
- Generative Models → Learn to create and generate

TABLE 1.1 Discriminative vs. Generative Models

Aspect	*Discriminative Models*	*Generative Models*
Objective	Predict labels	Generate new data
Learning Goal	Decision boundaries	Data distribution
Output Type	Class or value	New samples
Example Tasks	Spam detection, classification	Image generation, text generation

1.3.3 Why this Matters for Generative AI

The latest Generative AI systems are based on the concept of generative modeling. Unlike conventional AI which is restricted to data interpretation only, Generative AI can:

- Produce text indistinguishable from human writing
- Bring about images that look real
- Compose and produce music and videos
- Provide non-real data that is hard to distinguish from real datasets

The skill to produce rather than merely forecast is the reason why Generative AI is fundamentally distinct from its forerunner machine learning systems.

Discriminative models and generative models have separate functionalities in AI. Discriminative models, for instance, are great for making predictions and categorizing data, while generative models, on the other hand, are the very heart of today's creative AIs. One of the most pivotal advancements in the development of AI has been the move from discriminative to generative methods.

1.4 TYPES OF GENERATIVE MODELS

Generative AI technologies rely on multiple foundational modeling strategies; each being tailored for diverse data types and activities. The primary categories of generative models that drive current AI innovations are as follows as shown in Figure 1.4.

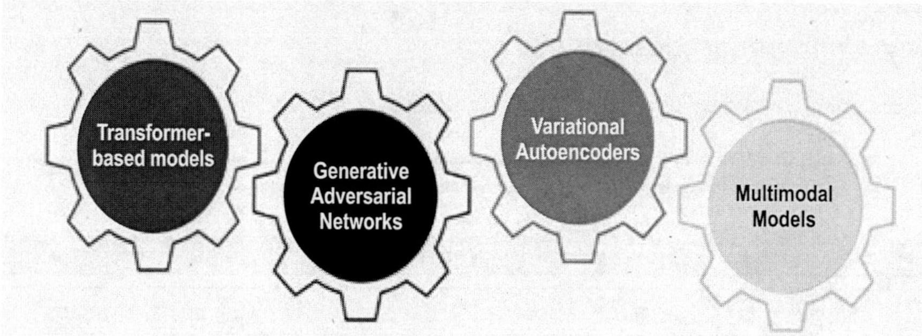

Figure 1.4: *Types of Generative AI Models.*

1.4.1 Transformers vs Autoregressive Models

Autoregressive models produce content sequentially, one element at a time, and the next element is predicted based on all previously generated elements. In text generation, this implies predicting the next word or token while keeping in mind the complete context of the earlier tokens.

The models in discussion are built upon the transformer architecture and use the self-attention mechanism that the latter offers, which is what enables them to capture the long-range dependencies and contextual relationships in the data. As a result, the models are very good at performing the following types of tasks:

- Generating text
- Generating code
- Answering questions
- Creating AI for conversation

Mathematically, they model the joint probability of a sequence $X = (x_1, x_2, ..., x_n)$ as:

$$P(X) = \prod_{i=1}^{n} P(x_i | x_1, x_2, ..., x_{i-1})$$

This means each new token depends on all earlier tokens.

Modern Large Language Models (LLMs) such as GPT use transformer architecture with self-attention to estimate this probability efficiently.

Self-Attention Mechanism

The core computation in transformers is:

$$\text{Attention }(Q, K, V) = \text{softmax}\left(\frac{QK^T}{\sqrt{d_k}}\right)V$$

where,

Q = Query
K = Key
V = Value

This mechanism allows the model to capture long-range dependencies in text.

1.4.2 Diffusion Models

Diffusion models belong to a new breed of generative models that have turned out to be very successful and in particular are the best choice for the case of image and audio generation.

The basic idea behind these models is to take completely random noise as the starting point and through a series of denoising steps gradually convert it to something meaningful. The model is trained to learn how to undo a procedure that adds noise to real data very slowly.

This method has been remarkably successful in the generation of outputs that look very real and are very detailed. Among the models that use diffusion principles are Stable Diffusion, DALL·E, and Midjourney, etc.

They are based on two processes:

(a) **Forward Process (Adding Noise)**
During training, real data is gradually corrupted with Gaussian noise ($\mathcal{N}$):

$$x_t = \sqrt{1 - \beta_t}\, x_{t-1} + \sqrt{\beta_t}\, \varepsilon$$

where
β_t controls noise level
$\varepsilon \sim \mathcal{N}(0, 1)$

(b) **Reverse Process (Denoising)**
The model learns to reverse this process and estimate:

$$p_\theta\,(x_{t-1} \mid x_t)$$

By repeatedly denoising, the model finally produces realistic data from pure noise.

1.4.3 Variational Autoencoders (VAEs) and Generative Adversarial Networks (GANs)

During the period when transformers and diffusion models were not yet on top of the charts, VAEs and GANs were the main actors in the world of deep learning for generative tasks.

Variational Autoencoders (VAEs) are constructed in a way such that they take the input data, compress it really well and then reconstruct it back. Thanks to the fact that the latent space is continuous and probabilistic, VAEs permit smooth interpolation among the samples generated. The particular areas where such a method is most beneficial are:

- Data compression
- Controlled generation
- Anomaly detection
- Synthetic data creation

VAEs are probabilistic generative models that learn a compressed latent representation of data.

They consist of two parts:

- Encoder: maps input x to latent variable z
- Decoder: reconstructs data from z

Objective Function

VAEs optimize the Evidence Lower Bound (ELBO):

$$\mathcal{L} = \mathbb{E}_{q(z|x)} [\log p(x|z)] - KL(q(z|x) \,||\, p(z)$$

where,

$q(z|x)$ is the learned latent distribution

$p(z)$ is a prior (usually Gaussian)

KL is Kullback–Leibler divergence

This encourages smooth latent spaces and controlled generation.

GANs work through a game-theoretic approach using two neural networks:

- Generator (G): Creates fake samples
- Discriminator (D): Tries to distinguish real from fake

GAN Objective Function

$$\min_G \max_D \mathbb{E}_{x \sim p_{\text{data}}} [\log D(x)] + \mathbb{E}_{z \sim p_z} [\log (1 - D(G(z)))]$$

The generator improves by trying to fool the discriminator, leading to highly realistic outputs.

The result of this rivalry is very realistic outputs, especially in the realm of image generation. But, at the same time, GANs might be hard to train and can suffer from problems such as instability and mode collapse.

Despite these challenges, GANs have been widely used in:

- Face generation
- Image enhancement
- Super-resolution
- Style transfer

1.4.4 Encoder–Decoder Models

Encoder–decoder models are meant for tasks that need the transformation of one form of data into another.

This architecture contains:

The encoder which is the first and main component that takes the input, processes it, and transmits it to an internal representation that is very compact.

The decoder which is the last component that takes this internal representation and produces the final output.

Encoder–decoder architectures transform one sequence into another.

They model conditional probability:

$$P(Y \mid X)$$

where,

X = input sequence

Y = generated output sequence

The encoder creates a representation $h = f(X)$, and the decoder generates:

$$Y = g(h)$$

These models are very much in the lead for tasks like sequence-to-sequence, for instance:

- Language translation
- Text summarization
- Speech recognition
- Image captioning

At the same time, they have updated their abilities by using the whole input which gives better understanding of the global situation contrasting with autoregressive-only models that output one token at a time.

Ensemble of the latest ones like T5, BART, and multimodal transformer models apply encoder–decoder architecture to tackle difficult generation tasks across domains.

1.4.5 Normalizing Flow Models

Normalizing flows are a group of generative models that focus on learning the exact data distributions via invertible transformations.

They apply a series of mathematical transformations to a simple probability distribution, and by that, they make it complex. This is why they are good for:

1. Estimating density
2. Generation based on likelihood
3. Modeling of scientific and medical data

Normalizing flows however, are less preferred in common usage compared to other models like transformers and diffusion, but they are still valuable in research and niche areas.

1.5 APPLICATIONS OF GENERATIVE AI

Generative AI denotes smart algorithms that can produce new content such as text, images, audio, and video. These deep learning models, which are based on architectures such as GANs and VAEs, are empowering industries through automation, creativity, and intelligent decision-making.

Generative AI has moved out of the research labs and is now being extensively applied in healthcare, finance, education, and entertainment, among others, as a real-world application as shown in Figure 1.5.

Major Domains of Generative AI Applications

The most important application areas of Generative AI include:

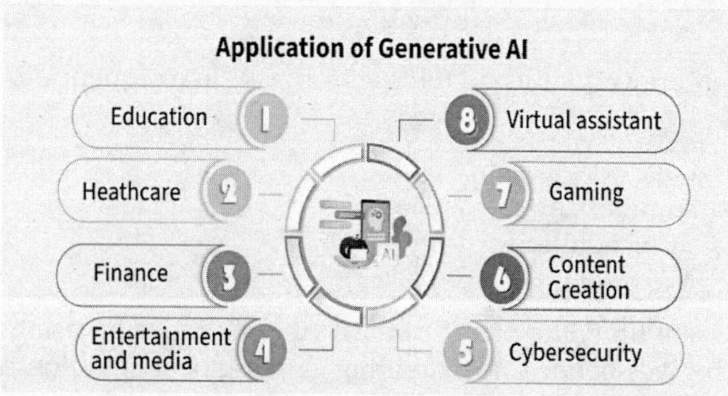

Figure 1.5: *Application of Generative AI.*

Each of these areas is discussed below with practical examples.

1.5.1 Healthcare Generative AI

Generative AI is a stimulus of the healthcare revolution by supporting doctors, researchers, and drug manufacturers.

Main use:

- **Drug Discovery:** AI models not only create new molecular structures but also make the whole process of discovering new medicines a lot faster compared to when traditional methods are used.
- **Personalized Medicine:** Generative AI has this capacity to recommend personal treatment plans via its analyses of patient history and genetics.
- **Synthetic Data Generation:** AI can produce fake patient data for the purpose of medical model training that does not risk confidentiality being breached.

  For instance: Insilico Medicine, Mayo Clinic.
- **Early Disease Detection:** An AI-based system has been developed to interpret medical images and identify the presence of diseases like cancer at their earliest stages.

  For instance: The SkinVision app, which is used for skin cancer detection, is an example of such a system.

1.5.2 Generative AI in Finance

Generative AI is always a step forward bringing the finance industry to a level of excellence with the inseparable trio of efficiency, security, and proper decision-making.

Applications:

- **Fraud Detection:** Artificial Intelligence is simulating the transactions in order to help the systems that are responsible for detecting fraud.
- **Risk Analysis:** The financial institutions forecast the risks using AI before they go ahead with the loan issuance or investment.
  Example: JPMorgan Chase makes use of AI when it comes to assessing investment-related risks.
- **Spending Pattern Analysis:** The AI system is responsible for tracking credit card activities in order to identify any doubtful cases.
  Example: American Express.

1.5.3 Generative AI in Entertainment and Media

This area in generative AI is among the most noticeable and artistic ones.

Applications:

- **Graphic Design:** AI assists in the creation of high-quality visuals by users effortlessly.
  Example: Features of Canva AI.
- **Music Generation:** AI services are capable of producing music on their own.
  Example: MusicFy.

1.5.4 Generative AI in Cyber Security

Generative AI is the key to safeguarding the digital landscape.

Applications:

- **Anomaly Detection:** Cyber-attacks are detected through abnormal behavior identification by AI in the network.
- **Phishing Detection:** Generative models driven by NLP perform fraud detection through email and message analysis.
- **Automated Incident Response:** AI handles security alert prioritization and action suggestion.

Cybersecurity systems become faster and more intelligent due to these capabilities.

1.5.5 Generative AI in Education

The way of studying by students is being revolutionized by generative AI.

Applications:

- Intelligent tutoring systems that create lessons suited to each individual.
- Generation of question papers automatically.
- Learning assistants based on AI who explain the concepts in an interactive way.
- Making real-world examples to ease the understanding of difficult topics.

AI provides a platform for students to have their own learning experiences based on their respective needs and pace.

1.5.6 Generative AI in Gaming

AI makes gaming even more fun by making it more interactive.

Applications:

- Player action-based storyline creation that is dynamic.
- Realism in virtual environments through designing.
- Creation of game characters that can adapt.

Examples:

- Pokemon Go—the mixing of real-world interaction with AI is what the game is about.
- Duolingo—gamification and AI-driven learning come together in this language-learning app.
- Fitbit—uses AI analytics to make fitness fun.

1.5.7 Generative AI in Virtual Assistants

Virtual assistants of contemporary times rely on generative AI for their functioning.

Applications:

- Customer communication like a human
- Individualized recommendations
- Systems for support that are automated

Instances:

- Amazon Alexa—a smart voice assistant
- Erica (Bank of America)—a virtual assistant for financial matters
- Duolingo AI Tutor—a personalized assistant for language learning

Incredibly, these systems are capable of comprehending the user's questions and producing relevant replies instantaneously.

1.5.8 Generative AI in Content Creation

Automated content generation is the most common application of generative AI.

Applications:

- Text Generation: blogs, reports, emails
- Visual and Video Creation
- Marketing Content Automation
- SEO Optimization

Real-World Examples:

- Netflix: AI recommends personalized content (80% of views come from it).
- Sephora Virtual Artist: AI-based AR makeup trials.
- StoryChief: AI tool for blog writing and SEO content.

Generative AI is a huge help for companies to increase the amount of content produced without sacrificing quality in the process.

1.6 CHALLENGES AND LIMITATIONS

Although they are highly capable, generative AI models still encounter various technical, ethical, and practical limitations. It is important to weigh these challenges thoroughly before putting the systems into practice in actual applications.

1.6.1 Precision and Dependability

One of the most significant issues with generative models is to provide their output with the highest level of correctness. Since the models generate content based on learned patterns and not by truly understanding the subject, they may sometimes output:

- non-factual information
- imaginary or invented details
- results that are misleading or inconsistent

In critical areas like health care, finance, or law, even the smallest inaccuracies could lead to significant problems such as wrong diagnosis, ill-informed decisions, or big monetary losses. Therefore, human validation and supervision continue to be very important.

1.6.2 Moral and Privacy Issues

Generative AI brings up major moral issues especially when it is used with sensitive or personal data. The most important concerns are:

- infringement of user privacy
- improper use of secret information
- production of content that is biased or discriminative
- making deepfakes and fake media

If the models get trained on biased datasets they might even unintentionally reinforce stereotypes or unfair practices. To counteract these risks, responsible data handling and strong ethical guidelines are required.

1.6.3 High Computational and Cost Requirements

Generative models come with high computational and financial demands for their training and deployment purposes:

- superior hardware (GPUs/TPUs)
- extensive storage and memory
- massive energy consumption

Such demands render generative AI costly and hard to be accepted by small firms or lone developers.

1.6.4 Dependence on Large-scale Quality Data

Training data quality is the most determining factor to generative models' performance. Nonetheless:

- the best datasets may be out of reach
- data particular to a certain field may be hard to come by
- cautionary data will give rise to cautionary outputs

The unavailability of trustworthy data will negatively impact the reliability and equity of generative AI applications.

1.6.5 Risk of Misinformation and Misuse

Since generative AI can produce nothing less than realistic text, images, and videos; it also opens up avenues for misuse:

- the spread of counterfeit information
- the creation of deceptive content
- opinion manipulation

Thus, the necessity of building safeguards, detection systems, and responsible usage policies.

The generative AI, which is a tremendous technology, comes with problems like the ones mentioned above that should be solved before anything else. Proper legislation, clearer communication, and human monitoring are all essential for the secure and advantageous usage of AI technologies.

1.7 OVERVIEW OF MODERN GENAI ECOSYSTEM

Currently, the Generative AI ecosystem is a vibrant and fast-growing atmosphere that consists of the superior algorithms, the excellent computing infrastructure and the actual applications. It showcases the integration of very diverse fields like artificial intelligence research, cloud computing, big data and human creativity as shown in Figure 1.6.

Large-scale AI models are the main components of this ecosystem including Large Language Models (LLMs), image generation models, and multimodal systems. Among the largest deep learning-based models,

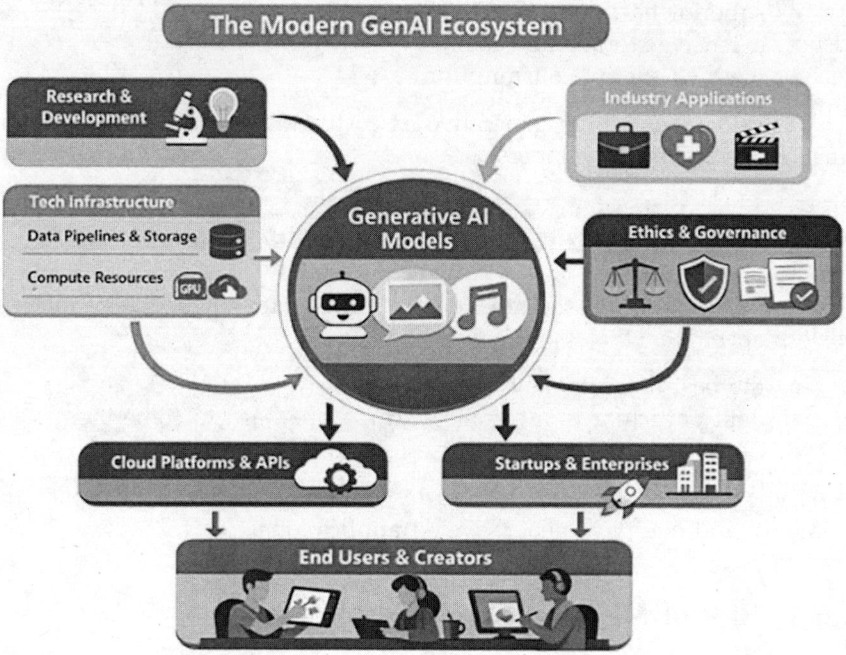

Figure 1.6: *Modern GenAI Ecosystem.*

researchers use hardware of the highest performance like GPUs and TPUs to train them on vast datasets. They are surrounded by an entire support system of tools, platforms, and frameworks that render generative AI accessible to the business and developer communities.

Today's GenAI is enabled by a multi-layered technology stack. The bottom layer is made up of data pipelines and storage systems which collect, clean, and manage the training data. Model development frameworks including TensorFlow, PyTorch, and Hugging Face which allow the researchers to design and train generative models lie above that. The deployment platforms, APIs, and cloud services that allow organizations to integrate the AI capabilities into the actual applications come after all these.

The ecosystem is also influenced by many different kinds of stakeholders:

- Research organizations that focus on AI creating cutting-edge models and techniques
- Cloud suppliers that give support for the training and hosting of the infrastructure
- New businesses that are developing innovative products powered by AI
- Companies incorporating GenAI in their operations for automation and decision support
- Consumers who are communicating through chatbots, assistants, and creative tools

Generative AI has now become a major part of several fields. In the corporate world, it is a good help with writing, customer services and decision making based on data. In the field of healthcare, it provides support in areas like imaging, drug discovery and personalized treatment planning. The same goes for education, where AI is present through smart tutors and customized learning paths. The creative world has also not been left out, as GenAI is being used in art, design, video production, and music composition.

Nonetheless, the ecosystem goes beyond tech—it involves governance, ethics, and regulation as well. The issues of data privacy, bias, misinformation, and responsible use have become major concerns within the GenAI landscape. For this reason, companies are paying more attention to AI safety, explainability, and compliance frameworks in order to support their trustworthy adoption.

All in all, the current GenAI ecosystem is a not-to-be-missed combination of models, platforms, applications, and users interconnected among them. It is changing very fast and is believed to be the main link in the chain that connects the future of innovation, automation, and human–machine collaboration together.

TEST YOUR KNOWLEDGE

1. What is Generative AI, and how does it differ from systems that only classify data?
2. Which probability does a model that classifies data learn, and which probability does a model that generates new data learn?
3. List the major stages in the evolution from early rule-based systems to AI that can create content.
4. How do models generate sequences step by step, and what is the formula for the probability of a sequence of elements?
5. Explain the process of adding noise and removing noise in models that generate data from randomness.
6. What is the main difference between a model that compresses and reconstructs data and a model that uses two networks competing against each other?
7. Give two examples of tasks where one system transforms one type of sequence into another.
8. Name three areas where AI-generated content is being used, with one real-world example for each.
9. List at least three major challenges faced when using AI to generate content in real applications.
10. What are the main layers and participants involved in the current AI ecosystem that generates content?

CHAPTER 2

Mathematical and Conceptual Foundations

Generative AI systems are grounded in solid mathematical and technical principles. Even though these models seem to be creative and smart, their actions are influenced by the concepts mapped out in a very precise manner from probability, statistics, optimization, and deep learning. To really understand the learning of generative models from data and their new content, it is necessary to comprehend these foundations first.

This chapter sets the stage for the main concepts to comprehend Generative AI from a technological viewpoint. It starts with the probability theory, which is the backbone of all generative modelling, then leads to the likelihood estimation and optimization techniques that are applied in training the models. Also, it clarifies some essential points taken from information theory like entropy and divergence measures in order to bring to light how the performance of the model is measured.

On top of that, the chapter navigates through loss functions, sampling methods, and the basic principles of neural networks which are the essentials of today's generative systems. Eventually, it takes the reader through the concepts of representation learning and evaluation which will assist them in judging the quality and efficacy of AI-generated results.

When the readers finish this chapter, they will have a strong mathematical and conceptual base that is necessary for the understanding of the advanced generative AI architectures that are going to be discussed in the upcoming chapters.

2.1 PROBABILITY THEORY FOR GENAI

The evolution of Machine Learning (ML) and Deep Learning (DL) has turned machines into data processing units that are capable of forecasting the future based on past data. Generative Modelling is one of the main applications of this technology that can produce new data points very similar to the original training data of the given model.

However, the question that comes up is:

What is the process of generative models in the creation of new data?

The answer is based on Probability Theory.

Generative AI models are not just replicating the training data. They get the hang of the probability distribution which is the basis of the data. By knowing this distribution, the models are able to deal with unpredictability, take variations into account, and produce super realistic new samples.

This part deals with the basic notion of probability distribution, its varieties, and its close connection with generative modeling.

2.1.1 What is a Probability Distribution?

A probability distribution is a mathematical function that characterizes the probability of various possible outcomes of a random variable.

To put it simply, it informs us:

"What is the probability of each and every possible value that a variable might take?"

There are two primary methods for displaying probability distributions:

- By means of probability tables
- By means of graphs or curves

EXAMPLE: Coin Toss

Consider flipping a fair coin. There are only two possible outcomes:

TABLE 2.1 Sample Dataset

Outcome	*Probability*
Heads	0.5
Tails	0.5

This table illustrates a basic probability distribution.

In the realm of statistics, one of the concepts that is frequently discussed is frequency distribution that illustrates the number of occurrences of specific values within the set of data. However, the probability distribution takes it one step further by attributing probabilities to the values.

Main characteristics of probability:

- Probability values are always in the range of 0 to 1.
- 0 represents impossibility.
- 1 represents certainty.
- The adding up of the probabilities of all the possible outcomes will always equal 1.

Types of Probability Distributions

Probability distributions are broadly classified into two categories:

1. Discrete Probability Distributions
2. Continuous Probability Distributions

Each type plays a crucial role in different kinds of generative models.

2.1.2 Discrete Probability Distributions

A discrete probability distribution is concerned with the cases when random variables assume no more than certain, enumerable values.

Here are some instances of discrete variables:

- Heads obtained in coin tossing
- Daily count of emails received
- Defective items in a batch

In the case of discrete distributions:

- There are just some potential outcomes.
- The others are considered impossible and thus, given zero probability.

For instance, during a dice throw, the results will be just:

1, 2, 3, 4, 5 or 6

Numbers such as 3.7 or 5.2 are impossible and thus excluded from the distribution.

TABLE 2.2 Discrete Distribution

Distribution	*Purpose*	*Example*
Bernoulli distribution	Models' success (1) or failure (0)	Single coin flip
Binomial distribution	Number of successes in n trials	Number of heads in 10 tosses
Poisson distribution	Events in a fixed interval	Emails received per hour
Geometric distribution	Trials until first success	Tosses until first head
Hypergeometric distribution	Sampling without replacement	Drawing coloured balls from a bag

These distributions are widely used in modelling categorical and count-based data as shown in Table 2.2.

2.1.3 Continuous Probability Distributions

Continuous distributions are associated with random variables that can assume any value in a given interval.

Some instances of continuous variables are:

- The height of a human being
- Heat
- Duration of a work procedure

There are infinite possible values between every pair of numbers.

For instance, within the range of [4, 5]:

4.1, 4.01, 4.001, ... plus an endless number of other values are present.

Among these, the Normal (Gaussian) Distribution is especially important in machine learning and deep learning as shown in Table 2.3.

TABLE 2.3 Common Continuous Distributions

Distribution	*Purpose*	*Example*
Uniform distribution	Equal probability in a range	Height between 5 and 6 feet
Normal distribution	Bell-shaped natural data	IQ scores, exam marks
Exponential distribution	Time between events	Time between customer arrivals
Log-normal distribution	Right-skewed data	Stock prices
Beta distribution	Probabilities in [0, 1]	Modelling success rates

2.1.4 Why Probability Theory Matters in Generative AI

Generative AI actually operates on probability at its core.

To be more specific, instead of learning via direct copying of the training data, the generative models are attempting to master:

P(X) – The probability distribution of the data.

The model is capable of selecting new data points from the distribution after that distribution has been learnt.

2.1.5 Major Applications of Probability in Generative Modeling

In generative AI, probability distributions serve the following purposes:

1. **Learning data distribution:** The main goal of generative models is to derive the actual data distribution that exists in the world, based on a limited number of training examples.
2. **Generating new samples:** Once the distribution is learned, models can create:
   - Images of the sort
   - Text of the sort
   - Audio of the sort
   - And synthetic datasets of the sort
3. **Model training and evaluation:** Metrics like:
   - Likelihood
   - Perplexity
   - KL Divergence
   - Wasserstein Distance

   are all probabilistic measures utilized for training and testing generative models.
4. **Dealing with uncertainty:** Data from the real world is often noisy and uncertain. The use of probability distributions allows the models to account for such variations and hence provide a range of different outputs.

Applications of Probability Distributions in Generative AI

Probability theory directly powers many modern AI applications:

Image Generation

Models like:

- GANs
- VAEs
- Diffusion Models

use probability distributions to create realistic images for:

- Design
- Art
- Medical imaging
- Gaming

Text Generation

Large Language Models (LLMs) such as ChatGPT generate text by estimating:

$$P(\text{"next word"} \mid \text{"previous words"})$$

This is purely a probabilistic process.

Applications include:

- Chatbots
- Content creation
- Code generation
- Summarization

Anomaly Detection

By learning the probability distribution of "normal" data, generative models can detect unusual patterns such as:

- Fraud transactions
- Network intrusions
- Medical abnormalities

Mathematical View of Generative Modelling

At a high level:

- Discriminative models learn

$$P(Y \mid X)$$

- Generative models learn

$$P(X) \quad \text{or} \quad P(X, Y)$$

This ability to model how data is generated is what makes generative AI fundamentally different from traditional AI.

Every generative model, be it a language model, image generator, or audio synthesizer, is based on the principles of probability for its operation.

We will gradually take a closer look at the very basics of likelihood, optimization, and information theory, which are directly influencing the way generative models are trained in the coming sections.

2.2 LIKELIHOOD AND OPTIMIZATION

In the earlier part, we saw that generative models are trying to figure out the hidden probability distribution of the data.

Still, one major question is left.

How does generative modeling work in the learning process?

The solution is found in two main ideas:

1. **Likelihood**—evaluating the degree to which a model is able to explain the data.
2. **Optimization**—the process of making the model better based on that evaluation.

The combination of these two ideas is what supports the training of all generative AI systems as shown in Figure 2.1.

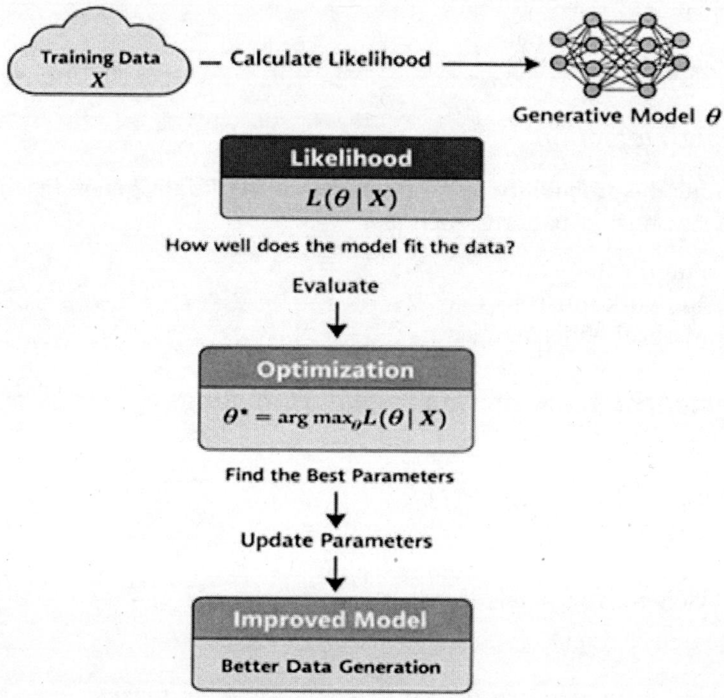

Figure 2.1 *Likelihood and Optimization.*

2.2.1 What is Likelihood?

Likelihood is a statistical phrase that lets us see the model's ability to explain the seen data.

Let's say you have:

- A dataset $X = \{x_1, x_2, ..., x_n\}$
- A generative model with parameters θ

The likelihood function is written as:

$$L(\theta | X) = P(X | \theta)$$

Meaning in Simple Terms

Likelihood poses the question:

If my model has parameters θ, how probable is it that this data was generated from it?

- High likelihood → the model is a good representation of the data
- Low likelihood → the model does not account for the data properly

Thus, likelihood serves as a scorecard for generative models.

2.2.2 Why Likelihood is Important in Generative AI

Generative models are fundamentally probabilistic. Their goal is to learn:

$$P_\theta(x) \approx P_{\text{data}}(x)$$

Likelihood is a measure for:

- distance between the model distribution and the real data
- quality of the current parameters
- constant checking of the model's progress

In the absence of likelihood, a mathematical means to assess a generative model's performance would not exist.

From Likelihood to Log-Likelihood

In real datasets, we have many samples.

The likelihood of the entire dataset becomes:

$$L(\theta | X) = \prod_{i=1}^{n} P(x_i | \theta)$$

Multiplying many small probabilities leads to extremely tiny numbers, which are hard to compute.

To solve this, we use log-likelihood:

$$\ell(\theta | X) = \sum_{i=1}^{n} \log P(x_i | \theta)$$

Log-likelihood is:

- easier to compute
- numerically stable
- widely used in machine learning

Most generative AI models are trained using log-likelihood instead of raw likelihood.

2.2.3 What Exactly does the Term Optimization Mean?

The model's quality is represented by the likelihood.

The model's quality is represented by the optimization.

Optimization in machine learning refers to:

Modifying the model's parameters gradually until the model's performance reaches its peak.

In the case of generative models, the optimization seeks to determine the parameters that yield the maximum likelihood:

$$\theta^* = \arg\theta\max \ell(\theta \mid X)$$

In simple words:

Find the parameter values that best explain the data.

Optimization as Loss Minimization

Most deep learning systems convert maximization into minimization.

Instead of maximizing log-likelihood, we minimize:

$$\text{Loss}(\theta) = -\ell(\theta \mid X)$$

This is called Negative Log Likelihood (NLL).

Training a generative model then becomes:

$$\theta^* = \arg \min_{\theta} \text{Loss}(\theta)$$

This idea connects classical statistics with modern deep learning.

2.2.4 How Optimization Works in Practice

Real generative models contain millions of parameters. We cannot compute optimal values directly.

Instead, we rely on iterative optimization algorithms such as:

- Gradient Descent
- Stochastic Gradient Descent (SGD)
- Adam Optimizer

These methods gradually update parameters using:

$$\theta_{\text{new}} = \theta_{\text{old}} - \eta \frac{\partial}{\partial \theta} \text{Loss}(\theta)$$

where,

- η is the learning rate
- the gradient tells the direction of improvement

This is how models like:

- ChatGPT
- Stable Diffusion
- DALL·E
- Variational Autoencoders

actually, learn from data.

Maximum Likelihood Estimation (MLE)

The integration of likelihood and optimization gives rise to one of the most significant uses:

Maximum Likelihood Estimation

MLE is a statistical technique that summarizes the concepts of:

$$\theta\hat{} = \arg\theta \max L(\theta \mid X)$$

In the domain of generative AI, MLE is a method for approximating the model parameters in such a way that they closely resemble the training data.

Example Intuition

Let us consider a scenario where we treat the data as a Gaussian distribution.

When using MLE, the estimations made then are:

- the mean
- the variance

and this is done in an optimal manner, mathematically and directly from the data.

A large number of generative models, especially the early ones, are based on this principle.

EXAMPLE: For Gaussian data:

$$x \sim \mathcal{N}(\mu, \sigma^2)$$

MLE gives:

$$\hat{\mu} = \frac{1}{n} \sum_{i=1}^{n} x_i$$

$$\hat{\sigma}^2 = \frac{1}{n} \sum_{i=1}^{n} (x_i - \hat{\mu})^2$$

This shows how classical statistics arises from likelihood optimization.

2.2.5 Role of Likelihood and Optimization in GenAI Models

Different generative models use these ideas in different ways (shown in Table 2.4).

TABLE 2.4 Role of likelihood and Optimization

Model Type	*Uses Likelihood and Optimization through*
Language Models	Cross-Entropy Loss
VAEs	ELBO Optimization
Diffusion Models	Noise Prediction Loss
GANs	Adversarial Optimization

Having comprehended the method generative models adopt in learning through likelihood and optimization, we will now proceed to the mathematical setup that quantifies information in probabilistic systems: Information Theory Basics.

2.3 INFORMATION THEORY BASICS

In order to comprehend the learning and assessment process of Generative AI models, one must resort to information theory concepts. Information theory supplies the mathematical instruments for the measurement of uncertainty, similarity, and efficiency in probabilistic models—the basis for the GenAI systems of today.

Why Information Theory is Important in GenAI

At their core, generative models are again and again probabilistic. They are intended to:

- Identify the actual data distribution
- Quantify the proximity of the model distribution to real data
- Eliminate uncertainty in output generation

Information theory supplies us with the precise measures to perform all these tasks as shown in Figure 2.2.

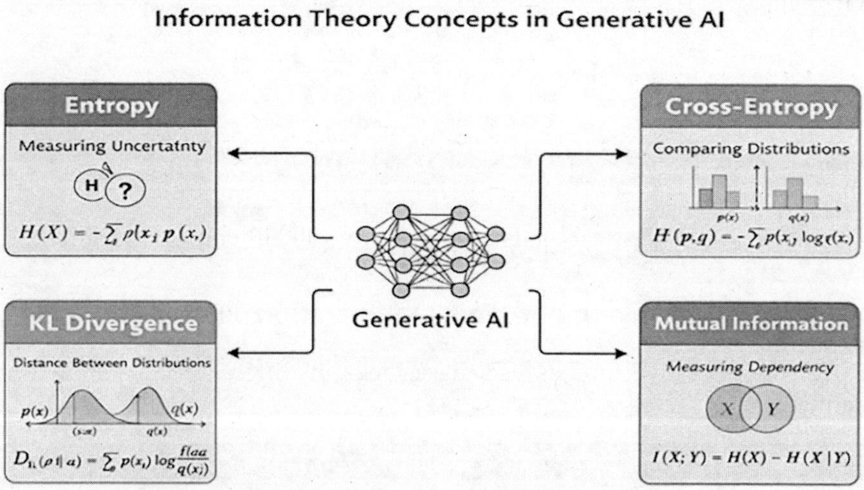

Figure 2.2 *Information Theory.*

1. Entropy—Measuring Uncertainty

Entropy quantifies the amount of uncertainty in a random variable.

$$H(X) = -\sum_{i} p(x_i) \log p(x_i)$$

- High entropy → more randomness
- Low entropy → more predictable data

EXAMPLE:

- A fair coin has higher entropy than a biased coin.
- In GenAI, entropy represents uncertainty in generated tokens, pixels, or features.

2. Cross-Entropy—Comparing Distributions

When training generative models, we compare:

- True data distribution $p(x)$
- Model distribution $q(x)$

This is done using cross-entropy:

$$H(p, q) = -\sum_i p(x_i) \log q(x_i)$$

Cross-entropy tells us:

- How well our model distribution approximates the real distribution.
- Most GenAI loss functions (like in language models) are directly based on cross-entropy.

3. KL Divergence—Distance between Distributions

In GenAI, the main problem is to bring the learned distribution closer to the original distribution. By doing that, it minimizes the gap. This gap is quantified: This gap measures a divergence such as Kullback-Leibler or other methods.

$$D_{KL}(p \parallel q) = \sum_i p(x_i) \log \frac{p(x_i)}{q(x_i)}$$

Properties:

- $D_{KL} \geq 0$
- Zero only when $p = q$
- Not symmetric: $D_{KL}(p \parallel q) \neq D_{KL}(q \parallel p)$

Many generative models such as VAEs (Variational Autoencoders) explicitly minimize KL divergence during training.

4. Mutual Information—Dependency between Variables

Mutual Information measures how much knowing one variable reduces uncertainty about another:

$$I(X; Y) = H(X) - H(X \mid Y)$$

In GenAI:

- Helps in representation learning
- Used in disentangled feature learning
- Important for understanding latent variables

Practical Consideration

- Training GenAI = minimizing information difference
- Better models = lower cross-entropy and KL divergence
- Evaluation = measuring information loss

Without information theory, modern generative modeling would not be mathematically possible.

2.4 LOSS FUNCTION IN GENERATIVE MODELS

In any machine learning model, learning is mainly driven by loss functions. In the case of generative AI, loss functions are even more influential, for the paradigm is not just to label predictions but also to capture whole data distributions and create convincingly new samples.

A loss function in generative models poses a straightforward yet powerful inquiry:

"What is the distance between the model-produced data and the actual data?"

The training invariably modifies the parameters of the model with the aim of reducing this gap by the adoption of optimization methods such as gradient descent.

Generative AI has different ways of looking at loss functions, but the most important ones are:

- To determine the degree of realism of the created samples
- To direct models to the true data distribution learning
- To assure training of complicated architectures
- To measure reconstruction quality
- To make a comparison between probability distributions

Generative AI losses paid less attention to traditional supervised learning aspects like:

- Probability distributions
- Image or text realism
- Latent space consistency
- Adversarial competition

Essential Loss Functions for Generative Models

Rather than discussing all the loss functions that could ever be used, we limit ourselves to these core ones that are present in the development of GANs, VAEs, Diffusion Models, and Transformers as shown in Figure 2.3.

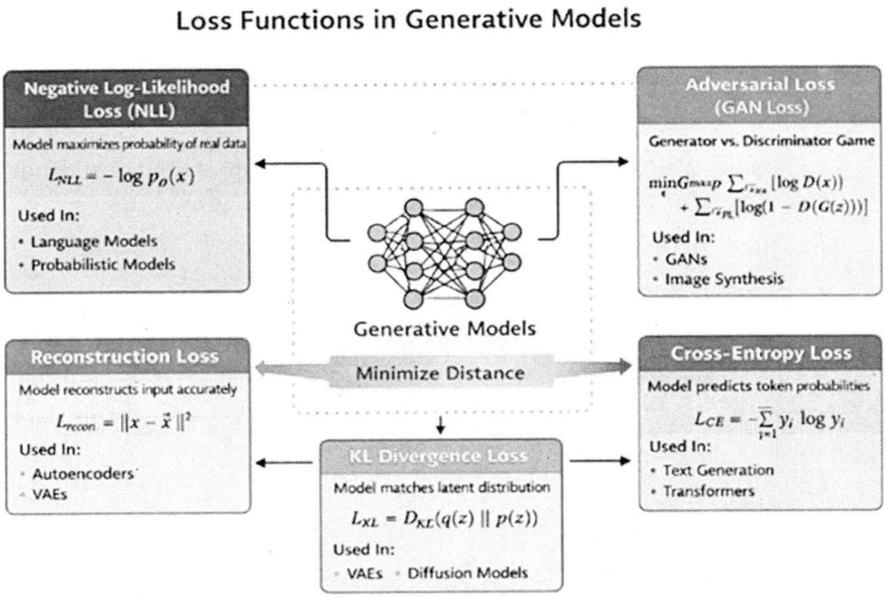

Figure 2.3: *Loss Function in GenAI.*

1. Negative Log-Likelihood Loss (NLL)

This is the most basic loss in generative modelling and is directly related to the concept of Maximum Likelihood Estimation (MLE).

Idea: The aim is to make the probability of real data under our model the highest.

Mathematically:

$$\mathcal{L}_{\text{NLL}} = -\log p_\theta(x)$$

where,

x = real data sample

$p_\theta(x)$ = probability assigned by the model

θ = model parameters

Minimizing NLL is equivalent to maximizing likelihood.

Used In:

- Language models
- Autoregressive text generation
- Probabilistic generative models

2. Reconstruction Loss (Autoencoder/VAE)

In Autoencoder and Variational Autoencoder (VAE)—like architectures, the precise reconstruction of input data is the main objective.

The loss quantifies the similarity between the original input and the reconstructed output:

$$\mathcal{L}_{\text{recon}} = \| x - \hat{x} \|^2$$

This is typically implemented using:

- Mean Squared Error (MSE)—for images
- Binary Cross-Entropy—for normalized data

Aim to used it:

- Ensures the model learns meaningful latent representations
- Forces generated output to remain close to real data

Used In:

- Autoencoders
- Variational Autoencoders
- Image generation and compression

3. KL Divergence Loss

Generative models often need to compare two probability distributions:

- True data distribution $p(x)$
- Model distribution $I(x)$

KL Divergence measures this difference:

$$D_{KL}(p \,||\, q) = \sum p(x) \log \frac{p(x)}{q(x)}$$

In VAEs:

KL divergence ensures that the learned latent space follows a structured prior (usually Gaussian):

$$\mathcal{L}_{KL} = D_{KL}(q(z|x) \;||\; p(z))$$

4. Adversarial Loss (GAN Loss)

GANs use a completely different learning paradigm based on competition between two networks:

- Generator G
- Discriminator D

The adversarial loss is defined as:

$$\min_G \max_D \mathbb{E}_{x \sim p_{\text{data}}}) [\log D(x)] + \mathbb{E}_{z \sim p_z} [\log (1 - D(G(z)))]$$

Concept:

- The generator's goal is to trick the discriminator
- The discriminator's work is to identify counterfeit samples
- This competition results in extremely realistic outputs

Used In:

- Image generation
- Style shifting
- Resolution enhancement
- Synthetic media

5. Cross-entropy Loss in Generative Models

Cross-entropy is widely used in:

- Language models
- Text generation
- Token prediction

For text generation:

$$\mathcal{L}_{CE} = -\sum_{i=1}^{n} y_i \log \hat{y}_i$$

where,

y_i = true token

$\hat{y}_i$ = predicted probability

This form backbone for:

- GPT models
- Transformers
- ChatGPT-style system

Key Takeaways

1. Loss functions determine the definition of good generation.
2. The generative AI losses are based on distributions, not on labels.
3. Different models imply different objectives in the very nature.
4. A consistent loss design is essential for successful training.
5. The majority of current generative systems utilize several losses.

Having comprehended the way generative models depict error through loss functions, the very next thing is to look at how models share and create samples from the learned distributions which takes us to the topic of: Sampling Techniques in Generative AI.

2.5 SAMPLING TECHNIQUES IN GENERATIVE AI

Sampling is one of the major concepts when it comes to Generative AI. After a generative model has gained learning on the probability distribution over the data, it is required to sample from that distribution to get new outputs. A generative model would compute probabilities only if it did not sample and it would never generate anything actually.

Two main stages can be pointed out in Generative AI where sampling happens:

1. Probabilistic models' sampling (training and inference)
2. Generation process' sampling (output creation)

They are both important though perform different functions.

In Generative AI, mainly in Large Language Models (LLMs), sampling decides how the model picks the subsequent token, word, or symbol in the course of text generation.

In essence, sampling addresses a very basic question:

"Taking into account everything that has been generated until now, how should the model pick the next one?"

The way this choice is made carries a direct effect on:

- Imagination
- Consistency
- Variety
- Trustworthiness
- Output's determinism

Given that different applications necessitate different sampling strategies, a chatbot, a creative writing aide, and a programming code generator each require one type of behavior respectively—and the sampling methods give us the power to define such behaviour as shown in Figure 2.4.

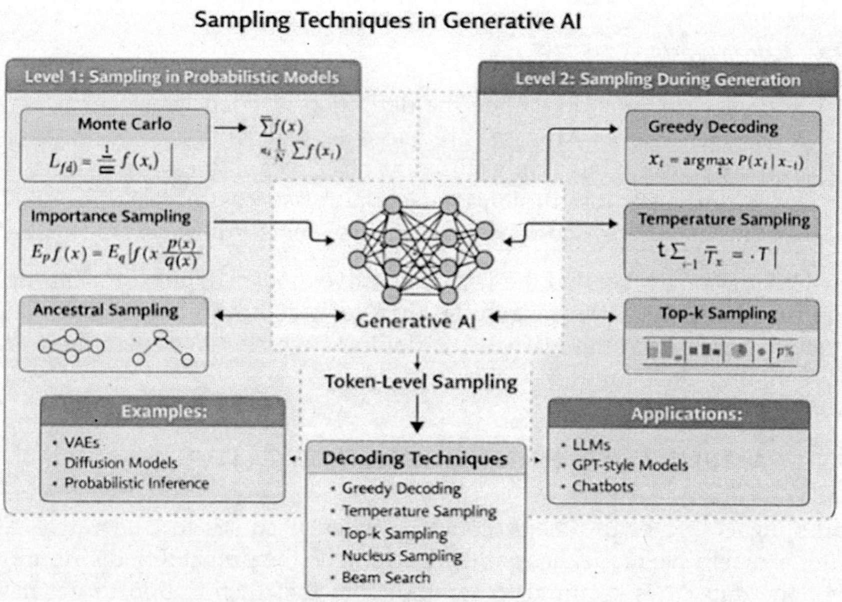

Figure 2.4: *Sampling Techniques in AI.*

2.5.1 Sampling in Probabilistic Models

Every generative model has a probability distribution at its center. Drawing samples from the complicated distributions that the training of such models needs is a common route, but sometimes it is impossible to calculate them directly. Statistical sampling methods come into play at this moment.

Why Sampling is Needed
Most generative models attempt to learn:

$$p(x)$$

or a conditional distribution:

$$p(x \mid z)$$

where, z is a latent variable.

That said, in the majority of real-life cases, these distributions would not be so straightforward. The process of dealing with computationally expensive methods for determining the exact probabilities or expectations is often impossible. Thus, the sampling method serves as the best solution for approximation.

2.5.2 Common Sampling Methods in Generative Modeling

Several mathematical sampling techniques are widely used:

1. **Monte Carlo Sampling:** Monte Carlo methods estimate expectations using random samples:

$$E[f(x)] \approx \frac{1}{N} \sum_{i=1}^{N} f(x_i)$$

   This idea is used extensively in Variational Autoencoders (VAEs) and diffusion models.
2. **Ancestral Sampling:** In models such as Bayesian Networks, samples are drawn sequentially following the dependency structure of variables.
3. **Importance Sampling:** When direct sampling from a target distribution $p(x)$ is difficult, samples are drawn from a simpler proposal distribution $q(x)$ and reweighted:

$$E_p[f(x)] = E_q\left[f(x)\frac{p(x)}{q(x)}\right]$$

   This technique is useful in VAEs and probabilistic inference.
4. **Markov Chain Monte Carlo (MCMC):** MCMC methods such as Gibbs sampling and Metropolis-Hastings allow sampling from very complex distributions by constructing a Markov chain whose stationary distribution is $p(x)$.

Role in Generative AI Models

Such statistical sampling approaches have their main application in:

- Latent space sampling in Variational Autoencoders
- Noise-based iterative sampling in diffusion models

- Probabilistic graphical models
- Bayesian deep learning

These methods are applied within the model during the entire process of training or inference.

1. *Sampling during Generation*

Once a generative model is trained, it must generate actual outputs such as text, images, or audio. This requires a different form of sampling—one that operates at the output level.

Autoregressive Generation

Most modern generative systems, especially Large Language Models (LLMs), generate data token by token using:

$$p(x) = \prod_{t=1}^{T} p(x_t \mid x_{1:t-1})$$

At each step, the model produces a probability distribution over possible next tokens:

$$p(x_t \mid x_{1:t-1})$$

Sampling techniques are then used to choose the next token from this distribution.

Why Output Sampling Matters

If we always select the highest-probability token, outputs become:

- Robotic
- Repetitive
- Lacking creativity

Controlled sampling allows generative models to balance:

- Coherence
- Diversity
- Creativity
- Accuracy

2. *Decoding Techniques for Generation*

These techniques control how the model selects tokens from its predicted probability distribution.

Greedy Decoding

The simplest strategy:

$$x_t = \arg\max p(x_t \mid x_{1:t-1})$$

The model always picks the most probable next token.

Advantages

- Fast
- Deterministic
- Good for factual tasks

Limitations

- No creativity
- Often repetitive
- Locally optimal, not globally optimal

3. *Temperature Sampling*

Temperature sampling introduces **controlled randomness** into token selection.

The probability distribution is modified as:

$$P'(x_i) = \frac{P(x_i)^{1/T}}{\sum_j P(x_j)^{1/T}}$$

where, T = temperature parameter

Effect of Temperature:

- $T < 1.0 \rightarrow$ distribution sharper $\rightarrow$ associated with safe and deterministic prediction
- $T = 1.0 \rightarrow$ distribution unchanged
- $T > 1.0 \rightarrow$ distribution flatter $\rightarrow$ More random outputs and creativity

Practical Interpretation:

- Lower temperature → formal, factual, conservative
- Higher temperature → creative, diverse, risky

Use Cases:

- Low T: Technical writing, summarization
- High T: Story creation, brainstorming

4. *Nucleus Sampling (Top–p Sampling)*

Nucleus sampling improves upon top-k by using a dynamic selection size.

Instead of fixing k, we define a probability threshold p.

The algorithm:

- Sort tokens by probability
- Keep adding tokens until cumulative probability $\geq p$

EXAMPLE: If $p = 0.9 \rightarrow$ keep most probable tokens that together make up 90% of the distribution.

Advantages:

- Adapts to context
- More flexible than top-k
- Produces natural and diverse text

This is currently one of the most widely used sampling methods in LLMs.

5. *Beam Search*

Beam search is not purely a sampling method but a sequence optimization strategy.

Instead of choosing one token at a time, beam search:

- Explores multiple possible sequences in parallel
- Keeps the best "B" sequences (beam width)
- Selects the highest probability sequence at the end

Objective:

Maximize overall sequence probability:

$$\arg\max_{x_{1:T}} P(x_{1:T})$$

Strengths:

- Produces highly coherent outputs
- Good for translation, summarization, and structured generation

Weakness:

- Less creative
- Can favor generic phrases

2.6 NEURAL NETWORK FUNDAMENTALS

Neural networks are the basic building blocks on which current AI and deep learning are devised. They are computational models that are built according to the human brain's anatomy and functioning. The same way biological neurons do signalling, artificial neural networks process data and learn from it.

Neural networks are at their heart formulated to detect data relationships and then utilize them for making predictions, classifications, or creating new information.

2.6.1 What is a Neural Network?

A neural network is a machine learning model that consists of interlinked processing units referred to as neurons as shown in Figure 2.5. The activity of these neurons leads to the conversion of raw input data into outputs that carry meanings.

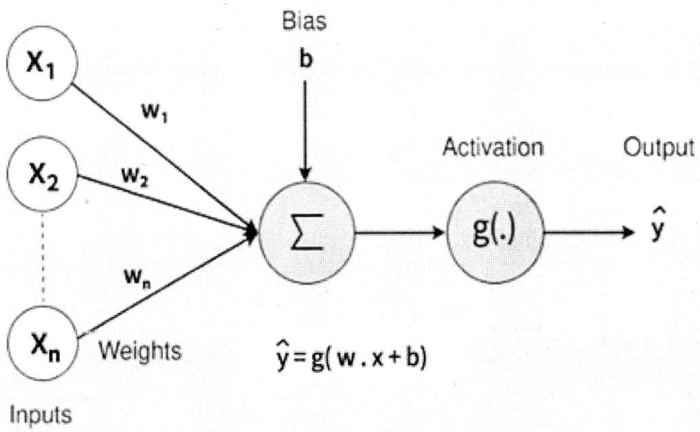

Figure 2.5: *Neural Network.*

Neural networks are not like traditional algorithms that stick to a fixed set of rules but rather they learn from data even more. As a result, they become very efficient for difficult tasks like:

- Recognition of images
- Processing of speech
- Understanding of languages
- Detection of patterns
- Analytics of predictions

The major advantage of neural networks is that they can freely and automatically dig out the really valuable features of the input data.

2.6.2 Core Components of a Neural Network

Every neural network is built from a few essential building blocks:

1. **Neurons:** Neurons stand as the most basic computation units of a neural network. Every single neuron:
   - Takes in input
   - Makes a computation out of them
   - Gives an output

   A single neuron does very simple math in its operating but millions of neurons working in concert can already represent the most intricate behaviors.
2. **Connections:** Neurons are linked through a system of pathways that transmit the information, one direction only, from neuron to neuron. Through these neuron-networks connections, data are transmitted across the network from one layer to another.
3. **Weights and Biases:** A weight, which is a number assigned to every connection, indicates the extent to which the input that is linked to this connection is significant.

   While the biases are decreased, it permits more flexibility in the adjustment of the output by the neurons.

   Neural network learning is literally the process of weights and biases tuning so that the network can produce more accurate outputs.
4. **Activation Functions:** Once the inputs are duly processed, the neurons resort to an activation function to gauge the likelihood and the intensity of their "firing".
   The most frequently used activation functions are:
   - ReLU
   - Sigmoid
   - Tanh

   The application of activation functions adds non-linearity to the process, which allows the neural networks to recognize complicated patterns instead of being stuck with just simple linear ones.

Neural Network Architecture

A neural network is structured by means of layers:

1. **Input Layer**
   - Gets unprocessed data
   - One feature per neuron
   - Computation is not done
2. **Hidden Layers**
   - Do the main part of the learning
   - Change the inputs into useful forms
   - There can be one or several hidden layers in a network

Generally, deep learning models have many hidden layers which enable them to detect patterns of different levels as shown in Figure 2.6.

3. **Output Layer:** The latest output of the model is processed by the final layer. Depending on the task at hand, this output might come in classifications, regressions, et cetera shown in Figure 2.6.

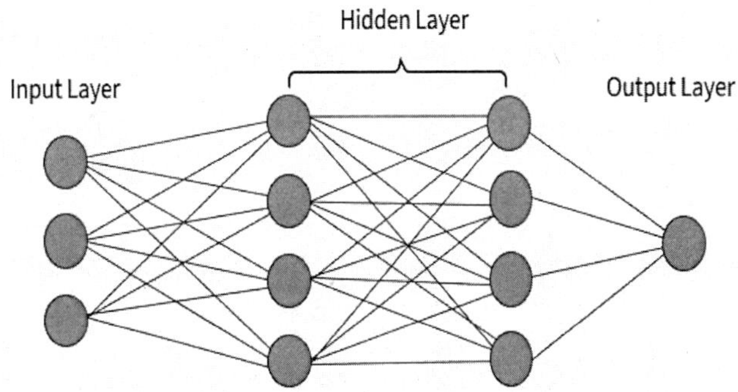

Figure 2.6: *Neural Network Architecture.*

Neuron Equation

The mathematical model of a neuron becomes:

$$a = f\left(\sum_{i=1}^{n} w_i x_i + b\right)$$

This equation defines how every neuron in a neural network operates.

From Single Neuron to Layers
A single neuron is limited in power. Neural networks combine many neurons together.

For a layer with multiple neurons, the computation is written in vector form:

$$a = f(Wx + b)$$

where,

x = input vector
W = weight matrix
b = bias vector
a = output vector

This matrix formulation allows efficient computation in deep learning frameworks.

Summary of Neuron Mathematics

The complete mathematical workflow of a neuron is:

1. Compute weighted sum

$$z = \sum w_i x_i + b$$

2. Apply activation

$$a = f(z)$$

3. Compare with target using loss

$$L(y, a)$$

4. Update weights using gradients

$$w_i = w_i - \eta \frac{\partial L}{\partial w_i}$$

2.6.3 Working of Neural Networks

The transformation of input data to output through the various mathematical operations performed in different layers is the way how neural networks get their learning. The functioning of neural networks is mainly based on two processes:

- Forward propagation—the process of prediction
- Back propagation—the process of correcting one's mistakes

These two processes are combined in such a way that the neural network gets better with each cycle.

1. *Forward Propagation*

Forward propagation is the process in which input data moves through the network to generate an output.

Step 1: Linear Transformation
Each neuron receives inputs, multiplies them by weights, adds a bias, and computes a weighted sum:

$$z = w_1x_1 + w_2x_2 + ... + w_nx_n + b$$

where,

x_i = input values
w_i = weights
b = bias
z = linear output

This equation forms the mathematical foundation of every neuron.

Step 2: Activation Function

The computed value is passed through an activation function:

$$a = f(z)$$

Common activation functions:

- ReLU: $f(z) = \max(0, z)$
- Sigmoid: $f(z) = 1/(1 + e^{-z})$
- Tanh: $f(z) = \tan h(z)$

Activation functions allow neural networks to model complex, non-linear relationships.

2. *Backpropagation—Learning Process*

After forward propagation, the network evaluates how accurate its prediction is.

Step 1: Loss Calculation

A loss function measures the difference between predicted output and actual output.

EXAMPLES:

- Mean Squared Error (MSE) — for regression
- Cross-Entropy Loss — for classification

The objective of training is:

Minimize Loss

Step 2: Gradient Computation

The network calculates how much each weight contributed to the error using derivatives:

$$\frac{\partial L}{\partial w}$$

This process determines the direction in which weights should be adjusted.

Step 3: Weight Update

Using an optimizer such as Gradient Descent:

$$w = w - \eta \frac{\partial L}{\partial w}$$

where, η = learning rate

This update process is repeated over many iterations until the network learns optimal parameters.

ILLUSTRATIVE EXAMPLE—Email Spam Classification

To understand neural network computation, consider a simple example.

Dataset Sample

TABLE 2.5 Dataset Sample

Email Content	*Label*
"Get free gift cards now!"	Spam (1)

We extract simple features:

- "free" → 1
- "win" → 0
- "offer" → 1

So, input vector:

$$[1, 0, 1]$$

Hidden Layer Computation

Assume two hidden neurons:

Weights:

Neuron H1: [0.5, –0.2, 0.3]
Neuron H2: [0.4, 0.1, –0.5]

Weighted Sum

For H1:

$$(1 \times 0.5) + (0 \times -0.2) + (1 \times 0.3) = 0.8$$

For H2:

$$(1 \times 0.4) + (0 \times 0.1) + (1 \times -0.5) = -0.1$$

Activation (ReLU)

H1: ReLU(0.8) = 0.8

H2: ReLU(–0.1) = 0

Output Layer Computation

Weights: [0.7, 0.2]

$$(0.8 \times 0.7) + (0 \times 0.2) = 0.56$$

Apply Sigmoid:

$$\sigma(0.56) = \frac{1}{1 + e^{-0.56}} \approx 0.636$$

Final Prediction

- Probability of spam = 0.636
- Since it is greater than 0.5 → Classified as Spam (1)

2.6.4 Advantages of Neural Networks

Neural networks have been adopted tremendously in various fields owing to their several practical strengths:

- **Flexibility:** Neural networks are capable of learning straight from the input data providing a solution to the problems in which the relations of input and output are complex or unknown.
- **Pattern Recognition:** They are very good at detecting subtle patterns in the data which results in image recognition, speech recognition, and processing, and also natural language understanding.
- **Simultaneous Computation:** One of the characteristics of neural networks is to carry out several computations at the same time which results in their speed and efficiency for performance on big tasks.
- **Ability to Model Non-Linear Relationships:** Activation functions give neural networks the ability to deal with intricate, non-linear relationships whereas traditional linear models would have failed.

2.6.5 Limitations of Neural Networks

Neural networks, however, have certain drawbacks that cannot be ignored:

- **High Computational Cost:** Time and significant computational resources are needed for deep neural networks training.
- **Black-Box Nature:** Very often the internal decision-making process is not clear, and this can be a problem in important applications.
- **Risk of Overfitting:** If proper regularization is not applied, neural networks may memorize the training data instead of being able to generalize to new data.

The foundation of generative AI and deep learning lies in neural networks. They can detect patterns from data and tackle complicated real-world issues through the automatic application of math transformations, activation functions, and training optimization methods.

It is necessary to master these basic concepts before proceeding to the next step, which is advanced generative models like GANs, VAEs, and Transformers.

2.7 REPRESENTATION LEARNING

Representation learning is one of the key cornerstones upon which modern Generative AI is built. It allows models to draw characteristically from the data, i.e., to learn automatically, to use the corresponding internal formats, or rather to transform the raw data into the desired internal formats. These learned representations are the grounds for the model's understanding, reasoning, and content generation.

2.7.1 What is Entitled Representation Learning?

The process of traditional machine learning saw the, sometimes, very expansive and meticulous, manual involvement of the domain experts to come up with features to be used in the training. Representation learning sets this manual work aside, for it makes it possible for the models to automatically discover the import features right from the data.

Representation learning's essential aim is to turn the complex and high-dimensional data like images, texts, or audios into smaller but still meaningful data representations which are easier and more efficient for the models to process and digest.

In the area of generative AI, representation learning supports models in the following ways:

- Grasping the quality and nature of the data
- Identifying the core patterns and links
- Being able to differentiate between the abstract features and surface-level details
- New sample data creation that is similar to the real data

2.7.2 Representation Learning in Generative Models

Generative models place a great deal of reliance on representation learning in their quest to model complex data distributions. Generator models like Vaes, GANs, and also new kinds of diffusions are all developing powerful internal representations of the data in learning process.

This development includes two major transformations to be accomplished:

1. **Data Representation Mapping (Encoding):** Generative models are performing the task of compressing the raw data into a less-dimensioned latent space. This latent space has the characteristics of being an abstract representation of the data:
   - The most similar points of data are located very close to one another.
   - The most significant features are preserved briefly.
   - Unwanted things such as noise and irrelevant details are minimized.

   For instance, the images of the same kind of objects (like different cats) might be mapped into nearby locations within the latent space, thus allowing the model to recognize their common structure.

2. **Mapping Representations Back to Data (Decoding):** Generative models can, once meaningful representations are learned, reverse the process and transform latent vectors into realistic data samples.

   This capability enables the models to:

   - Create new images, text, or audio from scratch
   - Change the original data by changing latent representations
   - Make gradual changes between samples to produce variations

   The combination of these two movements—encoding and decoding—constitutes the very foundation of generative AI technologies.

Representation Learning, a Vital Issue in GenAI

The effective representation learning opens the door to the following significant benefits:

1. **Better Generalization:** Models acquire the concept instead of just memorizing the data.
2. **Efficient Learning:** Smaller representations involve lesser computational power.
3. **Creative Generation:** The movement of latent features can be used to create new data.
4. **Cross-Domain Learning:** Representations learned from one task can often be reused for others.

Representation learning serves as the only interlink between the unprocessed data and intelligent creation. Generative AIs, through learning meaningful inner representations, implicitly understand the intricate data and produce new, realistic, and varied-content capabilities.

Representation learning, however, is the crucial layer that connects the raw materials (data) and AI-generated products (intelligent outputs).

2.8 EVALUATION CONCEPTS IN GENERATIVE AI

The assessment of generative AI systems is a vital procedure that guarantees the models' outputs to be correct, dependable, and beneficial. Generative models, in contrast to classical machine learning models, are generative in nature and hence, produce new content, e.g., text, images, audio or even video. Consequently, their evaluation calls for both the application of numerical measures as well as the exercise of subjective judgment.

1. *Why Evaluation is Important in GenAI*

Generative AI models are inherently creative and probabilistic. A single input can lead to several different results. This implies:

- Not just accuracy is the criterion.
- Outputs need to be assessed for:
    - Quality
    - Coherence
    - Relevance
    - Safety
    - Fairness

Correct evaluation assists in:

- Model comparison
- Model performance enhancement
- Bias and hallucination detection
- User satisfaction guarantee

Types of Evaluation Methods

Evaluation in Generative AI can be broadly divided into three categories:

1. Automatic Evaluation Metrics
2. Human Evaluation
3. Benchmark-based Evaluation

2. *Automatic Evaluation Metrics*

The automatic scoring methods rely on rigorous mathematical computations to evaluate the quality of resulting texts without any human input.

The evaluations are rapid, can be applied to a large scale, and serve as a progression aid during the model development process.

Metrics for Text Generation

(a) BLEU Score

- Bleu score is the principal metric for both text generation and machine translation.
- It indicates the degree of similarity between the output and the reference text.
- It uses the method of n-grams matching (word sequence).

The backbone of this:

Higher BLEU score → Human reference text has been matched more closely.

Drawback:

Does not reflect the inventiveness or significance very well.

(b) ROUGE score

- Utilized often for tasks concerning summary
- Rather, to emphasize recall than precision
- Quantifies the volume of crucial content coming from the reference that is found in the text produced

Subtypes:

- ROUGE-N → overlap of *n*-grams
- ROUGE-L → longest shared sequence
- ROUGE-S → bigram matching with skips

Ideal for:
Evaluating text summarization

(c) Perplexity

Perplexity measures how confident a language model is in predicting text.

- Lower perplexity = better model
- Indicates fluency and naturalness
- Used to compare different language models

Use Case:

- Evaluating chatbots
- Comparing LLM versions
- Checking coherence of generated content

Metrics for Image Generation

Text metrics are not suitable for images. Therefore, specialized metrics are used.

(a) Fréchet Inception Distance (FID)
FID is the most popular metric for evaluating AI-generated images.

- Compares real images vs generated images
- Uses a pre-trained neural network to extract features
- Measures similarity between feature distributions

Interpretation:

- Lower FID score = better image quality
- Indicates both realism and diversity

(b) Inception Score (IS)

Measures two aspects:

1. Image quality
2. Diversity of generated images

Higher Inception Score indicates better performance.

(c) CLIP Score

Used for text-to-image models.

- Measures alignment between:
    - Input text prompt
    - Generated image

Higher CLIP Score = Better semantic matching

Used in:

- DALL·E
- Stable Diffusion
- Text-to-image evaluation

Benchmark–based Evaluation

Standardized datasets and tests are used to compare AI systems objectively.
Popular benchmarks include:

- MMLU — General knowledge and reasoning
- GLUE/SuperGLUE — Language understanding
- BIG-bench — Complex reasoning tasks

These benchmarks help in:

- Fair comparison
- Measuring progress
- Ranking different AI models

Choosing the Right Metric

Different tasks require different evaluation methods (shown in Table 2.6):

TABLE 2.6 Choosing the right metric

Task	*Best Metrics*
Machine Translation	BLEU
Summarization	ROUGE
Chatbot Responses	Perplexity + Human Eval
Image Generation	FID, IS
Text-to-Image	CLIP Score
Speech Generation	MOS
Video Generation	FVD

The evaluation of Generative AI is a complex issue with several dimensions. There is no universal metric to evaluate all the aspects.

A proper evaluation strategy includes:

- Score charts
- Expert opinion
- Criteria for the specific task

It is only by the use of all these that we can effectively determine the actual performance of a generative AI system.

TEST YOUR KNOWLEDGE

1. Why do generative models rely on probability distributions instead of directly memorizing training data?
2. What is the practical difference between likelihood and log-likelihood in model training?
3. How does Maximum Likelihood Estimation help a model learn from data?
4. Why are entropy and cross-entropy important when training generative models?
5. What is the purpose of KL divergence in comparing probability distributions?
6. Why are loss functions essential in generative AI, and how do they guide model learning?
7. How do sampling techniques influence the quality and creativity of generated outputs?
8. Explain why activation functions are necessary in neural networks.
9. What role does backpropagation play in improving neural network performance?
10. Why is evaluating generative models more challenging than evaluating traditional machine learning models?

CHAPTER 3

Fundamentals of Large Language Models

The introduction of Large Language Models (LLMs) has completely changed machines' capability to interpret and produce human language in a more natural way. A variety of applications, such as smart chatbots, content creation, translation, and even virtual assistants, are all using LLMs today as their main technology. However, such incredibly sophisticated capabilities are rooted in a mixture of strong Natural Language Processing, deep learning, and neural networks. Thus, the chapter is giving a preview of the basic concepts that one has to know in order to get a grasp of the functioning and building of LLMs.

The first thing the chapter does is to take the reader back to the beginning of NLP, detailing the whole process of how machines understand, process, and analyze text data. Then it continues to deal with sequence models and transformers, the pair of technologies which are at the very core of contemporary LLMs. Going through the attention mechanism in detail refers to the doing of the case which one can view the model's focusing on the relevant parts of the input text. The reader will also be informed about key preprocessing concepts as these are very essential in changing the raw text into numerically meaningful representations..

Next step, the chapter tells about the training objectives that have been used in the development of large language models, and at the same time, presenting a list of the most liked LLM architectures like GPT, BERT, T5, etc. The last part of the discussion is dedicated to the major limitations and challenges indeed faced with LLMs tech which will ultimately give an idea of a balanced understanding of both the strengths and weaknesses of this dispensation. It is expected that at the end of the chapter the learners would be well equipped with the necessary conceptual foundation to take on the advanced topics in generative AI and language modeling.

3.1 BASICS OF NATURAL LANGUAGE PROCESSING

Natural Language Processing (NLP) can be characterized as a branch of Artificial Intelligence that makes it possible for machines to comprehend, decipher, and even produce human language. Human communication is very different from data in a structured format; it possesses the very high complexity, the very high degree of ambiguity, and dependence on the context. The aim of NLP is to eliminate the barrier that exists between human communication and machine comprehension.

NLP is fundamentally a fusion of the ideas of linguistics, computer science, and machine learning for processing and analyzing textual data. The old-style NLP systems were based on rules, which meant they relied on the painstakingly created grammatical rules and dictionaries. With the passing of time, statistics and machine learning methods gradually took over the work from the strict rules, thus enabling the NLP field to gain more versatility and scalability.

NLP's core goals

NLP has one major goal, which is to enable machines to:

- Get the message that is in the text
- Get language to give them the information that is useful
- Answer like humans do
- Do the language translation
- Communicate with the users in the most comfortable manner

These potentials are a must for the fields of search engines, virtual assistants, chatbots, sentiment detection, and machine translation, among others.

From a computational perspective, NLP can be defined as learning a function:

$$f: T \to Y$$

where,

T represents textual input (sentences, documents, conversations)

Y represents meaningful output such as classification labels, translations, summaries, or responses.

Unlike structured numerical data, natural language is highly unstructured, ambiguous, and context-dependent, making NLP one of the most challenging areas of Artificial Intelligence.

3.1.1 The Nature of the Challenge in NLP—Computationally Difficult

The human language is full of nonsense and problems that are different from the ones faced in traditional data processing:

1. **Ambiguity:** The same sentence can be understood in many different ways.
   For instance:
   "I saw her duck."
   Is it about a bird or an action?

2. **Context Dependence:** The meanings of words depend on other words.
   For example:

   "He went to the bank." (a money place)
   "He sat on the river bank." (next to a river)
3. **Variable-Length Input:** The length of sentences and documents varies, which is the opposite of fixed-size numerical data.
4. **Grammar and Semantics:** Human language is full of very complicated grammatical structures, idioms, sarcasm, and implicit meanings.

All these things make it necessary for NLP systems to do the hardest part of the work, which is to convert raw text into mathematical representations that are structured in such a way that they are ready for further intelligent processing.

3.1.2 Key Components of NLP

Two major components constitute the core of modern NLP systems:

1. **Natural Language Understanding (NLU)**
   The goal of NLU is to make the machines comprehend the human language. It is a combination of the following tasks:
   - Understanding who is saying what, where and why
   - Entities, relationships and their respective attributes are extracted
   - Context and meaning are interpreted
2. **Natural Language Generation (NLG)**
   NLG generates meaningful and grammatically correct sentences from structured or unstructured data. It finds its application in:
   - Responses to customer queries in chatbots
   - Production of automated reports
   - Summarizing text

NUEL and NUG together lay the ground for intelligent language-based systems.

3.1.3 Traditional NLP Pipeline

Before the era of deep learning and LLMs, NLP followed a structured multi-step pipeline.

Step 1: Text Normalization
Raw text is cleaned and standardized:

- Lowercasing
- Removing punctuation

- Removing special characters
- Handling spelling variations

EXAMPLE:

Input:

"Hello, World!!! NLP is Amazing."

Normalized Output:

"hello world nlp is amazing"

Step 2: Tokenization

Tokenization splits text into smaller meaningful units called tokens.

Mathematically, for a sentence:

$$S = [w_1, w_2, ..., w_n]$$

Tokenization function:

$$\text{Tokenize}(S) = \{w_1, w_2, ..., w_n\}$$

Step 3: Stopword Removal

Common words such as is, the, a, an often add little semantic value.

$$\text{Filtered Tokens} = \text{Tokens} - \text{Stopwords}$$

This reduces noise in text representation.

Step 4: Stemming and Lemmatization

Words are reduced to their base or root forms:

- running → run
- better → good

3.1.4 From Classical NLP to Machine Learning-based NLP

The first generation of natural language processing systems (NLP) made use of basic statistical techniques, like Bag of Words (BoW)—where text was represented in terms of a frequency count of words, TF-IDF—where the importance of words in a document was measured, N-grams—where local word patterns were captured.

Even though these approaches were helpful, they couldn't avoid the following major limitations:

- Lack of context understanding
- Inability to represent and understand the meaning of text
- Poor handling of word sequence
- Struggles with interpreting the meaning of words

The aforementioned problems were resolved by the introduction of machine learning and deep learning techniques.

3.1.5 The Advent of Neural NLP

The whole scenario of deep learning led to the complete adoption of neural networks in NLP:

- Using Word Embeddings (Word2Vec, GloVe, fastText), words could be depicted as continuous vectors of high dimension.
- Recurrent Neural Networks (RNNs) worked on the principle of text being a sequence of words.
- The Long Short-Term Memory and Gated Recurrent Unit networks made significant breakthroughs in their ability to manage the context of longer duration.
- The Sequence-to-Sequence models opened up the application of translating and summarizing by machine.

These techniques provided large improvements in performance but were still limited by factors like:

- Inability to grasp the dependencies over long ranges
- Restrictions on processing one after the other
- Shallow contextual comprehension

These problems demanded a more superior architecture.

3.1.6 Evolution from NLP to Large Language Models

The major turning point in NLP came with the introduction of Transformer architecture in 2017 as shown in Figure 3.1. Transformers replaced sequential processing with self-attention mechanisms, enabling models to:

- Understand long-range dependencies
- Capture rich contextual meaning
- Process entire sentences in parallel
- Scale efficiently to massive datasets

This innovation led to the development of Large Language Models (LLMs) such as:

- BERT
- GPT
- T5
- RoBERTa

Unlike traditional NLP models that were trained for specific tasks, LLMs are:

- Trained on massive amounts of text
- Capable of general-purpose language understanding
- Able to perform multiple tasks with minimal fine-tuning
- Context-aware and highly fluent

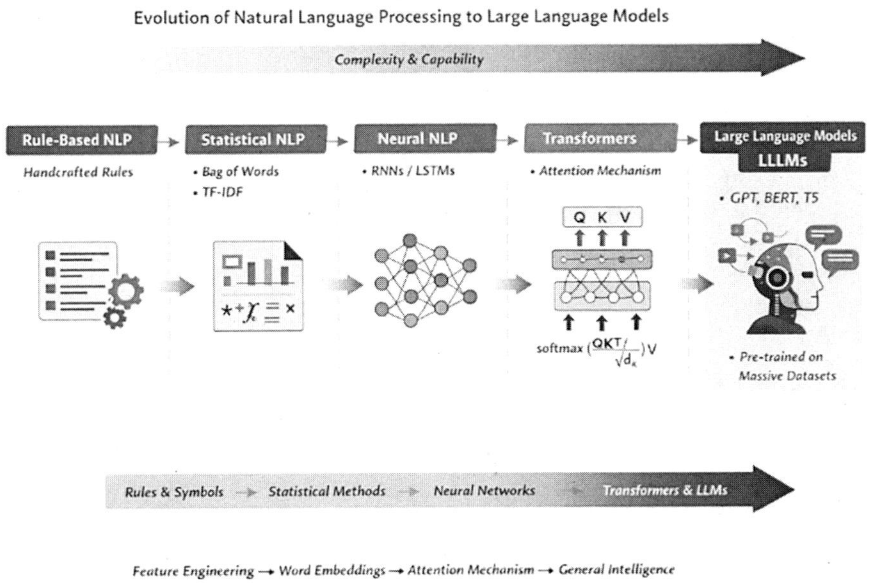

Figure 3.1: *Evolution of NLP to LLM.*

3.1.7 What is a Large Language Model (LLM)?

An LLM can be mathematically viewed as:

$$\text{LLM}(T, C) \rightarrow \text{Output}$$

where,

T = input text
C = context
Output = generated response

LLMs are trained using the objective:

$$P(w_t \mid w_1, ..., w_{t-1})$$

This is known as Next Token Prediction, the fundamental principle behind models like GPT.

3.1.8 NLP in the Era of LLMs

To date, NLP has gone beyond mere text processing and classic models. It has become the basis of:

- Chatbots
- Smart assistants
- Creation of content
- Information retrieval
- Code writing

Knowing conventional NLP ideas is still significant, but the main factor for modern NLP is the transformer-based LLMs.

Natural Language Processing has come a long way from basic rule-driven approaches to the very sophisticated Large Language Models that can understand and generate human-like text. This transition—from traditional means through neural networks and finally to transformers—has been one of the key features of modern AI-based language technology.

We will take a closer look at the technical foundations of LLMs in the next sections, starting with sequence models, transformers, and attention mechanisms.

3.2 SEQUENCE MODELS AND TRANSFORMERS

Language is essentially a sequential phenomenon at its core.

A sentence is not simply a random assortment of separate words—it has a hierarchical arrangement in which each word gets its meaning from the context provided by the previous and the next words. Thus, natural language processing necessitates the use of models that are capable of comprehending and retaining sequential dependencies.

This necessity led to the development of a type of model called sequence models.

3.2.1 What is Sequence Model?

Sequence models are basically machine learning models that are specifically created to work with the data that is ordered in such a way that:

- The order of elements is important
- The context of the previous elements has a great impact on the next ones
- The information has to be processed in a sequence

In the domain of Natural Language Processing, sequence models are trying to recognize patterns such as:

- Choosing the next word in a sentence
- Finding out how words relate to each other
- Getting long-term dependencies

For instance, in the above statement:

"The film which I saw yesterday was terrific."

The model must keep in mind that "terrific" is the attribute of "film," even if there are few words in between. This matter of relationships in between is the main issue of sequence modeling.

In NLP, sequence models attempt to learn the probability:

$$P(x_t \mid x_1, x_2, \ldots, x_{t-1})$$

This forms the mathematical basis of language modeling.

3.2.2 Traditional Sequence Models in NLP

Before the rise of Transformers, NLP systems primarily relied on three major architectures:

1. Recurrent Neural Networks (RNNs)
2. Long Short-Term Memory Networks (LSTMs)
3. Gated Recurrent Units (GRUs)

These models process text one token at a time, maintaining an internal memory (hidden state) that carries information forward.

Recurrent Neural Networks (RNNs)

RNNs were the first neural architectures specifically designed for sequential data. They process input sequentially and update their internal state at every step.

Mathematically:

$$h_t = f(W_h h_{t-1} + W_x x_t + b)$$

$$y_t = g(W_y h_t)$$

where,

x_t = input at time step t
h_t = hidden state
y_t = output

While RNNs introduced the idea of "memory" in neural networks, they had major practical problems:

- Difficulty in remembering long-term context
- Vanishing and exploding gradient issues
- Slow training due to sequential processing
- Poor performance on long sentences

LSTMs and GRUs—Improved Sequence Models

To overcome RNN limitations, more advanced gated models were introduced:

- LSTMs (Long Short-Term Memory)
- GRUs (Gated Recurrent Units)

LSTM Equations (Conceptual)

$$f_t = \sigma(W_f\ [h_{t-1}, x_t])$$
$$i_t = \sigma(W_i\ [h_{t-1}, x_t])$$
$$c_t = f_t * c_{t-1} + i_t * \tilde{c}_t$$

These models were able to:

- Retain information for longer durations
- Handle longer sentences better
- Reduce gradient problems

For many years, LSTMs became the backbone of NLP applications such as:

- Machine translation
- Speech recognition
- Text generation

3.2.3 The Need for a New Architecture

By around the middle of the decade 2010, Natural Language Processing had come to its limitation.

The scientists were in search of an architecture that would:

- Get the long-range dependencies
- Handle whole sequences simultaneously
- Possess high parallelization support
- Represent global context very well
- Be capable of working with extremely large datasets

This demand resulted in one of the most remarkable advancements in AI: Transformers

3.2.4 What are Transformers?

Transformers are a deep learning architecture introduced in 2017 through the paper:

"Attention is All You Need."

Unlike traditional sequence models, Transformers do not process text sequentially. Instead, they rely entirely on a mechanism called: Self-Attention.

Core Idea of Transformers

Rather than reading a sentence word by word, Transformers:

- Look at the entire sentence at once
- Learn relationships between all words simultaneously
- Understand global context directly
- Process data in parallel

This simple shift completely changed NLP.

EXAMPLE
Consider the sentence:

"The bank of the river was overflowing."

A Transformer can easily understand that:

- "bank" is related to "river"
- and not to finance

because it analyzes all words together and learns contextual relationships.

Traditional sequence models often failed at such disambiguation

3.2.5 Architecture of Transformers

At a high level, a Transformer consists of the following components as shown in Figure 3.2.

1. Input Tokenization
2. Token Embeddings
3. Positional Encoding
4. Self-Attention Layers
5. Feed-Forward Neural Networks
6. Normalization and Residual Connections

Why Positional Encoding?

Since Transformers process all words together, they do not inherently know the order of words.

To solve this, positional encodings are added so that the model understands:

- Which word came first
- Which came later
- The relative position of tokens

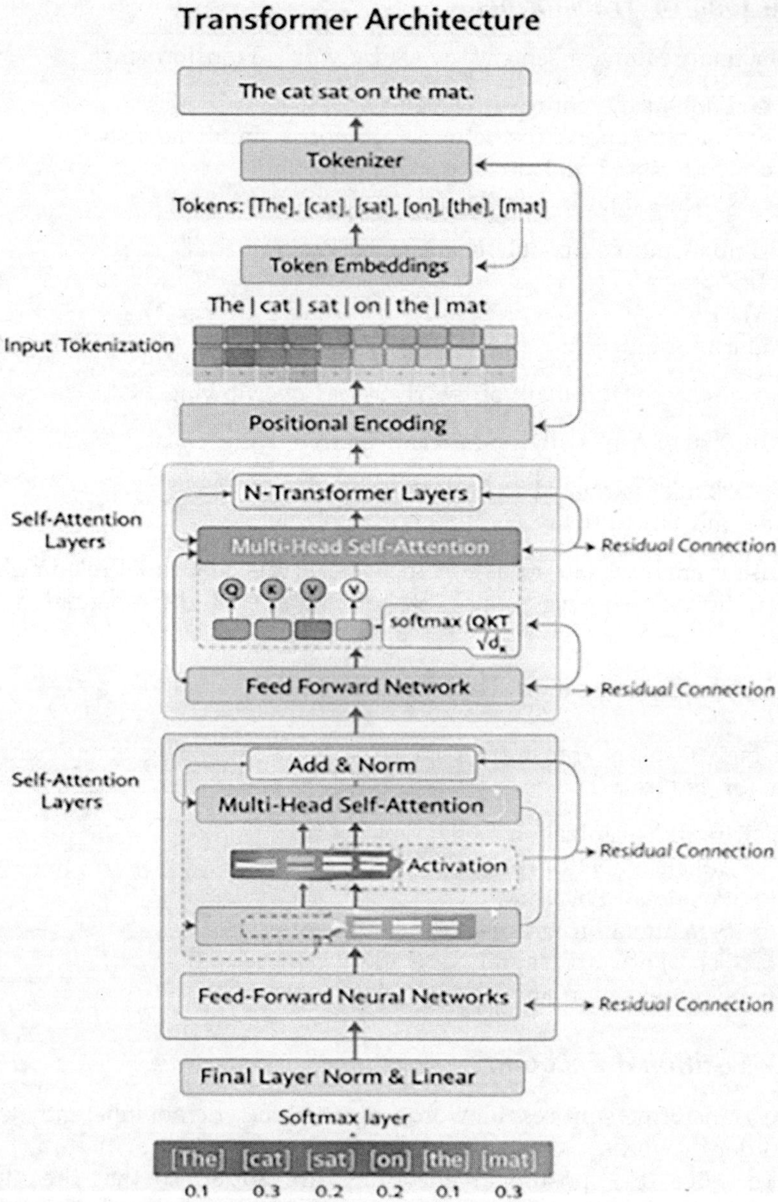

Figure 3.2: *Transformer Architecture.*

3.2.6 Sequence Model vs Transformer

This comparison explains why Transformers rapidly replaced older architectures in almost all NLP applications is shown in Table 3.1.

TABLE 3.1 Sequence model vs Transformer

Aspect	*Traditional Sequence Models*	*Transformers*
Processing Style	Word by word	Entire sequence together
Speed	Slow	Very fast
Parallelization	Difficult	Easy
Long Context	Weak	Strong
Scalability	Limited	Highly scalable
Current Usage	Rare	Industry standard

3.2.7 When to Use Transformer

When should Transformers be utilized as the best option?

- You have a requirement for processing big documents
- The comprehension of context is vital
- The datasets are huge
- The performance needs to be high
- The tasks are text generation or understanding

At present, Transformers are the driving force behind nearly every contemporary NLP system such as:

- ChatGPT
- Google Translator
- Tools for summarizing texts
- AI chatbots
- Systems for code generation

3.2.8 Real-World Examples

Some popular Transformer-based systems include:

- BERT—for text classification and search
- GPT models—for text generation
- T5 and BART—for summarization and translation
- Vision Transformers—for image processing
- Speech Transformers—for speech recognition

These examples show that Transformers are not limited to NLP—they are now a general-purpose AI architecture.

3.2.9 From Transformers to Large Language Models

Large Language Models (LLMs) are essentially:

Transformers Trained at Massive Scale

What changed from basic Transformers to LLMs:

- Huge training data
- Billions of parameters
- Large-scale computing
- Advanced training techniques

Thus, the journey has been:

Sequence Models → Transformers → Large Language Models

3.3 ATTENTION MECHANISM IN GENERATIVE AI

The attention mechanism is considered to be one of the most important conceptual innovations in modern machine learning and is at the heart of Generative Artificial Intelligence (GenAI) models like Transformers, BERT, and GPT, as well as other Large Language Models (LLMs). Attention, a widely used mechanism in modern AI, is responsible for the weakness of such models. It enables one to see the future by listening to the past.

The attention implementation in neural networks has a major effect on how long the token sequence is treated. In generative tasks like text creation, translating, shortening, and chat modeling, all input tokens do not have the same share of the final output. The attention mechanism settles this problem by giving the model the chance to concentrate on the information-rich tokens and to suppress the less relevant ones as shown in Figure 3.3. The ability to focus selectively is what allows today's models to deal with long-range dependencies, keep context coherence, and maintain semantic consistency throughout lengthy sequences.

3.3.1 Motivation for Attention in Generative Models

The aforementioned sequence-based architectures have been the Recurrent Neural Networks (RNNs) and their updated versions, Long Short-Term Memory (LSTM) networks, which have been compressing the entire input sequences into single fixed-length context vectors. The longer the input, the more significant the compression, leading to information loss and poor performance, particularly with long or difficult sequences.

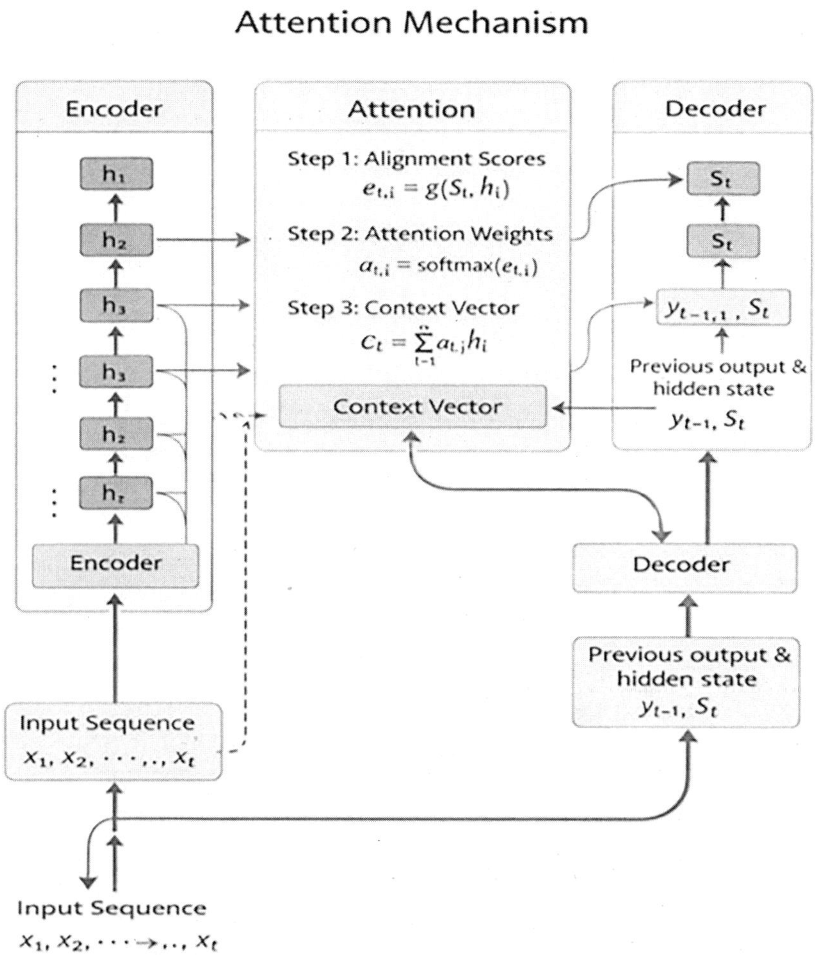

Figure 3.3: *Attention Mechanism.*

The attention mechanism, on the other hand, is able to do the following:

- To grant the entire input representations' unrestricted access to each generation step.
- To provide flexibility in context selection instead of frozen compression.
- To preserve gradient flow and learning stability.
- To make the model easier to interpret by showing which parts were given most attention via attention weights.

Gradually these points come together to create the situation where attention has become powerful and even essential in generative modeling and dealing with large-scale language comprehension.

3.3.2 Core Idea of Attention

The attention mechanism focuses on the alignment, which is weighted, between the elements of the input sequence and those of the output sequence. Rather than treating every token the same way, the model calculates the importance scores that measure how much the input token should impact the current output.

For this purpose, the model first creates three vectors from each input representation:

- Query (Q): It shows what the model is seeking at that moment.
- Key (K): It indicates the contribution of each input token.
- Value (V): It carries the information which will be combined.

These vectors are obtained through learned linear transformations:

$$Q = XW_Q,\ K = XW_K,\ V = XW_V$$

where, X is the input embedding matrix and W_Q, W_K, W_V are learnable parameters.

The degree of relevance between a query and the keys affects the value of the contextual representation formed by their combination.

3.3.3 Mathematical Formulation

Given query, key, and value matrices Q, K, and V, the attention operation is defined as:

$$\text{Attention}(Q, K, V) = \text{softmax}\left(\frac{QK^T}{\sqrt{d_k}}\right)V$$

where,

d_k is the dimensionality of the key vectors
The scaling factor stabilizes gradients
Softmax converts similarity scores into attention weights

This formulation forms the basis of self-attention used in Transformers and LLMs.

3.3.4 Self-Attention in Generative Models

Within self-attention, the query, key, and value vectors are all derived from one and the same sequence. This facilitates the attention of each token to all other tokens in the input, thus the model learns to recognize the internal dependencies within the whole sequence.

Self-attention plays a significant role in the case of generative AI due to the following reasons:

- It efficiently takes long-distance dependencies.
- It eliminates the sequential limitation of RNNs.
- It allows for complete parallelization during the training phase.

3.3.5 Multi-Head Attention

Instead of generating just a sole attention distribution, Transformer models perform multi-head attention, which is the case where there are several attention operations conducted concurrently in various representation subspaces:

$$\text{MultiHead}(Q, K, V) = \text{Concat}(\text{head1}, \ldots, \text{headh})\text{WO}$$

The different heads learn different relationships; thus, the model can capture the syntactic, semantic, and positional patterns together.

3.3.6 Attention in Encoder–Decoder Generative Models

In tasks of sequence-to-sequence generation like translation and summarization, attention acts as a bridge between the encoder and decoder:

- The encoder draws up concealed representations of the input sequence.
- Attention is utilized by the decoder to continuously choose applicable encoder states at every generation step.

The context vector created guarantees that the output tokens come from the input parts that are most relevant and not from a static summary representation.

3.3.7 Attention Mechanism Architecture

The classical attention mechanism is organized into three interacting components: Encoder, Attention Layer, and Decoder. Together, they enable dynamic context modeling and long-term dependency capture as shown in Figure 3.4.

1. *Encoder*

The encoder processes the input sequence $x_1, x_2, \ldots, x_T$ and transforms it into contextual hidden representations:

$$h_t = f(h_{t-1}, x_t)$$

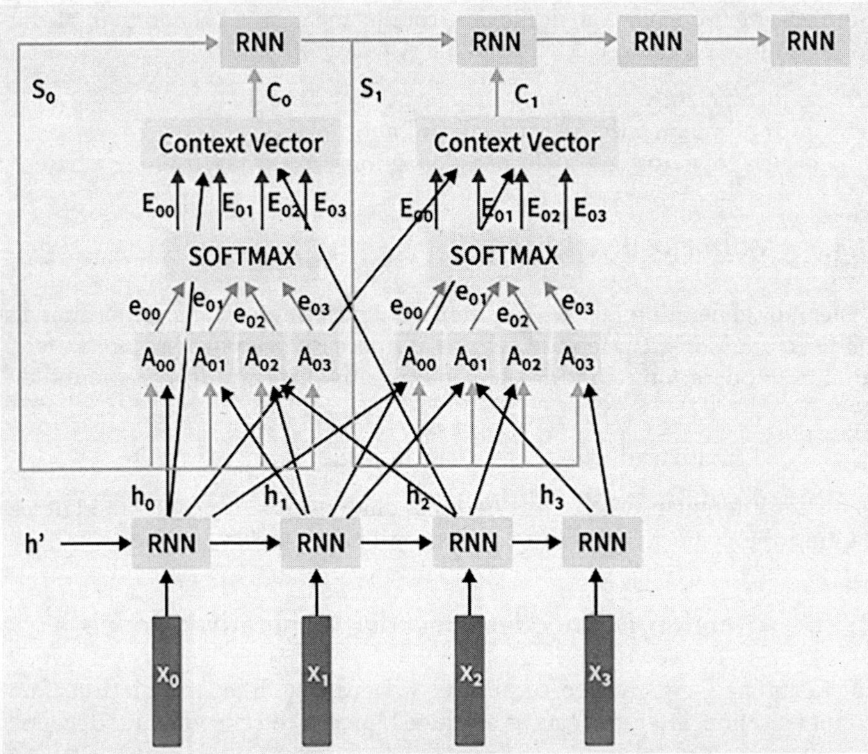

Figure 3.4: *Attention Mechanism Architecture.*

where,

h_t represents the hidden state at time step t

f may be an RNN, LSTM, GRU, or Transformer encoder

Each hidden state encodes both the current token and its surrounding context. These encoder outputs are forwarded to the attention layer.

2. *Attention Layer*

The attention layer determines which encoder states are most relevant for generating the current output token.

Step 1: Alignment Score Computation

$$e_{t,i} = g(S_t, h_i)$$

where,

S_t is the decoder hidden state

h_i is the encoder hidden state

g is a learnable alignment function

Step 2: Attention Weight Normalization

$$\alpha_{t,i} = \frac{\exp(e_{t,i})}{\sum_{k=1}^{T} \exp(e_{t,k})}$$

These weights represent the importance of each input token.

Step 3: Context Vector Formation

$$C_t = \sum_{i=1}^{T} \alpha_{t,i} h_i$$

The context vector dynamically summarizes the most relevant information from the input sequence.

3. *Decoder*

The decoder generates output tokens by combining:

- The previous output token
- The decoder hidden state
- The attention-derived context vector

$$y_t = \text{Decoder}\,(y_{t-1}, S_t, C_t)$$

This process repeats iteratively until the full output sequence is generated.

3.3.8 Role of Attention in Generative AI and LLMs

In the case of the Generative AI models, attention is an essential component and not an auxiliary one—that it is the fundamental computational mechanism of the system. Transformers use only self-attention networks stacked one on top of the other completely without any recurrence for modeling language.

Attention makes it possible to:

- Model the global context over long sequences
- Carry out parallel computation in the course of training
- Achieve very strong scalability with up to billions of parameters
- Gain better coherence in the produced text

The shift in architecture is the main reason for the success of the likes of GPT, BERT, T5 and other foundational models.

3.3.9 Advantages of Attention Mechanisms

- Models properly the dependencies of the long ranges.
- Eliminates the information bottlenecks that arise with fixed-length vectors.
- Improves interpretability by means of attention weights.
- Facilitates parallelization (as opposed to RNNs).
- Has a positive impact across NLP and multimodal tasks.

3.3.10 Limitations

- Complexity of computations that is quadratic in relation to the length of the sequence.
- Memory usage that is high with long inputs.
- Attention weights can lose their interpretability in extremely deep models.

The attention mechanism has fundamentally altered the way machines work with sequential data. Attention makes it possible for models to see through the human-like contextual understanding and at the same time, take advantages of fast and huge scale computation. Its adoption in the architecture of Transformers has altered the NLP to be geared towards Generative AI and Large Language Models, which is a significant change in the process of evolution.

3.4 TOKENIZATION AND EMBEDDINGS IN GENERATIVE AI

Tokenization and embeddings constitute the basic interface between human language and generative models. All Large Language Models (LLMs), such as GPT, BERT, and T5, depend on these two processes to change the raw text into a structured numerical representation that is then suitable for processing and generating by the neural networks.

In the case of generative AI, tokenization is the factor that determines what the model perceives, whereas embeddings are the factor that determines the model's comprehension of meaning.

3.4.1 Tokenization: Structuring Language for Models

Tokenization means breaking down raw text into little parts, which are then called tokens. These tokens are the smallest elements that statistical and artificial neural network models can work with. In contrast to humans, machines are not able to access text and therefore cannot process it the same way; they work with numbers that stand for each discrete symbol.

A token can embody:

- The entire word
- A part of the word
- A single character
- A sequence of bytes

Today, sub-word tokenization is the main method used in generative models because it does not only limit the size of the vocabulary but also ensures that the language can express meanings and that it can handle even unseen words is shown in Figure 3.5.

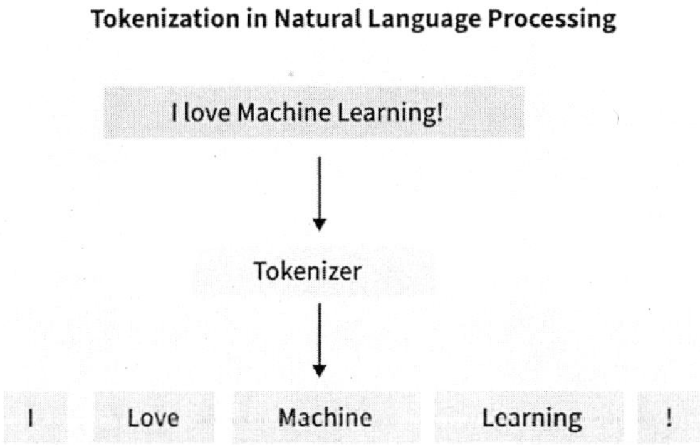

Figure 3.5: *Tokenization in NLP.*

3.4.2 Why Tokenization Matters in Generative AI

Tokenization has a direct impact on:

- Vocabulary size and memory consumption
- Model generalization for rare or non-existent words
- Training being stable and inference being efficient
- Output being fluent and controllable

If the tokenization is bad, the meaning will be fragmented, the sequences will be longer, and the quality of generation will be lower.

3.4.3 Tokenization as a Mathematical Mapping

Formally, tokenization can be viewed as a mapping:

$$\mathcal{T}: \mathcal{X} \rightarrow \{1, 2, \ldots, V\}$$

where,

$\mathcal{X}$ is the space of raw text

V is the vocabulary size

each token is assigned a unique integer index

A sentence such as:

Generative models learn language may be mapped to:

[1245, 982, 317, 2048]

These indices are not semantic by themselves; meaning emerges only after embedding.

3.4.4 Types of Tokenization

Types of Tokenization as shown Figure 3.6.

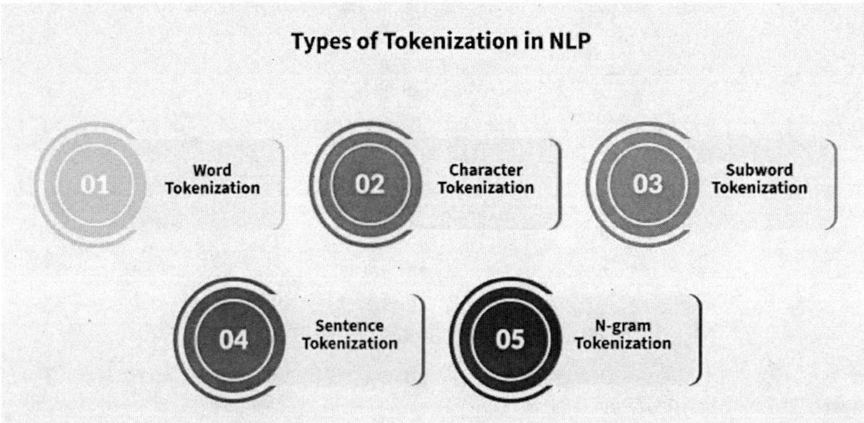

Figure 3.6: *Types of Tokenization.*

- **Word Tokenization:** The entire text is processed in such a way that each word is treated as a separate entity.
- **Character Tokenization:** The text is cut into pieces and transformed into a continuous line of single characters.
- **Sub-word Tokenization:** It takes the middle ground between word and character tokenization by splitting the text into pieces that are larger than one character but smaller than a whole word.
- **Sentence Tokenization:** It separates paragraphs or big sets of sentences into individual sentences which are then used as tokens.
- **N-gram Tokenization:** Words are broken down into parts of predetermined size (size = n), thus resulting in fixed-sized chunks.

3.4.5 Tokenization Strategies in Modern LLMs

Generative AI (GAI) or Generative Models systems predominantly apply data-driven tokenization techniques that are inclusive of the following as shown in Figure 3.7.

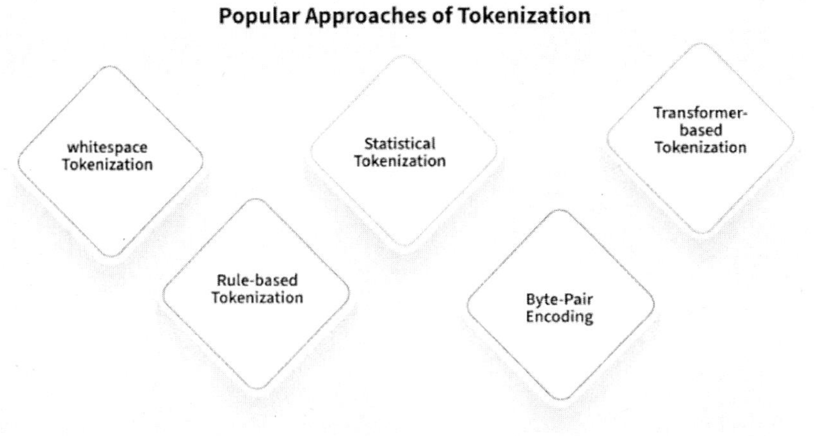

Figure 3.7: *Tokenization Strategies.*

- **BPE (Byte Pair Encoding):** It keeps on merging the widely used character pairs iteratively.
- **WordPiece:** It varies the likelihood of token sequences optimizing them.
- **SentencePiece:** It is language-independent, and its operation is directly on the raw text.
- **Byte-level tokenization:** It covers all the characters of the Unicode text.

All these methods enable the models to deal with:

- Uncommon words
- Texts in different languages
- Special vocabularies of specific domains

3.4.6 Embeddings: Representing Meaning Numerically

Once text is tokenized, each token is transformed into a dense numerical vector known as an embedding. Embeddings allow models to encode semantic, syntactic, and contextual relationships between tokens as shown in Figure 3.8.

An embedding map a discrete token ID to a continuous vector:

$$\varepsilon : \{1, \ldots, V\} \rightarrow \mathbb{R}^d$$

where,

V is vocabulary size

d is embedding dimension

Each token is represented as:

$$\mathbf{e}_t \in \mathbb{R}^d$$

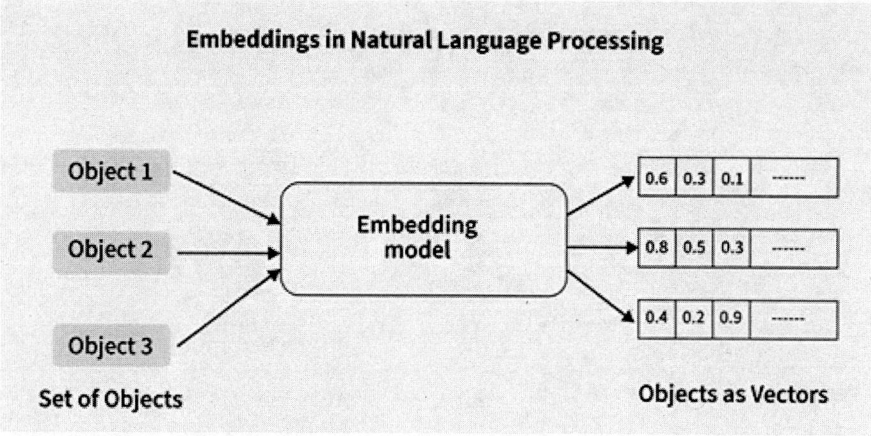

Figure 3.8: *Embedding in NLP.*

3.4.7 Why Embeddings are Critical for Generative Models

Models can be enabled by embeddings to (shown in Figure 3.9).

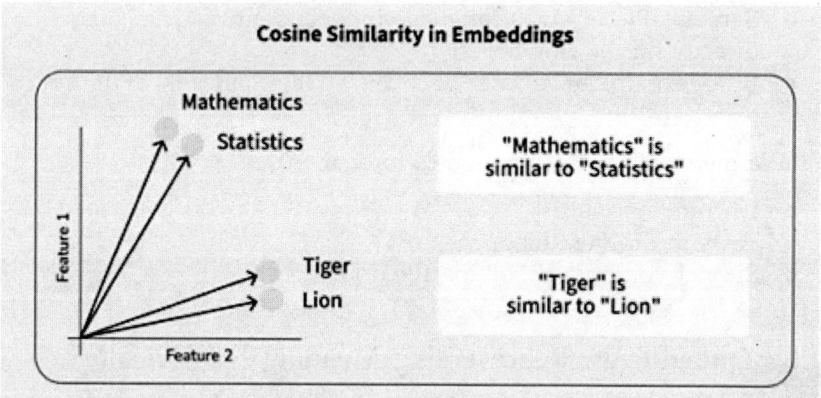

Figure 3.9: *Cosine Similarities in Embedding.*

- Seize the meaning similarity (e.g., king ≈ queen)
- Acquire grammatical structure
- Extend their learning across different situations
- Carry out gradual interpolation in latent space

In the case of generative AI, embeddings are the semantic foundation from which new text is produced.

3.4.8 From Static to Contextual Embeddings

Back in the day, static embeddings were the only option for NLP systems, so a specific and unique vector representation was used for each word. Generative models, on the other hand, exploit contextual embeddings, which change a token's representation according to the other tokens around it.

Conceptually,

$$\mathbf{e}_t = f(t, \text{context})$$

This really opens up the door for a word to convey multiple meanings depending on the context, which is imperative for consistent and logical generation.

3.4.9 Embeddings inside LLM Architectures

In transformer-based generative models:

1. Token IDs are mapped to embeddings
2. Positional information is added
3. The resulting vectors flow through attention and feed-forward layers.

Embeddings are learned jointly with the model, optimized to maximize the likelihood of generating correct next tokens.

3.4.10 Relationship between Tokenization and Embeddings

Tokenization and embeddings are tightly coupled:

Tokenization defines the *symbolic space*, while embeddings define the *semantic geometry* of language shown in Table 3.2.

TABLE 3.2 Tokenization vs Embedding

Aspect	*Tokenization*	*Embeddings*
Purpose	Structural decomposition	Semantic representation
Output	Discrete token IDs	Continuous vectors
Role	Defines input units	Encodes meaning
Context awareness	No	Yes (in LLMs)
Mandatory	Always	Essential for deep models

3.4.11 Importance in Generative AI Systems

In generative AI, tokenization and embeddings determine:

- What the model can generate
- How fluently it generates text
- How well it generalizes across domains
- How efficiently it scales

They are not preprocessing steps but core architectural components that shape the behavior and capabilities of the entire model.

Tokenization breaks down a language into its elements.

The process of creating embeddings translates the elements into meanings.

The two steps allow generative models to acquire, reason, and produce languages in a mathematically grounded and scalable way—thus, the real basis of today's Large Language Models.

3.5 TRAINING OBJECTIVES OF LARGE LANGUAGE MODELS

The training of Large Language Models (LLMs) is done with great care and through objectives that exceed the mere prediction of text. These objectives determine the model's learning, its generalization, and its expected performance in real-world application scenarios. It is necessary to be aware of these training aims for understanding the impressive performance of LLMs in various NLP and Generative AI tasks002E.

The goals for LLM training can be broadly summarized as the extraction of linguistic knowledge, reasoning power, and versatility from huge volumes of unstructured text data, all the while ensuring the models remain scalable and robust as shown in Figure 3.10.

3.5.1 Learning to Understand and Generate Human-Like Language

One of the main goals for an LLM is to represent natural language. The process of feeding large amounts of text into the model and letting it learn how to choose the most likely next token based on previous ones is quite simple but it does give the model a lot of implicit knowledge about:

- Grammar and syntax (sentence structure)
- Semantics (meaning of words and phrases)
- Pragmatics (context-dependent meaning)
- Discourse-level coherence (flow across sentences and paragraphs)

Through optimizing this objective for billions or trillions of tokens the model is able to produce fluent, coherent, and contextually appropriate text and so it can be used for applications like text generation, summarization, dialogue systems, and content creation.

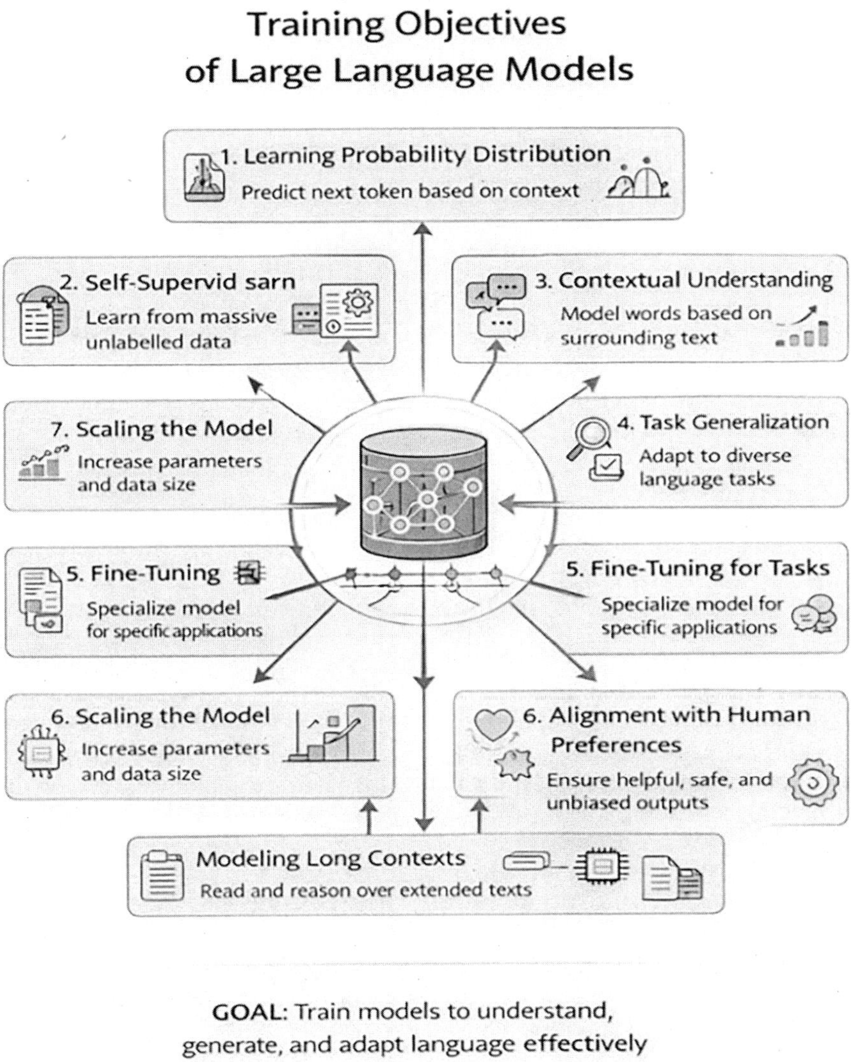

Figure 3.10: *Training Objectives of LLM.*

3.5.2 Capturing Linguistic Patterns, Semantics, and Context

Most of the time, LLMs undergo training with massive amounts of unlabelled text data from various sources, which include books, articles, code repositories, and web data. One of the main training purposes is implicitly to unearth linguistic statistical and semantic patterns.

The model, through this training, acquires:

- Word relationships and semantic similarity
- Syntactic dependencies even in very long sentences

- Contextual meaning of words (polysemy)
- Long-range dependencies across paragraphs or documents

In contrast to conventional NLP systems that depend on manually created rules or fixed features, LLMs automatically build up multi-layered language representations through learning, which rapidly enhances their flexibility and generality.

3.5.3 Generalization across Tasks through Pretraining

Task generalization is another crucial aim that is an integral part of the training of large language models (LLMs). They are not trained for one specific task but rather in a task-agnostic way and mostly at the beginning, which allows them to switch the learned knowledge to a lot of downstream applications.

This leads to:

- Zero-shot learning (doing tasks without being provided with explicit examples)
- Few-shot learning (having a small number of examples to learn from)
- Cross-domain adaptation (language, code, science, reasoning)

Thus, this very learning objective grants the power to transfer between different types of learning and makes LLMs the right choice for various tasks such as translation, question answering, sentiment analysis, reasoning, and code generation.

3.5.4 Task Adaptation through Fine-Tuning and Alignment

Pretraining gives LLMs a wide spectrum of linguistic knowledge, but they are still fine-tuned with task-optimized objectives to make them fit for particular tasks or behaviors.

These objectives consist of:

- Supervised fine-tuning with datasets specifically designed for the tasks
- Instruction tuning that enables the models to obey natural language commands
- Alignment objectives that aim at creating outputs that are helpful, safe and reliable
- Reinforcement learning from human feedback (RLHF)

Fine-tuning is the process that links the language comprehension of the models with their practical usability, making sure that the outputs of the models are in line with human requirements and the requirements of the application.

3.5.5 Learning Long-Context and Sequential Reasoning

One of the most important goals in the training of related contemporary LLMs is their capability to deal with long contexts. In contrast to previous models that could not do much with long inputs, the present LLMs are capable of not only processing but also retaining an understanding of thousands of tokens worth of information.

This goal is a major contributor to:

- Document-level understanding
- Multi-turn dialogue consistency
- Long-form reasoning and analysis
- Code and scientific text comprehension

Models like GPT-4 and Gemini 1.5 give high priority to this goal and thus become amazingly fit for very complex and real-life scenarios that require prolonged and precise awareness of the context.

3.5.6 Robustness, Reliability, and Deployment Readiness

The training objectives for LLMs include factors like performance, but robustness and stability come first as well. The model should manage inputs with noise, queries that are not clear, and partial information, all this without having a total failure.

When doing this, you need to:

- Cut down on the occurrences of hallucinations
- Enhance the consistency of facts
- Manage rare situations in a sophisticated way
- Show stable behavior when different prompts are used

All the listed objectives are very important for the use of LLMs in real-time systems like search engines, assistants, medical help, and enterprise software.

Putting together the training objectives of LLMs make it possible to develop models with the following features:

- Linguistically fluent and semantically rich
- Context-aware and capable of long-range reasoning
- General-purpose yet adaptable to specific tasks
- Scalable, robust, and deployment-ready

Instead of doing the training of LLMs for a specific task, they are trained as foundational models, which are the source that gives rise to many different AI applications, making them versatile and adaptable.

3.6 POPULAR ARCHITECTURES OF LARGE LANGUAGE MODELS (LLMS)

Large Language Models (LLMs) are algorithmically mainly dependent on the Transformer architecture which was introduced by Vaswani and colleagues in 2017. The present LLMs are of different scale, strategy of training and area of application but most of them belong to a few basic architectural categories. To comprehend today's generative AIs, it is very important to know such architectures as shown in Figure 3.11.

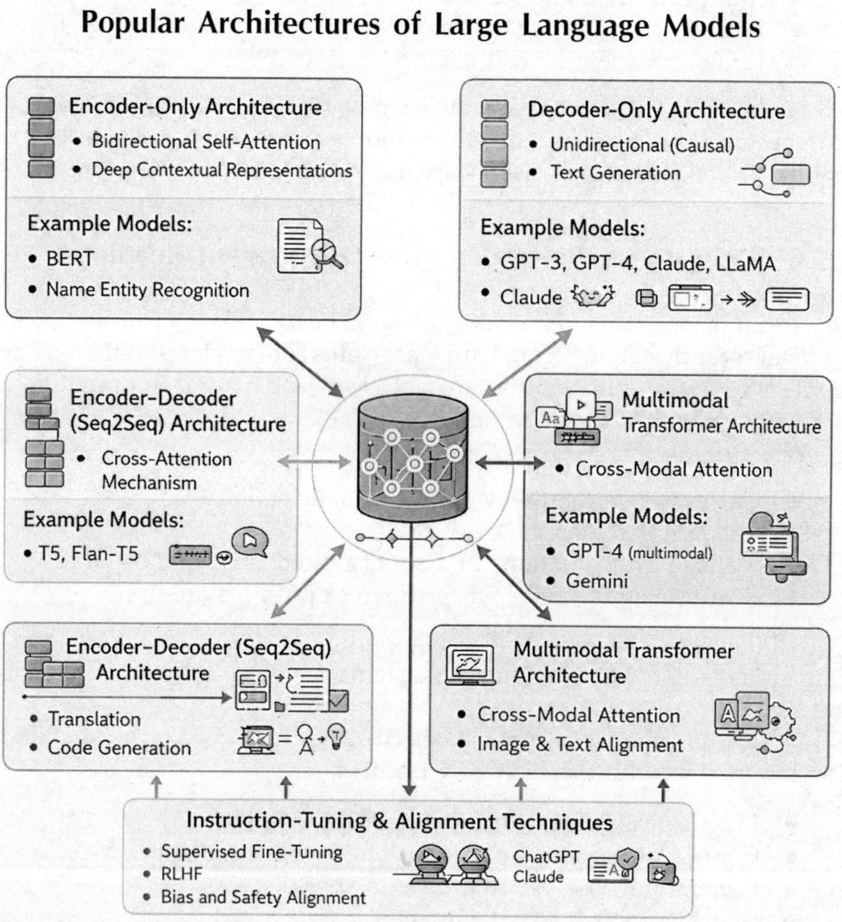

Figure 3.11: *Popular Architectures of LLM.*

This part of the study describes the LLM architectures that are most frequently used and are of greatest importance to academics, giving attention to their design philosophy, learning objectives and practical significance.

3.6.1 Encoder-Only Architecture

The Transformer encoder stack is what composes encoder-only models entirely. These models are intended to grasp the language instead of producing long sequences. They, however, create profound representations that are contextual in both directions and thus represent the text in a more meaningful way.

Key Characteristics

- Bidirectional self-attention (each token attends to both left and right context)
- Strong contextual embeddings
- Optimized for language understanding tasks

Representative Model

- BERT (Bidirectional Encoder Representations from Transformers)

Applications

- Text classification
- Named Entity Recognition (NER)
- Question answering (extractive)
- Sentiment analysis

Typically, encoder-only models are trained by means of Masked Language Modeling (MLM), during which certain input tokens are concealed, and the model is taught to guess their identity by means of the context that is surrounding them. This process makes it possible to develop a profound understanding of semantics but at the same time puts a restriction on the generation of text in a free-form manner.

3.6.2 Decoder-Only Architecture

The decoder-only models make use of the Transformer decoder exclusively and are fine-tuned for the autoregressive text production process. Such structures are the fundamental elements of the majority of today's generative AI applications.

Key Characteristics

- Unidirectional (causal) self-attention
- Predicts the next token given previous tokens
- Highly scalable

Representative Models

- GPT family (GPT-2, GPT-3, GPT-4)
- LLaMA
- Claude
- Falcon

Applications

- Text generation
- Code generation
- Chatbots and virtual assistants
- Creative writing and summarization

Decoder-only models are trained using next-token prediction, learning the probability distribution:

$$P(x_t \mid x_1, x_2, \ldots, x_{t-1})$$

This simple yet powerful objective allows these models to exhibit emergent abilities such as reasoning, in-context learning, and few-shot generalization when scaled to billions or trillions of parameters.

3.6.3 Encoder–Decoder Architecture (Seq2Seq Transformers)

Encoder–decoder models incorporate both the Transformer parts and are therefore very appropriate for the sequence-to-sequence tasks where the input and output structures differ.

Key Characteristics

- Encoder processes the input sequence
- Decoder generates output conditioned on encoder representations
- Explicit modeling of input–output alignment

Representative Models

- T5 (Text-to-Text Transfer Transformer)
- Flan-T5

Applications

- Machine translation
- Text summarization
- Question answering
- Text transformation tasks

These models are trained in a text-to-text format, where all tasks are framed as transforming one text sequence into another. This unified formulation simplifies multi-task learning and improves transferability across tasks.

3.6.4 Multimodal Transformer Architecture

The multimodal large language models (LLMs) provide a way of going beyond the traditional text-based model limitations and including the processing of various data modalities, e.g. images, sound, and video apart from text.

Key Characteristics

- Shared or aligned embedding spaces across modalities
- Cross-attention between modalities
- Unified reasoning across heterogeneous inputs

Representative Models

- GPT-4 (multimodal variant)
- Gemini
- PaLM-based multimodal systems

Applications

- Visual question answering
- Image captioning
- Multimodal reasoning
- Human–computer interaction systems

The foundation of multimodal models consists of the integration of modality-specific encoders and a central Transformer backbone. The application of attention mechanisms facilitates the alignment of visual or audio features with the corresponding linguistic tokens, thus resulting in a deeper semantic comprehension.

3.6.5 Instruction-Tuned and Aligned Architectures

Beyond raw architecture, modern LLMs are enhanced through instruction tuning and alignment techniques, which significantly improve usability and safety.

Key Techniques

- Supervised fine-tuning on instruction datasets
- Reinforcement Learning from Human Feedback (RLHF)
- Preference optimization

Representative Models

- ChatGPT
- InstructGPT
- Claude

These techniques do not change the core architecture but reshape the model's behavior, making outputs more helpful, truthful, and aligned with human intent.

3.6.6 Architectural Comparison Summary

What primarily distinguishes modern large language models is not only the number of their parameters but also the design of their architectures, which significantly influence the processing, representation, and generation of information as shown in Table 3.3. It is through the study of these ground architectural paradigms that the students and researchers get the basic and solid ground for exploring advanced topics such as scaling laws, prompt engineering, fine-tuning strategies, and multimodal AI systems.

TABLE 3.3 Architectural Comparison Summary

Architecture Type	*Primary Goal*	*Typical Models*	*Strength*
Encoder-only	Language understanding	BERT	Deep contextual embeddings
Decoder-only	Text generation	GPT, LLaMA	Scalable generative power
Encoder–decoder	Seq2Seq tasks	T5	Structured text transformation
Multimodal	Cross-modal reasoning	GPT-4, Gemini	Unified multimodal intelligence
Aligned models	Safe and helpful AI	ChatGPT	Human-centered interaction

This architectural viewpoint has also made it easier to see the reason for different LLMs triumphing in different tasks even though a common Transformer backbone connects them.

3.7 LIMITATIONS AND RISKS OF LARGE LANGUAGE MODELS

Large Language Models (LLMs) and Generative AI systems show great success in various natural language processing tasks but have several basic limitations which need to be thoroughly understood before the widespread usage. These limitations are due to architecture, training, deployment, and ethical issues. A detailed analysis of these matters is important for both the researchers and the practitioners who work with LLM-based systems as shown in Figure 3.12.

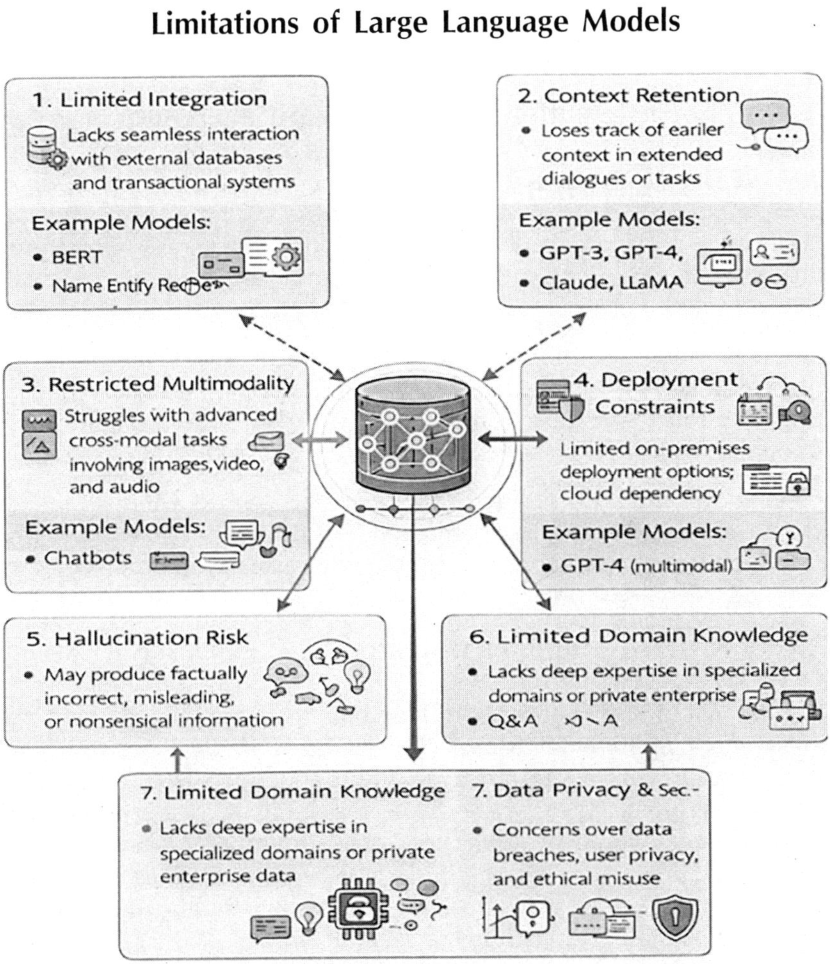

Figure 3.12: *Limitation of Large Language Models (LLMs).*

3.7.1 Limited Integration with External and Transactional Systems

The LLMs are mainly created as stateless text generators and do not come with the direct interaction with the transactional or operational systems (like databases, payment gateways, ERP tools, or real-time workflow engines) as a feature. As a consequence, activities that demand state control, data coherence, or transactional reliability are left out of the main functionality of LLMs.

The above-mentioned restriction seriously limits the areas of application of LLMs in the e-commerce, banking, and enterprise customer support sectors, where complete automation of the process from beginning to end is a must. Indeed, by generating instructions or responses, the LLMs will still look for the external orchestration layer or API to act out the world actions, thus increasing the overall system complexity and the risk of failure at several points.

3.7.2 Context Retention and Long-term Coherence

Today, LLMs are up to the task of dealing with the expanded input sequences but still are not so good at maintaining long-term contextual consistency, especially when it comes to prolonged dialogues or multi-step reasoning tasks. The longer the context window is the more the earlier information may fade away and thus have no effect:

- Repetition of information that has already been stated
- Inconsistent replies
- Key constraints that were introduced earlier in the communication may be lost.

The above limitation is due to the restricted context window and the stochastic nature of next-token prediction which does not guarantee either persistent memory or symbolic reasoning over extensive periods.

3.7.3 Restricted Multimodal Reasoning Capabilities

The traditional LLMs are mainly text-based models. Even though there have been advances, multimodal extension still remains a hard problem when it comes to reasoning across text, images, audio, and video. Deep cross-modal understanding—is an area where visual reasoning, spatial interpretation, or audio-context alignment—tasks still suffer from inaccuracies.

This limitation makes it hard for LLMs to be used in places like medical imaging, autonomous systems, fashion design, and multimedia analytics, where non-textual information is the main actor.

3.7.4 Deployment Constraints and Infrastructure Dependence

The majority of the leading-edge LLMs are available only as cloud services, with little or no possibility of on-site deployment. This situation is difficult

for which regulatory, compliance, or data sovereignty requirements are strict and organizations impact those fields along with industry regulation.

Data control in terms of storage, processing and usage is the main concern in healthcare, finance, and defence industries. Therefore, the unavailability of a self-hosted deployment option can slow down LLM acceptance in sensitive or regulated environments.

3.7.5 Reliability, Hallucination and Factual Accuracy

LLMs do not use validated knowledge bases to output but pick their results based on the statistical patterns derived from large corpora. They cause hallucinations, which are the fluent, but factually incorrect or misleading responses, when they are not the whole picture.

This shortcoming is most pronounced in high-stakes sectors such as:

- Legal advisory systems
- Medical decision support
- Scientific research assistance

Since LLMs lack built-in truth verification or real-time knowledge validation capabilities, their outputs will still need to be monitored closely and we will be relying on external verification systems to strengthen their reliability.

3.7.6 Limited Domain and Enterprise-specific Knowledge

It is true that LLMs can generalize quite well across rather different domains, but they still tend to be somewhat shallow in terms of the specific domain knowledge, as well as in understanding of an organization's-specific policies, workflows, and even proprietary data. Once again, without fine-tuning or retrieval-augmented mechanisms, LLMs find it difficult to cater to specialized enterprise use cases that require contextual knowledge beyond what is generally available in public training data.

Thus, the limitation serves as a reminder of the importance of not just relying on LLMs, but rather, combining them with domain adaptation techniques, private knowledge bases, or task-specific models.

3.7.7 Data Privacy, Security, and Ethical Risks

The use of Large Language Models (LLMs) that require extensive data access for training and inference operation is bound to raise the issue of data privacy, security, and even misuse. Apart from that, using cloud-based deployment models can also lead to the risks of data being exposed to unauthorized persons, breaching compliance, and suffering attacks from adversaries.

Moreover, LLMs might have the unintended consequence of perpetuating the biases that exist in the training data, creating toxic content, or even being used as a tool for either misinformation or disinformation campaigns. To deal with such risks, the application of strong governance frameworks, alignment techniques, and human-in-the-loop monitoring systems is required.

3.7.8 Summary of Limitations

In conclusion, Large Language Models (LLMs) although a revolutionary development in artificial intelligence are not a one-size-fits-all solution. The areas where they fall short like integration, contextual reasoning, multimodality, deployment flexibility, accuracy, domain specificity, and security not only highlight the necessity of hybrid AI architectures but also point out that LLMs should be integrated with rule-based systems, knowledge graphs, retrieval engines, and domain-specific models.

To be able to come up with trustworthy, ethical, and scalable AI systems for real-world applications, the constraints imposed by the technology have to be perfectly understood.

TEST YOUR KNOWLEDGE

1. Why does next-token prediction enable emergent abilities such as in-context learning and reasoning, even though the objective itself is statistically simple?
2. Explain why transformers do not inherently understand word order and how positional encoding compensates for this limitation without introducing recurrence.
3. Compare encoder-only and decoder-only architectures from a representation learning perspective rather than from task usage.
4. Why do attention mechanisms scale quadratically with sequence length, and what fundamental trade-offs does this impose on long-context modeling?
5. How does contextual embedding fundamentally differ from static embedding in terms of semantic representation, and why is this difference critical for generative coherence?
6. In what ways does tokenization influence not only vocabulary size but also the reasoning capability and bias behavior of an LLM?
7. Why are LLMs prone to hallucinations despite being trained on massive and diverse datasets, and why does scaling alone not fully solve this issue?

8. Explain why LLMs struggle with long-term consistency in multi-turn dialogues even when the full conversation is within the context window.
9. From an architectural standpoint, why are LLMs considered stateless systems, and how does this impact their integration with real-world transactional applications?
10. Why is attention considered the *core* computational primitive of transformers rather than just an optimization over recurrent models?

CHAPTER 4

Prompt Engineering and LLM Interaction

The focus of prior chapters was primarily on the internal aspects of Large Language Models (LLMs) and, in this chapter, the user engagement and control via prompt engineering will be discussed. Prompt engineering is the input instruction structured design that controls the model's behavior and allows it to do many different things without explicit retraining.

New LLMs are capable of performing the new tasks just by using the well-crafted prompts; the zero-shot and few-shot learning are consequently introduced. These techniques allow one to build up models that can generalize with very few or even no task-specific data. This chapter also deals with Chain-of-Thought reasoning, which offers logical consistency through the promotion of step-by-step reasoning, and instruction tuning, which makes model outputs compatible with human intent.

Moreover, the practical prompt design strategies will be discussed along with handling hallucinations methods and prompt effectiveness evaluation. The combination of these topics leads to a formal understanding of how prompt engineering acts as an important interface between human requirements and LLM capabilities. Thus, it is indispensable for the person working with generative AI systems to master this skill.

4.1 CONCEPTS OF PROMPT

Large Language Models (LLMs) are not fully automated systems, but rather their actions are primarily influenced by the user's input or prompt. A prompt is the most important medium to transfer human's will to the model. LLMs behave in a probabilistic manner to natural language input, thus making prompt a very important factor in determining model performance, a total opposite of traditional software systems which are governed by strict rules or clear algorithms.

Theoretically speaking, a prompt is a formalized text input that exerts control over the model's creation process. It tells what to do, how to do it and what the output will look like. As LLMs are trained to produce the next token based on previous context, even slight variations in phrasing of the prompt can result in major differences in the quality of the output produced.

Prompt Engineering can thus be characterized as the technique of creating, improving, and testing prompts to draw out the correct, clear, and corresponding to task responses from large language models—through just changing the parameters of the model as shown in Figure 4.1.

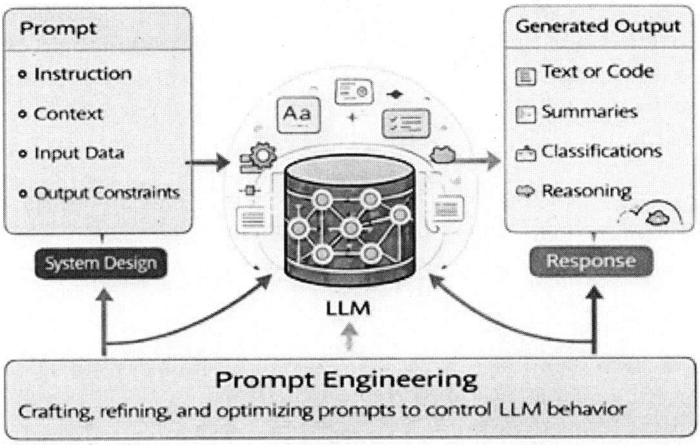

Figure 4.1 *Concept of Prompt Engineering.*

4.1.1 Functional Role of Prompts in LLMs

An LLM works like three people when a prompt is put into it:

Task Specification

The prompt specifies the task which is to be executed and it can be any of the following: summarization, translation, reasoning, code generation, or question answering. Learning systems do not have to be LLM-specified to be retrained; rather, the task is directly inferred from the prompt.

Context Conditioning

Prompts act as the model's and provide context that narrows down the response. This context can be background knowledge, assumptions, constraints, or prior conversation history. Good context conditioning diminishes the overlooking of the main point and raises the relevance, particularly in complicated or multi-step tasks.

Output Guidance

Prompts can really determine output in any way such as requiring bullet points, mathematical derivations, pseudocode, or even formal explanations.

This enables LLMs to change their responses according to the setting which could be academic, industrial, or conversational.

4.1.2 Core Components of a Prompt

From a system-design standpoint, a prompt that is well-structured usually contains the following elements:

- **Instruction:** The instruction expresses the goal of the task. Instructions that are clear and to the point diminish the difference in model outputs and increase reproducibility.
  Example: "Describe the transformer architecture focusing on self-attention."
- **Context:** Context gives necessary background information that the model is to take into account when creating the answer. This is particularly significant when working with domain-specific or restricted knowledge.
- **Input Data:** Input data is the term for the particular material that the model is to handle, which may be in the form of text passages, tables, code snippets, or datasets.
- **Output Specification:** This part of the prompt specifies the format of the response or the criteria for evaluation. Having clear output specifications makes the process easier and lessens the need for post-processing.

As a result, these elements work together to turn a prompt from a mere question into a powerful but simple programming interface for LLMs.

4.1.3 Prompts as a Control Mechanism

To speak more broadly, the prompts are the control over the pretrained models. Considering that the parameters of the LLM are not changed during inference, prompts are the only means through which the model's run-time behavior can be changed. Consequently, prompt engineering is likened to programming with natural language, with prompts serving as soft constraints that guide the model's internal representations towards the desired results.

This change in thinking—from parameter tuning to prompt-driven control—constitutes the basis for the development of such innovative methods as zero-shot learning, few-shot learning, and reasoning-based prompting, which are discussed in the subsequent sections of this chapter.

4.1.4 Prompt Engineering as a Control Paradigm

Prompt Engineering has changed the way intelligence is controlled in AI systems and represents a new paradigm. Model weights are not altered by retraining or fine-tuning, but rather users control the model's behavior through natural language inputs that are carefully crafted. This new method allows for quick and easy adjustments, lower power consumption, and the simultaneous use of the technology in different areas.

The use of LLMs is on the rise and their scaling up making them more powerful thus effective prompt engineering is a must for getting the most out of them. To direct more sophisticated prompting strategies—e.g., zero-shot learning, few-shot learning, reasoning-based prompts, and instruction tuning—building upon the very basic concepts presented in this section and discussing them in the following sections of this chapter.

4.2 ZERO-SHOT AND FEW-SHOT PROMPTING IN LARGE LANGUAGE MODELS

Zero-shot and few-shot prompting serve as the basic interaction paradigms that allow Large Language Models (LLMs) to apply their knowledge to new tasks during inference. These methods, in contrast to conventional supervised learning paradigms, take advantage of the pre-trained representational capacity of LLMs, as well as their ability to do in-context learning, where comprehension of the task develops through the prompt and not through parameter updates as shown in Figure 4.2.

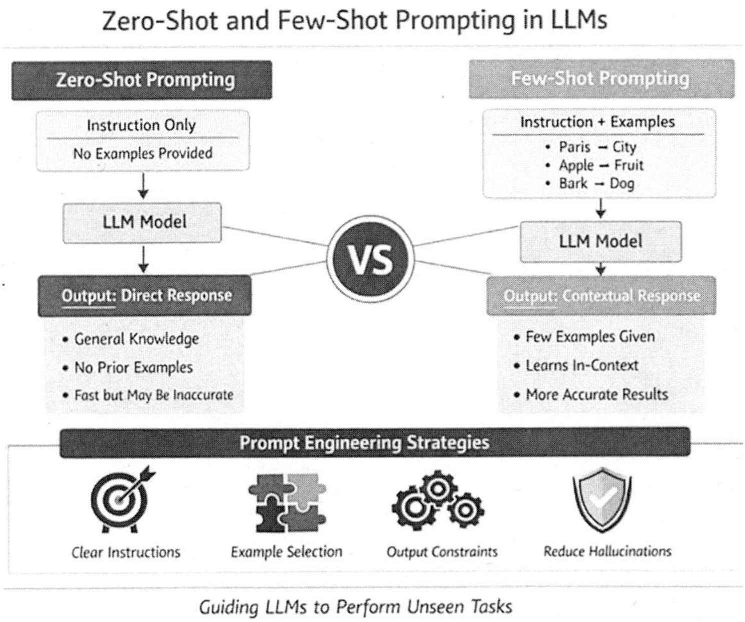

Figure 4.2 *Zero shot and Few Shot Learning.*

Moreover, these techniques are based on the transformer's self-attention mechanism, which makes it possible for the model to discover the patterns, commands, and relations among the tokens present in the prompt and then convert them into a probabilistic output distribution.

4.2.1 Zero-Shot Prompting

Zero-shot prompting signifies the capability of a large language model (LLM) to complete an assignment without being given any instance of that assignment in the prompt. The model solely depends on its pre-trained understanding, which was acquired through vast corpora, and the explicitness of the instruction given.

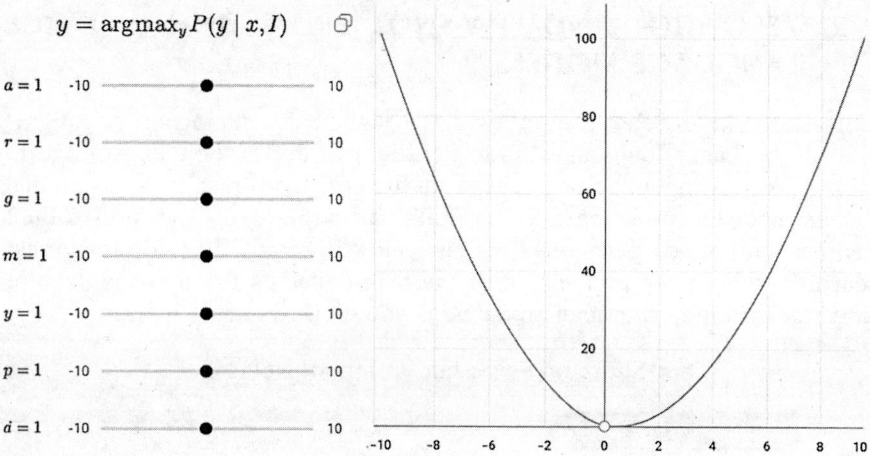

Figure 4.3 *Zero Shot Prompting.*

In the case of zero-shot prompting, the model is given solely the task instructions without any demonstration. The effectiveness of zero-shot prompting is primarily determined by the degree to which the instruction corresponds to the patterns the model came across during pretraining.

Formally, for an input x and instruction I, the model estimates:

$$P(y \mid x, I) = \prod_{t=1}^{T} P(y_t \mid y_{<t}, x, I)$$

where,

x represents the task input (e.g., a sentence),
I represents the instruction defining the task,
$P(y \mid x, I)$ is the conditional probability learned during pretraining.

This formulation highlights that:

- The instruction I becomes part of the conditioning context.
- Any ambiguity in I propagates through the entire generation process.

Key Insight

Zero-shot prompting works best when:

- The task is semantically common (classification, summarization, explanation).
- The instruction is explicit, constrained, and unambiguous.

However, as task complexity increases, the model may:

- Hallucinate unsupported facts
- Misinterpret task boundaries
- Produce inconsistent outputs across runs

Practical Example

In the case of sentiment classification, a zero-shot prompt could be:

Identify the sentiment of the text below as Positive, Negative, or Neutral:

"I had a wonderful day at the beach."

Even though the LLM was not specifically trained on this classification task, it applies its general knowledge of language and sentiment to come up with the right label.

Strengths

- Need not prepare any example
- Very resource-saving
- Ideal for quick prototyping and exploratory tasks

Limitations

- For complex, ambiguous, or very specific tasks, performance gets worse
- Depends on the wording of the instructions
- Has lower consistency compared to methods guided by examples

4.2.2 Few-Shot Prompting: In-Context Learning Dynamics

The implicit supervision comes from the examples that are directly embedded in the prompt and the few-shot prompting provides it to the model. The crucial point is that the model does not acquire new parameters; rather, by recognizing the statistical patterns in the given examples, it derives the task. Basically, few-shot prompting is a pattern of providing the model with a small number of inputs–output examples before the actual query that will make task performance better. The model is then indirectly shown how the task is done, thus leading it towards the expected reasoning pattern and output format as shown in Figure 4.4.

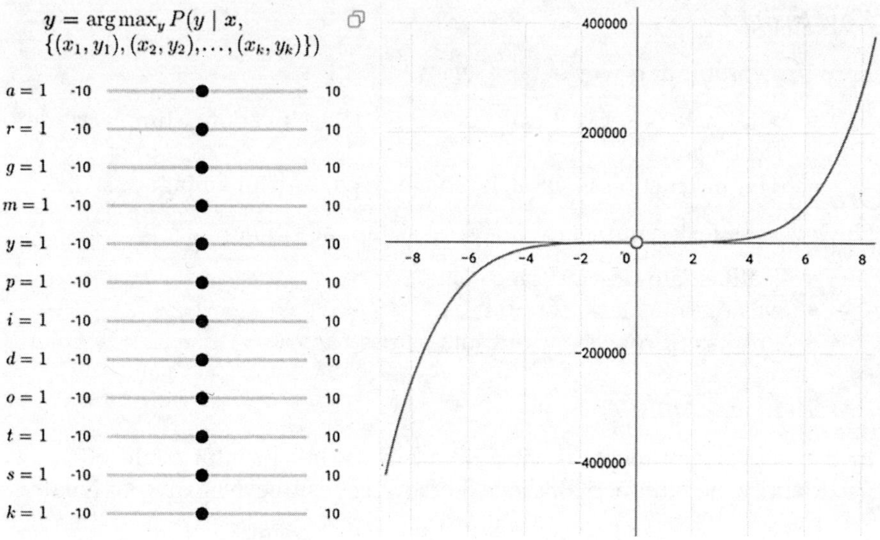

Figure 4.4: *Few Shot Prompting.*

Given a set of demonstrations $D = \{(x_1, y_1), \ldots, (x_k, y_k)\}$, prediction becomes:

$$y^* = \arg\max_y P(y \mid x, D)$$

where,

(x_1, y_1) are example input–output pairs (shots),
k is typically small (1–10),
No parameter updates occur; learning is purely contextual.

Just to clarify, you are using a few-shot sentiment prompt for classification.

Here are the text samples with their corresponding sentiments:

- Text: "It was the worst movie I've ever seen." → Sentiment: Negative
- Text: "What an incredible performance!" → Sentiment: Positive
- Text: "It was okay, nothing special." → Sentiment: Neutral

Now classify: "I could not have asked for a better vacation."

With the help of the examples, the model learns the task structure and label mapping, hence it is capable of making more accurate predictions.

The Reason behind Few-Shot Working

Few-shot prompting makes use of LLM's in-context learning capacity, where the transformer architecture through attention mechanisms recognizes patterns and relationships among the examples without any weight's adjustment.

From a transformer perspective:

- Examples influence attention weights
- Output tokens are conditioned on pattern repetition
- Label consistency reinforces task mapping

Ordering Effect

Empirical studies show that:

- Example order affects performance
- Recent examples receive higher attention
- Contradictory examples degrade output quality

Strengths

- More accurate and stable predictions
- Output format more controlled
- Wide domain-specific applications

Drawbacks

- The accuracy of the performance is highly dependent on the quality and order of the provided examples
- Restricted by the size of context window
- If poor examples are given, the model may be misled

4.2.3 Failure Modes in Zero-Shot and Few-Shot Prompting

Despite their power, both prompting approaches suffer from systematic weaknesses:

- Instruction underspecification → vague outputs
- Example bias → overfitting to demonstration patterns
- Context window limits → truncation of important examples
- Semantic drift → gradual deviation from task intent

These limitations motivate structured prompt engineering strategies, discussed next.

4.2.4 Prompt Engineering Strategies for Zero-Shot and Few-Shot Prompting

The skill of prompt engineering is the very painstaking and systematic design of prompts to gain the maximum trustworthiness, correctness, and controllability of the model. In the case of zero-shot and few-shot settings, prompt engineering can be considered as an alternative to the model fine-tuning technique.

Clarity of Instructions and Designation of Responsibility

Stating the model's role in a clear-cut way enhances the alignment of the task with the model:

"You are a data analyst. Conduct an analysis of the text below, then classify the sentiment..."

This method reduces the range of possible outputs by encouraging the activation of domain-relevant representations that were learned during pretraining.

Task Decomposition

Complex tasks should be decomposed into smaller reasoning steps:

$$\text{Task} \rightarrow \{\text{Subtask}_1, \text{Subtask}_2, \ldots\}$$

This reduces cognitive load on the model and minimizes hallucination, especially in zero-shot scenarios.

Example Selection in Few-Shot Prompts

The most effective few-shot examples should exhibit the following qualities:

- They should truly represent the actual inputs;
- They should be varied in terms of edge cases;
- They should have the same format and labeling throughout.

The use of badly-selected examples leads to example-induced bias, a situation where the model gives preference to the structure of the demonstration rather than the correctness of the task.

Output Constraints and Formatting Control

The imposition of output constraints serves to heighten determinism:

"Answer using just one word: Positive, Negative, or Neutral."

In mathematical terms, constraints lead to the reduction of the effective output space:

$$Y' \subset Y$$

resulting in better precision and more seamless integration in downstream applications.

Temperature and Sampling Control

While not part of the textual prompt, decoding parameters interact with prompt design:

- Low temperature → deterministic outputs
- High temperature → creative but unstable outputs

Prompt engineering must consider both prompt content and generation settings.

Defensive Prompting to Reduce Hallucinations

Prompts can explicitly discourage fabrication:

"If the answer is unknown, respond with 'Insufficient information'."

This strategy shifts probability mass away from unsupported generations and improves trustworthiness.

4.2.5 Conceptual Difference from Classical Few-Shot Learning

It is important to distinguish few-shot prompting in LLMs from few-shot learning in traditional machine learning as shown in Table 4.1.

TABLE 4.1 Few Shot Learning LLM vs ML.

Aspect	*Few-Shot Prompting (LLMs)*	*Few-Shot Learning (ML)*
Learning type	In-context	Parameter update
Model training	No retraining	Requires training
Data usage	Prompt examples	Support and query sets
Computation	Inference-time	Training-time

In classical few-shot learning, a support set S and query set Q are used, often relying on similarity metrics such as cosine similarity:

$$\text{sim}(x_q, x_s) = \frac{x_q \cdot x_s}{\| x_q \| \, \| x_s \|}$$

In contrast, LLM few-shot prompting embeds examples directly into the prompt, enabling task adaptation without explicit similarity computation.

4.2.6 Practical Significance in Real-World Applications

Zero-shot and few-shot prompting significantly reduce the need for expensive fine-tuning, making LLMs practical for real-world deployment in:

- **Healthcare:** Rare disease classification with limited annotations.
- **Cybersecurity:** Detection of novel attack patterns.
- **Customer Support:** Intent classification without retraining.
- **Data Analytics:** Ad-hoc text analysis and summarization.
- **Education:** Personalized content generation.

These techniques demonstrate how LLMs transfer general linguistic knowledge to new tasks efficiently, making them a cornerstone of modern Generative AI systems.

4.3 CHAIN-OF-THOUGHT REASONING

The use of Large Language Models (LLMs) in various complicated tasks such as logical reasoning, multi-step problem solving, code generation, and analytical decision-making is increasing; thus, the inadequacy of direct question-answer prompting has become a clear issue. LLMs might yield smooth and coherent answers; however, their answers could be logically inconsistent, opaque, or weak when the tasks skilled reasoning.

Chain-of-Thought (CoT) reasoning solves this problem and allows the models to break down the main issue into minor reasoning steps that eventually lead to the final solution. Instead of considering reasoning as a latent mental activity, CoT prompting reveals the entire reasoning process, thus enhancing the accuracy, interpretability, and reliability as shown in Figure 4.5.

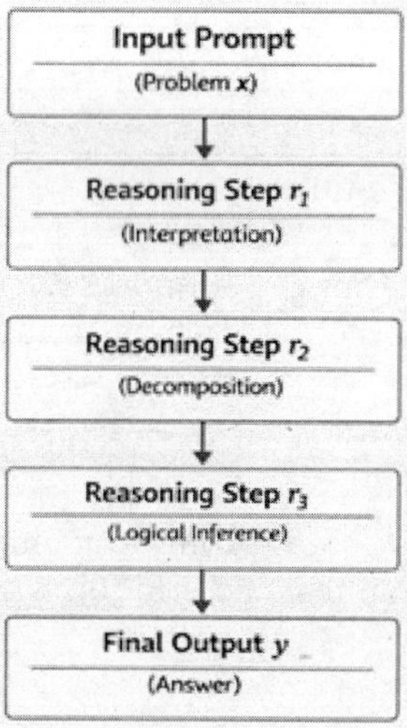

Figure 4.5: *Chain of Thought Reasoning.*

4.3.1 Concept of Chain-of-Thought Reasoning

Chain-of-Thought reasoning is a prompting approach where the large language model (LLM) is directed to create the intermediate reasoning steps which logically connect the problem statement with the final answer.

In traditional prompting only:

- The model directly maps an input to an output.
- Reasoning is still implicit and not clear.

In CoT prompting:

- The model gets encouraged to verbalize a series of logical steps.
- Each step is based on the previous one, and together they create a reasoning chain that is clear.
- The final answer is reached easily through this structured procedure.

This method is very similar to the way humans deal with analytical problems—they don't just give the answer straight away but they reason by taking one step at a time.

4.3.2 Formal Definition

Let an input problem be represented as:

$$x = (x_1, x_2, \ldots, x_n)$$

and the desired output as:

$$y$$

Traditional prompting models the conditional probability directly as:*

$$P(y \mid x)$$

In Chain-of-Thought prompting, reasoning steps are introduced as latent variables:

$$r = (r_1, r_2, \ldots, r_k)$$

The model instead learns to generate:

$$P(y, r \mid x) = P(y \mid r, x) \cdot P(r \mid x)$$

This decomposition encourages the model to:

- First generate a valid reasoning sequence r
- Then derive the final answer from that reasoning

4.3.3 Why Chain-of-Thought Works

In terms of modeling, CoT takes advantage of the huge training data that modern LLMs are exposed to, which consists of explanations, proofs, tutorials, and stepwise solutions. The model can thereby trigger these reasoning patterns, which it has learned, when given the right prompt, making its output more trustworthy.

The main reasons why CoT is able to enhance performance are:

- Elimination of logical shortcuts that often result in wrong answers
- Superior processing of multi-hop reasoning tasks
- Closer correspondence between intermediate reasoning and final output

Several research studies have demonstrated that the application of CoT prompting leads to a significantly better performance in tasks involving arithmetic reasoning, symbolic manipulation, logical inference, and algorithmic problem solving.

4.3.4 Types of Chain-of-Thought Prompting

1. *Zero-Shot Chain-of-Thought*

Zero-shot CoT does not in any way ask for example demonstrations. However, a minimal instruction does accompany the prompt to promote stepwise reasoning.

Typical features:

- Very easy to use
- No extra prompt engineering cost
- Good for fairly complex reasoning tasks

Illustrative structure:

- Description of the task
- Instruction leading to step-by-step reasoning

Zero-shot CoT relies on a minimal instruction that activates reasoning behavior:

$$P(y \mid x, \text{“step-by-step reasoning”})$$

Zero-shot CoT is especially advantageous when there is a need for quick deployment or when no task examples are available.

2. *Manual (Few-Shot) Chain-of-Thought*

Manual co-t was the method that required the user to give an example of the question with the reasoning steps before actually asking the question.

In few-shot CoT, demonstrations are provided:

$$(x^{(1)}, r^{(1)}, y^{(1)}, \ldots, (x^{(m)}, r^{(m)}, y^{(m)})$$

This allows the model to learn a reasoning distribution:

$$P(r \mid x) \approx \sum_{i=1}^{m} P(r^{(i)} \mid x^{(i)})$$

Features:

- More precise results for difficult tasks
- Weaker control over the reasoning style
- More extended prompts and design efforts

This method is apt for:

- Reasoning confined to a specific domain (e.g., law, medicine, technical analysis)
- Teaching and learning systems
- Tasks involving decisions with significant impacts

4.3.5 Practical Use Case: Analytical Text Evaluation

The task requires researchers to identify bias present in news articles.

A direct prompt leads to an answer which lacks depth because it only provides minimal evidence. The CoT-based prompt leads the model to complete different tasks which include:

- The task requires researchers to identify all emotionally charged words.
- The task involves determining which facts have been left out and which information has been selectively shown.
- The task requires researchers to analyze how different viewpoints have been presented in the material.
- The task requires researchers to combine all evidence to create a logical conclusion.

The structured evaluation process produces results which show:

- The system outputs become more understandable
- The results become simpler to examine
- The final results show improved matching with human methods of analytical thinking.

4.3.6 CoT in Algorithmic Problem Solving

For algorithmic tasks, CoT helps the model select optimal strategies.

EXAMPLE: Shortest path in a grid.

The reasoning chain often includes:

1. Problem classification → graph traversal
2. Constraint identification → unweighted edges
3. Algorithm selection → BFS

Mathematically, BFS guarantees shortest path length:

$$d(v) = \min\{\text{number of edges from } s \text{ to } v\}$$

CoT allows the model to justify this choice before implementation.

4.3.7 Advanced Chain-of-Thought Techniques

Self-Consistency

Instead of a single reasoning chain, the model samples multiple chains:

$$\{r^{(1)}, r^{(2)}, \ldots, r^{(n)}\}$$

Final answer is selected using majority voting:

$$y^* = \arg\max_{y} \sum_{i=1}^{n} I(y^{(i)} = y)$$

This reduces variance and improves robustness.

4.3.8 Automatic Chain-of-Thought (Auto-CoT)

It creates reasoning demonstrations through its three-step process.

- The system uses questions for sampling.
- The system creates reasoning paths through its process.
- The system uses the created paths as an implicit part of its reasoning process.

The system needs less manual work for prompt development because it maintains the advantages of CoT.

Chain-of-Thought Reasoning provides two advantages for organizations and academic institutions.

- The system achieves better results through its ability to handle complex multi-step reasoning problems.
- Enterprise systems and academic systems need explainability as their main requirement.
- The system allows users to trace their work through multiple stages to find faults.
- The system produces more reliable AI results through its enhanced output credibility.

Limitations

- Increased token usage
- Not required for simple factual queries
- Reasoning may still be logically flawed despite appearing coherent

Hence, CoT must be applied selectively.

The process of Chain-of-Thought reasoning enables LLMs to develop into structured problem-solving systems through its method of expressing, intermediate reasoning steps. The combination of mathematical decomposition with algorithmic proof and logical order enables CoT to function as a basic method for developing advanced prompt engineering systems and dependable AI implementation methods.

4.4 INSTRUCTION TUNING FOR LARGE LANGUAGE MODEL

The development of Large Language Models (LLMs) reached its highest point through instruction tuning which improves their ability to comprehend and execute human commands. Instruction tuning develops a model's ability to handle multiple tasks through natural language commands whereas standard fine-tuning methods restrict a model to performance on specific tasks.

The process of instruction tuning changes a general language model into a system that follows instructions while executing various tasks which include question answering and summarization and reasoning and coding and dialogue within one integrated framework.

4.4.1 Motivation and Need for Instruction Tuning

Through their pre-trained state LLMs acquire language skills by learning to forecast upcoming words based on existing word sequences. The objective enables learners to develop strong linguistic skills yet it fails to ensure that they will fulfill their specific user requirements. The model produces fluent output which results in excessive wordiness and produces content that fails to meet the required response structure and relevant material requirements.

The model requires instruction tuning because it needs explicit guidance on how to execute tasks according to given commands as shown in Figure 4.6.

The primary objectives of the study include the following two goals:

1. The system develops outputs which accurately match user requests for different answer types including short and long responses.
2. The system enables one model to execute multiple tasks without requiring new training dedicated to each task.

The system produces dependable results because it requests users to provide structured instructions which lead to well-defined answers instead of creating random or mistaken information.

4.4.2 Conceptual Framework of Instruction Tuning

Instruction tuning reframes language modeling as a conditional generation problem, where the model learns a mapping:

$$\text{Instruction } (I) \rightarrow \text{Desired Output } (Y)$$

Given a pre-trained model with parameters θ, instruction tuning optimizes the conditional likelihood:

$$\mathcal{L}(\theta) = -\sum_{(I,Y)} \log P_{\theta}(Y \mid I)$$

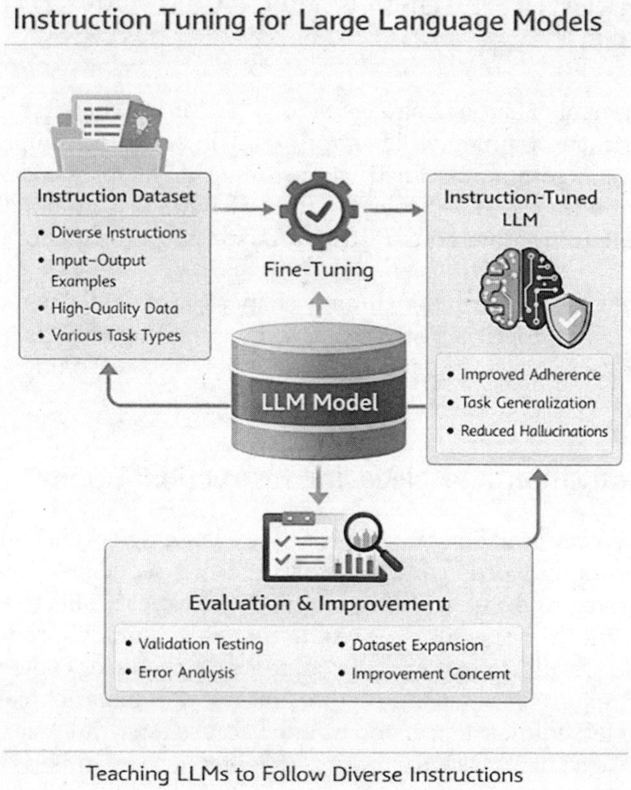

Figure 4.6: *Instruction Tuning for LLM.*

where,

I is a natural language instruction,

Y is the target response,

P_θ represents the model's probability distribution.

This objective encourages the model to condition its generation explicitly on the instruction, rather than relying solely on implicit task inference.

4.4.3 Instruction Tuning Process

The instruction tuning pipeline typically consists of three stages:

(a) *Instruction Dataset Construction*

A diverse dataset of instruction–output pairs is curated. The instructions require different levels of difficulty because they involve tasks with various complexities, which include:

- Simple factual queries
- Multi-step reasoning tasks

- Transformations (translation, summarization)
- Open-ended generation

The system requires diverse input because it needs results that can generalize across various situations.

(b) *Supervised Fine-Tuning*

The pre-trained LLM is fine-tuned using supervised learning. The model learns to execute instructions correctly when it reduces the loss between its produced outputs and the corresponding reference responses during training.

(c) *Evaluation and Iteration*

The model is evaluated on unseen instructions to test:

- Instruction adherence
- Output correctness
- Consistency across similar prompts

The solution requires additional data and training iterations because existing weaknesses need resolution.

4.4.4 Instruction Tuning vs Multi-Task Fine-Tuning

Although both approaches improve model versatility, they differ fundamentally in objective and design philosophy.

Instruction tuning prioritizes flexibility and alignment, making it more suitable for conversational and interactive AI systems as shown in Table 4.2.

TABLE 4.2: Instruction Tuning vs Multi-Task Fine tuning.

Instruction Tuning	*Multi-Task Fine-Tuning*
Learns to follow explicit natural language instructions	Learns predefined task-specific behaviors
Emphasizes generalization to unseen tasks	Focuses on optimizing known tasks
Instruction-driven interaction	Task-label-driven interaction
Better suited for open-ended systems	Better for specialized pipelines

4.4.5 Characteristics of Instruction-Tuning Datasets

High-quality instruction-tuning datasets share the following properties:

- **Natural Language Instructions:** Humans use natural language to create their questions and commands.

- **Clear Input–Output Mapping:** The system establishes specific response requirements through its instructions.
- **High-Quality Outputs:** The output delivers precise information which the user receives in an organized format.
- The system needs to manage four different task categories which include reasoning tasks and generation tasks and transformation tasks and dialogue tasks.

The system will experience performance problems when users provide substandard instructions or substandard outputs.

4.4.6 Representative Instruction-Tuning Datasets

Several benchmark datasets have driven progress in instruction tuning:

- The FLAN dataset provides a large-scale multi-task instruction dataset which researchers use to improve their zero-shot generalization capabilities.
- Super-Natural Instructions show how users can complete complex tasks through human-like instructions which exist across multiple assignments.
- Alpaca shows that smaller models can reproduce the performance of larger models through their use of synthetic instructional data.
- OpenAssistant shows how users can follow instructions through conversational interactions.
- The Self-Instruct system uses large language models to create automated instruction-response pairs which help decrease the costs of annotation work.

The datasets demonstrate how instruction tuning can scale to different situations while maintaining adaptable performance across multiple scenarios.

4.4.7 Challenges and Limitations

The method of instruction tuning functions effectively but it brings multiple challenges through its application.

- **Data Quality Sensitivity:** Noisy or ambiguous instructions lead to unreliable behavior.
- **Overfitting Risk:** Excessive tuning on specific patterns may reduce generalization.
- **Bias Propagation:** Biases present in instructions can be amplified.
- Scalability constraints require the use of substantial data sets together with high processing capacity.
- Models demonstrate different response patterns when they receive semantically identical instructions.

Researchers continue to work on solutions for these challenges.

4.4.8 Practical Applications

The developed AI system is designed to handle different interactive AI projects according to its instruction following capabilities. The developed AI system is designed to handle different interactive AI projects according to its instruction following capabilities. The developed AI system is designed to handle different interactive AI projects according to its instruction following capabilities. The developed AI system is designed to handle different interactive AI projects according to its instruction following capabilities.

Instruction tuning establishes a new method for teaching machines in which they learn from generic instructions instead of specific tasks. The process of instruction tuning enables Large Language Models to improve their performance because it teaches them how to implement instructions instead of learning specific tasks.

4.5 PROMPT DESIGN STRATEGIES

4.5.1 Designing Effective Prompts for Large Language Models

Proper construction of prompts for Large Language Models (LLMs) serves as the basic requirement which enables users to create precise and dependable results that meet production standards. High-quality prompting needs structured development which undergoes multiple testing phases to assess its effectiveness. The field of prompt engineering functions as a distinct engineering discipline which requires practical application instead of theoretical work as shown in Figure 4.7.

Formally, an LLM can be viewed as a function:

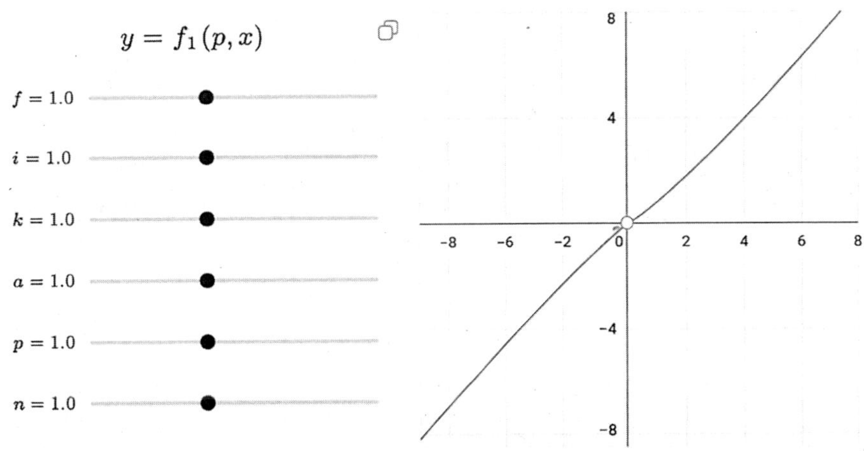

Figure 4.7: *Prompt Design.*

where,

p = prompt (instructions + constraints),
x = input data,
y = generated output,
θ = model parameters.

Since θ is fixed at inference time, prompt design becomes the primary control mechanism for influencing model behavior.

1. *Co-Design Prompts with the LLM*

The Co-Design of Prompts with LLMs enables users to create their prompts when they ask LLMs to create their own prompts.

Approach

- The user must provide a basic task description together with its limitations.
- The LLM needs to enhance the existing prompt by creating a new version which makes the content easier to understand and complete.
- The process of developing the prompt begins with testing to collect user feedback which leads to subsequent improvements.

The process leads to better results for:

- The process enhances the logical structure of content.
- The process enables generalization of content across different input types.
- The process enables users to identify both hidden details and contradictory regulations.

The system operates because LLMs learn to identify both patterns and abstract concepts. The model generates broader and more flexible prompts than can be produced through manual writing when it needs to create a new version of a task.

2. *Use Self-Evaluation for Quality Control*

LLMs produce answers which meet acceptable standards but do not deliver optimal results. The solution requires implementing a self-evaluation system which needs to be built into the prompt system.

Technique

The model should create a response which needs to receive a quality score $q \in [1,10]$ which ranges from 1 to 10. The answer needs to be either refined or retried when $q < T$ occurs, with T representing a predefined threshold value that usually equals $T = 9$.

$$\text{Accept output if } q \geq T$$

This technique significantly improves:

- Precision-critical tasks
- Rule compliance
- Consistency in production pipelines

3. *Combine Structure with Targeted Examples*

The provided output structure describes the expected appearance of responses which the included examples demonstrate to show proper filling of that structure.

Best practices

- Use one or two high-quality examples only.
- Avoid excessive examples to reduce token overhead.
- The preferred data format for use is machine-readable formats which include XML and JSON.

Example Structure

```
<items>
<item>
<sub_item>Text</sub_item>
</item>
</items>
```

This approach is especially effective for nested outputs, API responses, and downstream automation.

4. *Break Complex Tasks into Simple Steps*

The performance of LLMs improves through the process of breaking down complex tasks into smaller tasks which need to be completed in order to achieve the main goal.

The document needs to go through:

- Proofreading prompt
- Translation prompt
- Summarization prompt
- Formatting prompt

This method helps people think better because it decreases their mental load while it prevents mistakes from spreading to other areas as shown in Figure 4.8.

If we denote each step as f_i, the workflow becomes:

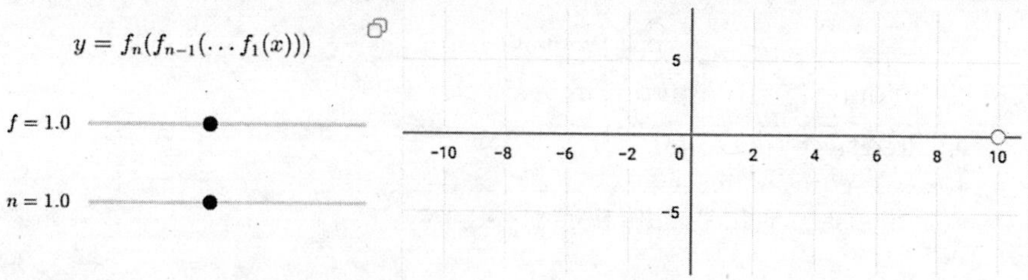

Figure 4.8: *Break Complex Tasks.*

Frameworks such as LangChain enable efficient orchestration of such multi-step pipelines.

5. *Request Explanations which Help You Create Better Prompts*

The most efficient method to debug an LLM when it generates unexpected results requires the user to request an explanation of its output from the model.

The explanations which LLMs provide show multiple reasoning pathways which they use to solve problems because they do not use symbolic reasoning.

This method of using explanations for prompt creation proves beneficial during:

- the development stage
- the pre-production testing stage
- the initial production monitoring phase.

4.5.2 Prompt Design Feedback Loop

The process of using LLMs resembles working with an expert assistant who lacks experience because LLMs deliver high performance and rapid results while showing flexible capabilities that need exact training methods. The bridge between both sides of the situation can be crossed through effective prompt engineering as shown in Figure 4.9.

The strategies discussed—co-designing prompts, enforcing self-evaluation, structuring outputs, task decomposition, and explanation-based refinement—transform basic prompting into a robust engineering practice.

Prompt engineering requires more than writing instructions. The process requires knowledge about how models understand language which guides designers to build their models. The process of creating better prompts results in improved model performance even though the model remains unchanged.

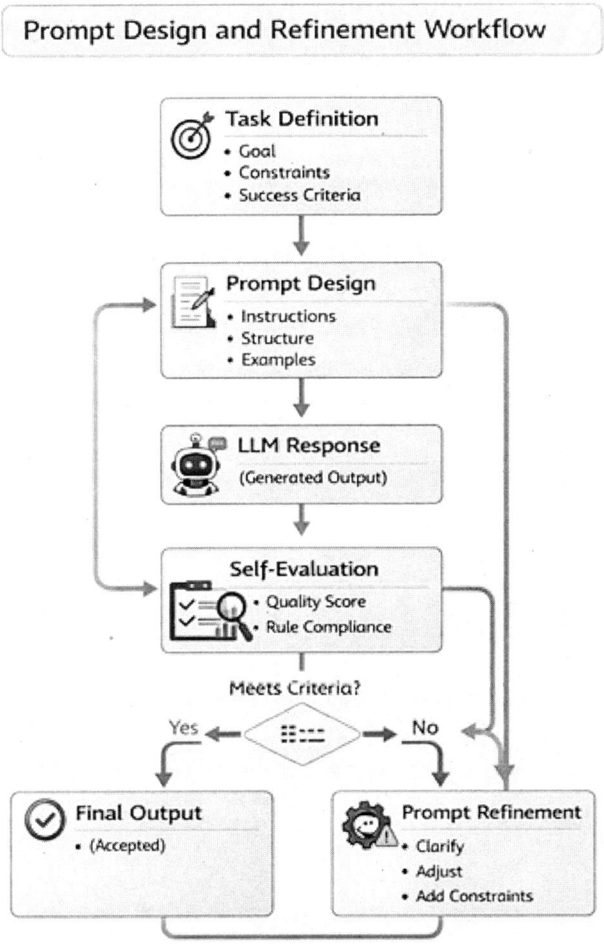

Figure 4.9: *Iterative prompt engineering loop showing prompt creation, evaluation, and refinement for reliable LLM outputs.*

4.6 HANDLING HALLUCINATIONS IN LARGE LANGUAGE MODELS

Large Language Models (LLMs) can produce fluent text which contains rich contextual information. The models produce outputs which contain incorrect information and misleading content and nonsensical results while displaying high confidence. This phenomenon is known as hallucination. The process of managing hallucinations stands as a vital requirement for trustworthy LLM usage in situations which demand exact information and dependable results.

4.6.1 What are Hallucinations?

LLMs produce hallucinations when their models generate information that lacks basis in actual facts and present context and logical thinking. The output of a system displays language errors as authentic-looking results which make it difficult to detect software defects in the system as shown in Figure 4.10 and 4.11.

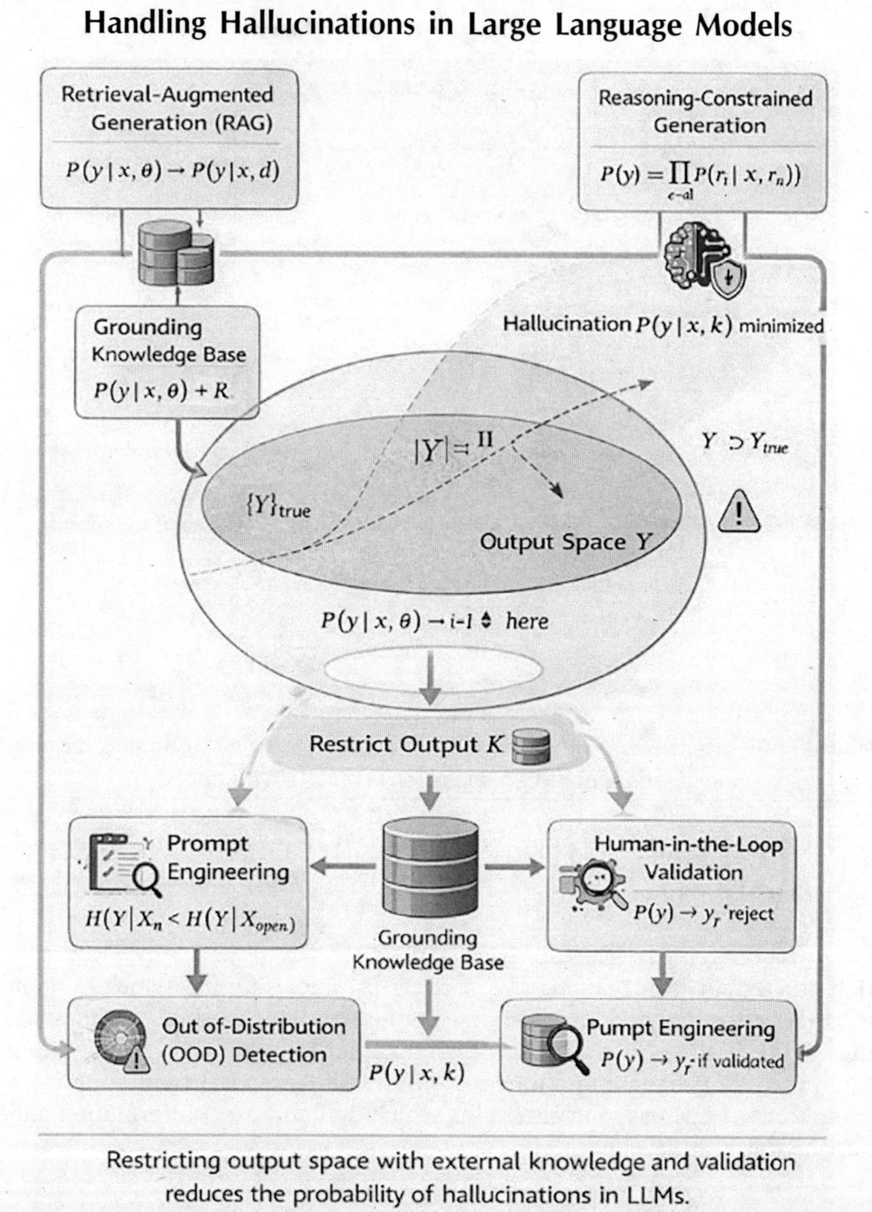

Figure 4.10: *Hallucinations.*

Formally, an LLM generates output y for an input prompt x by maximizing:

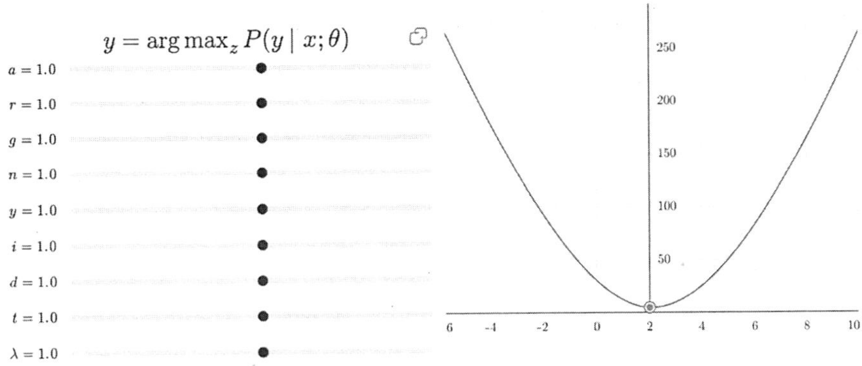

Figure 4.11: *Handling Hallucinations.*

where θ represents model parameters.

Hallucination occurs when:

$$P(y \mid x;\, \theta) \text{ is high but } y \notin \mathcal{Y}_{\text{true}}$$

where, $\mathcal{Y}_{\text{true}}$ denotes the set of factually or logically valid responses.

Formally, hallucination occurs when:

$$P(\text{Output} \mid \text{Input}) \text{ is high, but Truth (Output)} = \text{False}$$

This mismatch between confidence and correctness makes hallucinations particularly dangerous.

4.6.2 Types of Hallucinations

Hallucinations can be categorized based on the nature of the error:

1. **Factual Hallucinations:** The model generates incorrect facts, such as wrong dates, fabricated statistics, or non-existent entities.

   $$y \notin \mathcal{F}_{\text{true}} \text{ (violates factual constraints)}$$

2. **Contextual Hallucinations:** The response deviates from the given prompt, solving a different or assumed problem instead of the intended one.

   $$P(y \mid x) \gg P(y \mid x_{\text{intended}})$$

3. **Commonsense Hallucinations:** Outputs violate basic real-world logic or physical constraints, despite being grammatically correct.
4. **Reasoning Hallucinations:** The facts may be correct, but the conclusions drawn from them are logically invalid or unsupported.

   $$(p_1, p_2, \ldots, p_n) \nRightarrow c$$

Among these, reasoning hallucinations are the most difficult to detect because they often appear logically structured.

4.6.3 Root Causes of Hallucinations

Hallucinations arise due to several interacting factors:

- Likelihood-based training objectives
  Models are trained to minimize cross-entropy loss:

  $$\mathcal{L} = -\sum_{t} \log P(w_t \mid w_{<t})$$

  which rewards fluency, not truth verification.
- Incomplete or biased training data
- Ambiguous or underspecified prompts
- Absence of external grounding during inference
- Overgeneralization beyond training distribution

These factors collectively increase uncertainty, which the model resolves by generating plausible completions.

4.6.4 Mathematical View of Hallucination Reduction

The probability of hallucination can be conceptually reduced by constraining the output space:

$$P(y \mid x, k), \text{ where } k \in \mathcal{K}_{\text{verified}}$$

Here, k represents verified external knowledge. Techniques that introduce k or restrict y reduce hallucination risk.

4.6.5 Techniques for Handling Hallucinations

1. *Retrieval-Augmented Generation (RAG)*

RAG systems use external knowledge sources to enhance their inference operations. The system generates responses through retrieved documents and databases which obtain information beyond its internal model memory.

RAG conditions generation on retrieved documents d:

$$P(y \mid x) \rightarrow P(y \mid x, d)$$

This grounding ensures that outputs are anchored to verifiable sources, significantly reducing factual hallucinations.

2. *Reasoning-Constrained Generation*

Chain-of-Thought prompting enforces intermediate reasoning steps:

$$P(y) = \prod_{i=1}^{n} P(r_i \mid x, r_{<i})$$

By explicitly modeling reasoning steps r_i, logical inconsistencies become less likely.

3. *Prompt Engineering with Guardrails*

Well-defined prompts reduce entropy in the output distribution:

$$H(Y \mid X_{\text{constrained}}) < H(Y \mid X_{\text{open}})$$

Lower entropy leads to more deterministic and reliable outputs.

4. *Out-of-Distribution (OOD) Detection*

OOD methods detect when inputs fall outside the model's confident domain and flag responses for review instead of generating unreliable outputs.

When input $x \notin \mathcal{D}_{\text{train}}$, uncertainty increases:

$$\text{Var}(P(y \mid x)) \uparrow$$

OOD detectors flag such cases, preventing unreliable generation.

5. *Human-in-the-Loop Validation*

Human control remains necessary for applications that have critical importance. The practice of reviewing only high-risk outputs leads to better system reliability while maintaining ability to expand.

For high-impact decisions, outputs are verified by humans:

$$y_{\text{final}} = \begin{cases} \text{y}, & \text{if validated} \\ \phi, & \text{otherwise} \end{cases}$$

This provides a safety layer beyond automated checks.

4.6.6 Impact of Hallucinations in Real Applications

Hallucinations can pose serious risks in real-world systems:

- **Healthcare and Legal Systems:** Incorrect advice or interpretation can lead to severe consequences.
- **Data Analytics:** Fabricated insights can distort decision-making.
- **Compliance and Reporting:** Confident but incorrect outputs can cause regulatory violations.
- **Business Intelligence:** Hallucinated explanations can misguide strategic planning.

Therefore, hallucination handling is not merely a model-level problem but a system design challenge.

Probabilistic language models cannot avoid hallucinations which exist as their fundamental restriction. The solution needs prompt design together with external grounding and validation mechanisms and human oversight to function effectively. Decision-making processes benefit from using LLMs as intelligent assistants instead of treating them as independent truth sources.

4.7 PROMPT EVALUATION STRATEGIES: TOOLS AND FRAMEWORKS

The process of prompt evaluation assesses how well a prompt directs a Large Language Model (LLM) to create task-specific outputs which meet predetermined requirements. The evaluation of prompts centers on assessing how well prompts perform their intended purpose while model evaluation tests an LLM's ability to perform different tasks as shown in Figure 4.12.

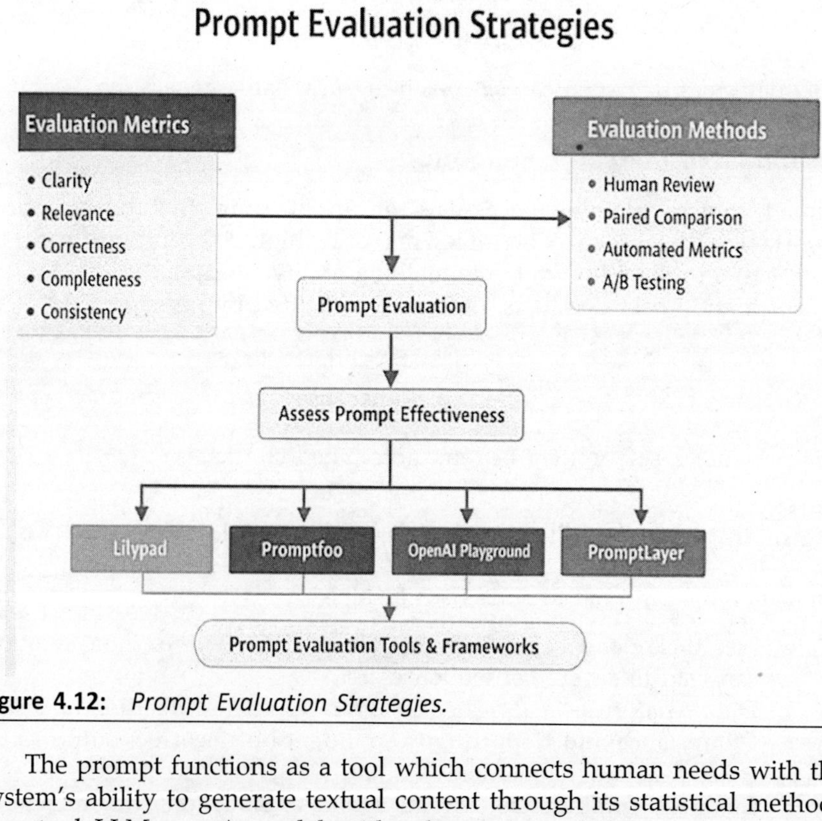

Figure 4.12: *Prompt Evaluation Strategies.*

The prompt functions as a tool which connects human needs with the system's ability to generate textual content through its statistical methods in actual LLM use. A model with advanced capabilities fails to deliver effective results when the prompt used needs more details or when it does not match the required task. The process of prompt evaluation exists as a vital procedure which guarantees that real-world systems like chatbots and recommendation engines and content generation tools and decision-support systems will function with reliability and correctness and consistent performance.

4.7.1 Why Prompt Evaluation is Necessary

LLMs generate text by modeling a conditional probability distribution:

$$P(y \mid x, \theta)$$

where,

x represents the input prompt,
y is the generated output,
θ denotes the model parameters.

Prompt evaluation aims to determine whether a given prompt x reliably steers the distribution toward desired outputs $y^{\backslash *}$, rather than irrelevant, incorrect, or hallucinated responses.

A poorly designed prompt increases entropy in the output space, leading to:

- Unclear or off topic responses
- Inconsistent tone or structure
- Factual inaccuracies and hallucinations
- Embedded bias from underspecified instructions

Thus, evaluating prompts is a form of control and alignment over the model's probabilistic behavior.

4.7.2 Core Prompt Evaluation Metrics

The evaluation of prompt effectiveness requires the use of both qualitative metrics and quantitative metrics.

Clarity

The clarity assessment tests whether the prompt delivers its intended task information without any confusion. A clear prompt reduces uncertainty in the model's interpretation which leads to a more focused output distribution.

The conditional entropy $H(Y \mid X)$ rises when a prompt lacks clarity because vague prompts create unpredictable output results.

EXAMPLE:

- **Weak:** "Help the user."
- **Strong:** "Ask the user about their billing issue and provide step-by-step resolution options."

Relevance

Relevance evaluates how well the generated output aligns with the intent of the prompt.

Formally, relevance can be approximated using semantic similarity:

$$\text{Relevance}\,(y, y^{\backslash *}) \approx \cos(\vec{y}, \overrightarrow{y^{\backslash *}})$$

where vectors are obtained from embedding models.

Low relevance often indicates that the prompt does not sufficiently constrain the task.

Correctness

Correctness measures factual and logical accuracy. This is especially critical in domains such as healthcare, law, finance, and education.

Correctness can be evaluated via:

- Human expert review
- External fact-checking systems
- Retrieval-based verification (RAG)

Completeness

Completeness assesses whether the response fully addresses all aspects of the prompt.

A response may be correct yet incomplete if it omits implicit sub-questions or contextual requirements. Human evaluation is typically required for this metric.

Consistency

Consistency ensures uniformity in tone, structure, and reasoning across multiple runs of the same prompt.

Inconsistent outputs often arise due to:

- High sampling temperature
- Poorly constrained prompts
- Lack of formatting or role instructions

4.7.3 Prompt Evaluation Frameworks and Tools

Several tools and frameworks have been developed to support structured prompt evaluation at scale.

Lilypad

Lilypad handles prompts as versioned artifacts which can be traced through their entire history instead of treating them as unchanging text.

The system automatically monitors and assesses each prompt while it undergoes performance-based evaluation and optimization process.

Key features

- Prompt versioning and traceability
- LLM-as-a-judge evaluation (pass/fail)
- Collaborative UI for domain experts
- Regression detection during prompt updates

Instead of scoring multiple independent metrics, Lilypad often uses a binary evaluation:

$$\text{Eval}(y) \in \{\text{Pass, Fail}\}$$

This simplifies decision-making and reduces ambiguity in borderline cases.

Promptfoo

Promptfoo enables users to test multiple prompt variants simultaneously across various models through its batch testing feature.

The system provides these capabilities:

- The system automatically generates test cases together with their required assertions.
- The system enables testing through red team exercises and adversarial testing methods.
- The system provides continuous integration and continuous delivery capabilities.
- The system provides dashboard tools for comparing different prompts.
- The system proves effective in discovering regression issues when users change their existing prompts.

OpenAI Playground

The OpenAI Playground enables users to test prompts in real time through its interactive environment.

The system provides prompt feedback to users in two ways:

1. The system allows users to adjust two specific parameters which are temperature and maximum token count.
2. The system works best for users who want to design their first prompt.

The system has two main drawbacks:

1. The system supports only OpenAI models.
2. The system does not support evaluation of large-scale testing.

PromptLayer

The software functions as a middleware solution which records user prompts together with their responses without requiring any changes to the existing application code.

Advantages

- The system provides automatic logging together with versioning capabilities.
- The system enables A/B testing experiments.
- Technical and non-technical staff members can work together through the system.

The system provides value to production environments because it enables organizations to track prompt changes through an auditing process.

Promptimize

The software uses a test-driven development (TDD) framework to create its prompt engineering tests.

Features

- The system generates test cases which evaluate prompt performance.
- The system automatically assigns rank to different prompt variations.
- The system evaluates costs by testing only specific areas through its selective re-testing feature.
- The system allows human reviewers to participate in the assessment process.

4.7.4 Frameworks vs Custom Evaluation Pipelines

While general-purpose frameworks accelerate development, they may not fully capture domain-specific requirements.

For specialized applications, custom evaluation pipelines are recommended. These pipelines allow:

- Tailored metrics
- Domain-specific constraints
- Integration with proprietary knowledge bases

A hybrid approach—combining frameworks for baseline evaluation and custom logic for domain accuracy—often yields the best results.

4.7.5 Methods for Evaluating Prompt Effectiveness

Human Evaluation

Human reviewers assess outputs for correctness, tone, bias, and completeness. Although expensive, this method remains the gold standard.

Paired Comparison

Evaluators compare outputs from multiple prompt variants and select the superior one. This method is effective for detecting subtle quality differences.

Automated Metrics

Common automated metrics include:

- BLEU/ROUGE for lexical overlap
- Cosine Similarity for semantic alignment
- Perplexity, defined as:

$$\text{Perplexity} = \exp\left(-\frac{1}{N}\sum_{i=1}^{N} \log P(w_i)\right)$$

Lower perplexity indicates higher fluency and coherence.

A/B Testing

Different prompt variants are deployed in real user settings, and performance is measured using engagement or satisfaction metrics.

Context-Specific Metrics

In structured tasks, precision and recall are used:

$$\text{Precision} = \frac{TP}{TP + FP}, \text{Recall} = \frac{TP}{TP + FN}$$

These metrics are especially useful in information extraction and classification-based prompting.

4.7.6 Best Practices for Prompt Evaluation

- Combine automated metrics with human judgment
- Iterate continuously through controlled experiments
- Version prompts systematically
- Account for ethical, cultural, and bias-related risks
- Avoid over-optimizing for a single metric

Prompt evaluation should be treated as an iterative optimization problem, similar to model tuning rather than a one-time validation step.

The process of evaluating prompts serves as an essential aspect of prompt engineering which maintains the accuracy and relevance of LLM outputs while meeting the requirements of specific tasks. The combination of qualitative judgment with quantitative metrics and structured frameworks enables developers to make systematic improvements to their prompts which will function effectively in actual deployment. The ongoing development of LLM applications requires prompt evaluation to establish reliable systems while enhancing operational safety and system efficiency.

SUMMARY

This chapter establishes prompt engineering as the main control interface for Large Language Models because it enables users to direct system operations through natural language commands instead of changing model parameters. The system begins with an introduction to prompt fundamentals before explaining zero-shot and few-shot prompting methods which allow inference-time learning and Chain-of-Thought reasoning techniques which solve problems by providing structured multi-step solutions. The chapter further explains instruction tuning as a scalable method for aligning model outputs with human intent across diverse tasks. The section discusses practical prompt design strategies which include task decomposition and self-evaluation and structured outputs and defensive prompting to enhance system reliability and controllability. The comprehensive study of hallucinations explains their different origins and types and associated dangers and provides methods to handle them through retrieval augmentation and constrained reasoning and human-in-the-loop validation. The chapter presents prompt evaluation as an iterative process to optimize results by using both qualitative and quantitative metrics and contemporary evaluation systems which show prompt engineering functions as a precise engineering discipline needed to establish trustworthy LLM systems for practical use.

TEST YOUR KNOWLEDGE

1. How does increasing prompt ambiguity mathematically affect the conditional entropy of an LLM's output distribution, and why does this lead to hallucinations?
2. In what situations can few-shot prompting reduce performance compared to zero-shot prompting, despite providing examples? Explain using attention and example bias.

3. Why is Chain-of-Thought prompting ineffective or even harmful for simple factual queries, and how does this relate to token usage and reasoning overfitting?
4. Compare few-shot prompting in LLMs with classical few-shot learning in machine learning from an optimization and inference-time perspective.
5. Explain how output constraints reduce the effective hypothesis space of an LLM and why this improves downstream system reliability.
6. Why does instruction tuning generalize better to unseen tasks than multi-task fine-tuning, even when both are trained on multiple objectives?
7. Describe a real-world scenario where reasoning hallucinations are more dangerous than factual hallucinations, and explain why they are harder to detect.
8. How does retrieval-augmented generation (RAG) alter the conditional probability distribution of generated outputs, and what failure modes still remain?
9. Why is self-consistency in Chain-of-Thought prompting able to reduce variance but not necessarily eliminate systematic bias?
10. Design a prompt evaluation pipeline for a healthcare application and justify which metrics must be automated and which must remain human-evaluated.

CHAPTER 5

Retrieval Augmented Generation (RAG)

Large Language Models (LLMs) operate as effective text generation systems which need pre-existing knowledge because they lack the capability to learn new information. The systems face difficulties when they need to access current data which includes specialized knowledge and factual details because this limits their ability to provide accurate answers. The Retrieval Augmented Generation (RAG) system enables language models to access external knowledge sources which they use to obtain necessary information during their text creation process.

The chapter presents the basic principles of Retrieval Augmented Generation through the introduction of embeddings and vector search methods and vector databases and RAG system architecture. The chapter examines various components, including knowledge grounding, hybrid retrieval techniques, actual uses of RAG, and its main challenges. The chapter provides a concise and structured understanding of how RAG enhances the accuracy, relevance, and trustworthiness of generative AI systems.

5.1 NEED FOR EXTERNAL KNOWLEDGE

Large Language Models (LLMs) acquire their linguistic abilities through training on extensive text collections which include their fundamental structural elements and all their generalizable language patterns. The system maintains its original knowledge base from training which prevents it from acquiring new knowledge about published works and specific field advancements and organizational expertise. This limitation becomes particularly significant in specialized domains such as healthcare and biomedical research and scientific documentation because these fields require precise and current information.

The National Library of Medicine (NLM) oversees extensive and continuously expanding biomedical information which includes clinical terms and research articles and medical databases that have been specially compiled. The internal knowledge of language models within these spaces does not fulfill all requirements for effective performance. The biomedical

Named Entity Recognition (NER) process and document indexing and knowledge discovery activities demand access to both authoritative sources and specific field knowledge resources for accurate results. By connecting external information sources to their systems language models can produce results that match established medical concepts and standardized vocabulary systems.

The system retrieves essential information from external databases during inference instead of embedding all domain expertise within its model parameters. The system enables better scalability while reducing model retraining needs and allowing organizations to update their knowledge base without needing to modify the language model.

The requirement for external knowledge establishes safeguards against unreliable information. LLMs produce incorrect information that seems plausible when they operate without external data verification, which creates problems for fields that require high-stakes accuracy like healthcare and scientific research. Retrieval-based approaches allow generated responses to be anchored in trusted sources, which leads to better transparency and trustworthiness of the results.

Retrieval Augmented Generation uses this principle to link language models with external knowledge retrieval systems. The architecture enables generative systems to function successfully in knowledge-intensive environments by producing responses that combine fluent language with accurate factual information.

5.2 EMBEDDINGS AND VECTOR SEARCH

5.2.1 Vector Embeddings

Vector embeddings function as mathematical models which represent data elements through continuous vector space mappings that show their related meanings. The system uses this method to transform an object which can be a word or a sentence or a document into a vector representation.

$$v = [v_1, v_2, \ldots, v_n]$$

The system represents every dimension through learned semantic data which shows specific contextual attributes.

Embedding models require large dataset training to achieve their goal of placing semantically similar items in close proximity within the vector space. The system creates closer vectors for items that share related meanings while it positions their unrelated items at greater distances. The system shows that documents which share identical technical topics will create their respective embeddings with minimal distance between them.

The architectural design process uses embeddings to create a connection between unstructured data and both retrieval systems and generation systems. The system begins with the transformation of raw text into embeddings which later serve as storage and indexing and comparison tools. This abstraction enables system design which scales up and operates with modular components.

5.2.2 Similarity Measurement in Vector Space

The process of calculating item similarity begins after data transforms into vector representation. The vector-based systems utilize cosine similarity as their primary similarity measure which is defined through the following equation. Cosine similarity measures the angle between two vectors rather than their magnitude. The similarity between two items shows strong similarity when the value approaches 1 and shows weak relationship between two items when the value approaches 0. The measure operates effectively because it measures semantic connection between two elements through their shared meaning instead of their physical dimensions.

$$\text{cosine\_similarity}\,(a, b) = \frac{a \, . \, b}{||a|| \; ||b||}$$

The precise mathematical expression becomes secondary to basic understanding because similar content shows through similar directional paths which vectors create. The principle allows for data evaluation through meaning-based measurement which enables both ranking and comparison.

5.2.3 Vector Search

Vector search functions as a retrieval system which employs vector embeddings together with similarity measurements to discover pertinent information. The system retrieves results through vector search because it determines matches based on semantic similarity instead of requiring exact term matches which traditional keyword-based search systems need.

The vector search process typically involves the following steps:

- **Embedding Generation:** The system transforms documents or data entries into vector embeddings.
- **Indexing:** The system stores embeddings inside a structure which enables efficient similarity search.
- **Query Embedding:** The user query is converted into an embedding using the same model.
- **Similarity Computation:** The system uses similarity measures including cosine similarity to compare the query vector against stored vectors.
- **Ranking and Retrieval:** The system ranks the most similar vectors to deliver them as search results.

Vector search enables systems to acquire relevant information because it understands fundamental meaning behind search queries which use different terms from existing database records.

5.2.4 Role of Embeddings and Vector Search in RAG

In a Retrieval Augmented Generation architecture, embeddings and vector search form the retrieval layer. When a user submits a query, vector search retrieves the most relevant documents or knowledge fragments from an external knowledge base. These retrieved items are then provided as contextual input to the language model.

Mathematically, this process can be viewed as selecting a subset of documents:

$$D_{\text{retrieved}} = \arg\max_{D} \text{similarity}(q, d)$$

where, q is the query embedding and represents document embeddings.

By grounding the generation process in retrieved data, RAG systems reduce hallucinations, improve factual accuracy, and enable access to up-to-date or domain-specific knowledge without retraining the model.

5.2.5 Architectural Perspective

The system design architectural framework uses three components which include semantic representation through embeddings and vector search for similarity-based retrieval and the language model for contextual generation. The system achieves scalable and maintainable performance through its design which separates operational functions needed to establish dependable generative AI technologies in actual business environments.

5.3 VECTOR DATABASES AND THEIR INTEGRATION WITH LARGE LANGUAGE MODELS

5.3.1 Role of Vector Databases in Modern AI Systems

Modern AI architectures depend on vector databases because these databases provide efficient storage and retrieval solutions for high-dimensional vector embeddings. The moment text or documents get converted into embeddings traditional relational databases become useless for conducting similarity searches. Vector databases are specifically designed to address this challenge by supporting fast semantic retrieval at scale as shown in Figure 5.1.

Vector databases integrated with Large Language Models (LLMs) enable the model to access information beyond its original training data. They provide access to specialized domain knowledge that includes proprietary information and ongoing updates which scientists require to create trustworthy AI systems used in real-world scenarios.

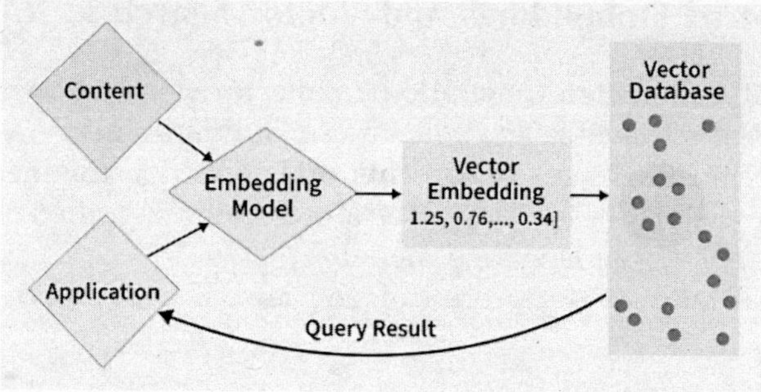

Figure 5.1: *Vector Database.*

5.3.2 Enhancing LLMs Using External Vector-based Knowledge

Large language models (LLMs) face two main problems because they do not have access to current information and they produce false information. Vector databases enable the retrieval of relevant contextual information which helps users find specific information before they generate answers. The integration of these systems enables LLMs to generate outputs which demonstrate greater accuracy through their ability to ground information and understand contextual details.

The integration of vector databases with large language models (LLMs) provides two main advantages for their combined operations.

- The system enables users to access both domain-specific information and up-to-the-minute data.
- The system reduces hallucinations because it uses actual information to establish facts.
- The system supports semantic search which goes beyond basic keyword matching.
- The system allows knowledge updates to proceed without requiring model retraining.

The system establishes the fundamental structure for Retrieval-Augmented Generation systems.

5.3.3 Retrieval-Augmented Generation Using Vector Databases

The primary architectural pattern of vector databases connects to LLMs through Retrieval-Augmented Generation (RAG). The RAG pipeline retrieves relevant documents from a vector database through semantic similarity which serves as input for the language model.

The RAG workflow consists of:

- The process to transform documents into vector embeddings.
- The process to store embeddings with their matching metadata inside a vector database.

- The process to create an embedding for the user query.
- The system uses similarity search to find the most pertinent vectors.
- The system provides retrieved context information to the LLM.
- The system produces a response which establishes verifiable links to external sources.

RAG generates better responses because it selects only essential information and thus uses fewer tokens.

5.3.4 Core Components of Vector Database

- A vector database system consists of multiple architectural components which form its main framework.
- The system uses embedding storage to save high-dimensional vectors which are created from text and image and other data sources.
- Metadata Storage maintains associated information such as document IDs, timestamps, source references, or access permissions.
- The system uses an indexing mechanism which organizes vectors through specialized data structures to enable users to perform fast approximate nearest-neighbor searches.
- The Similarity Engine calculates similarity between query vectors and stored vectors through distance and angle-based measurement methods.

The architecture of vector databases enables them to find semantically similar items instead of requiring exact item matches.

5.3.5 Role of Vector Databases in RAG Systems

Vector databases form the retrieval layer in Retrieval Augmented Generation architectures. Upon receiving a user query, the system retrieves the most relevant documents or knowledge fragments using vector search. These retrieved results are then passed as contextual input to the language model.

Formally, the retrieval step selects a subset of documents:

$$D_{\text{retrieved}} = \{d \mid \text{similarity}(q, d) \geq \tau\}$$

where, q represents the query embedding and τ is a relevance threshold.

By supplying only relevant context to the language model, RAG systems improve factual accuracy, reduce hallucinations, and make more efficient use of model input tokens.

Illustrative Use Case: Research Assistant System

Consider a research assistant designed to answer queries related to ethical issues in AI surveillance. When a user submits a query, the vector database retrieves relevant academic papers, policy documents, and reports related to AI ethics. These retrieved sources are then passed to the language model, which synthesizes them into a coherent and well-supported response.

This architecture enables the system to reference authoritative sources, maintain factual accuracy, and adapt to newly published research without modifying the language model.

5.3.6 Integration Approaches

There are two primary approaches for integrating external knowledge with LLMs as shown in Table 5.1:

TABLE 5.1 Integration Approaches

Approach	*Description*	*Use Cases*
Retrieval (RAG)	External knowledge retrieved at inference time	Chatbots, Q&A systems, search
Injection	Knowledge embedded into model parameters	Narrow, domain-specific models

Among these, Retrieval-Augmented Generation is preferred due to its flexibility, scalability, and lower maintenance cost.

Vector databases function as the main foundation which supports both semantic search and Retrieval-Augmented Generation systems. The combination of these systems with Large Language Models produces AI applications which deliver precise results at large scales while understanding specific contextual information. The system architecture establishes a separation between knowledge storage and language generation processes which enables systems to develop over time while sustaining operational dependability.

5.4 ARCHITECTURE OF RETRIEVAL-AUGMENTED GENERATION (RAG) SYSTEMS

5.4.1 Overview

Retrieval-Augmented Generation(RAG) functions as an architectural framework which provides Large Language Models(LLMs) with enhanced abilities through its connection to external knowledge databases. The main idea is simple but powerful: the system starts by retrieving relevant information from a vector database which it uses to create more precise and context-aware responses instead of relying on the LLMs pre-existing knowledge.

RAG systems require two components which work together as one architectural system:

1. **Retriever Component**—responsible for finding the most relevant external knowledge.
2. **Generator Component**—the LLM that uses the retrieved knowledge to produce the response.

The system enables modularity through its design because retrieval systems undergo separate updates while the LLM maintains its current state and accesses fresh external knowledge as shown in Figure 5.2.

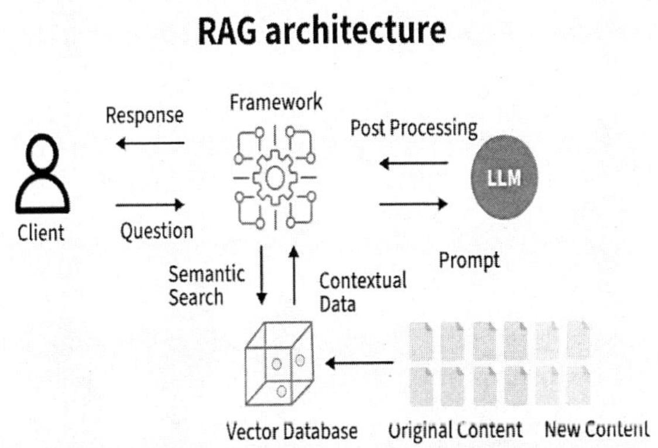

Figure 5.2: *RAG Architecture.*

5.4.2 Retriever Component

The retriever transforms the user query into a vector embedding which it uses to search the vector database for matching documents and knowledge fragments.

Key steps

1. **Query Embeddings:** The user question or prompt gets converted into vector form through a pre-trained embedding model.
2. **Document Embedding:** Documents in the knowledge base are pre-encoded into vectors:

$$d_i = \text{Embed}(\text{doc}_i)$$

3. **Similarity Search:** The retriever compares the query vector with all document vectors using a similarity metric (commonly cosine similarity):

$$\text{similarity}\,(q, d_i) = \frac{q \cdot d_i}{\|q\|\;\|d_i\|}$$

4. **Top-k Retrieval:** The system retrieves the top-k most relevant documents to provide as context for generation.

Approximate nearest neighbor (ANN) indexing is often used to make retrieval scalable for millions of vectors.

5.4.3 Generator Component

The generator system uses a transformer-based large language model which generates answers by combining two input sources, the retrieved context and the original query. There are two primary methods which organizations use to connect their obtained data with their current operations.

Fusion-in-Decoder (FiD)

The system maintains two distinct processes which separate retrieval from generation until the decoding phase.

- The LLM generates output by focusing on specific documents which it has retrieved.
- The system provides greater operational freedom together with superior output quality, although its processing speed is slightly reduced.

Fusion-in-Encoder (FiE)

- The system processes the combined query and retrieved documents as a single unit in the encoder.
- The system achieves operational efficiency through its ability to handle retrieved sources, although it sacrifices freedom to work with multiple documents as shown in Table 5.2.

TABLE 5.2 Compare FID vs FIE

Aspect	*FiD*	*FiE*
Fusion Point	Decoding	Encoding
Retrieval-Generation Separation	Yes	No
Efficiency	Moderate	High
Quality	High	Slightly lower

5.4.4 End-to-End Workflow

The RAG architecture establishes a pipeline system which operates through three main components:

- **Query Preprocessing:** Normalization of text is performed while all extraneous elements are removed.

- **Query Embedding:** The query undergoes conversion into vector representation.
- **Vector Search:** The system extracts its top-k relevant documents from the vector database.
- **Context Injection:** The retrieved documents serve as input materials for the LLM system.
- **Response Generation:** The LLM generates its output by integrating its internal knowledge with the retrieved context.

Python Snippet for Process Workflow

```
# Convert query to vector
query_vector = embed_model.encode(user_query)
# Retrieve top-k relevant documents from vector database
top_docs = vector_db.search(query_vector, k=5)
# Pass context to LLM to generate response
response = llm.generate(query=user_query, context=top_docs)
print(response))
```

The pipeline enables the model to access current domain-specific information because it does not require retraining for new data as shown in Figure 5.3.

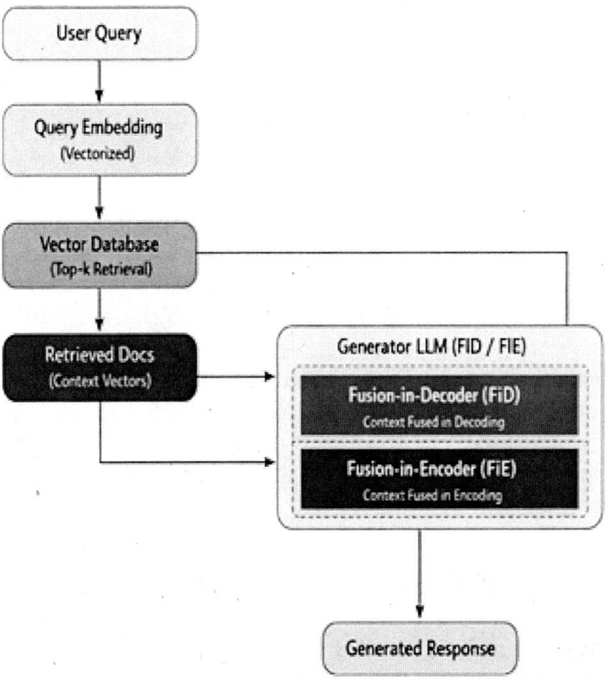

Figure 5.3: *Workflow of RAG Architecture.*

5.4.5 Advantages of RAG Architecture

- The system provides current answers through its ability to fetch external information during operation.
- The system produces fewer false outputs because it bases its results on verified information.
- The system enables organizations to access their specific knowledge without needing retraining.
- The system updates external knowledge in real time without requiring expensive fine-tuning procedures.

5.4.6 Design Considerations

- The system requires optimal chunk size because document sections need to be divided into smaller parts which help with more accurate information retrieval.
- Domain-specific embeddings function better than other options because they increase model performance in particular domains.
- The system achieves better search results by using both vector search and keyword filters to perform hybrid search operations.
- The system maintains operational capacity for large systems through its use of ANN indexing together with its ability to store vectors efficiently.

5.5 KNOWLEDGE GROUNDING

5.5.1 Concept of Knowledge Grounding

Knowledge grounding establishes factuality and reliability for Large Language Model (LLM) outputs through validation from recognized external sources. LLMs produce coherent text but they generate false information because their knowledge base contains information from past times. The system establishes grounding through its ability to connect generated answers with external sources of verified information which include vector databases and documents and structured data repositories.

The process of knowledge grounding enables artificial intelligence systems to perceive reality through connections to external information which they use to confirm their results instead of depending solely on their training data.

5.5.2 The Role of Knowledge Grounding in RAG Systems

The knowledge grounding process functions as a fundamental component within Retrieval-Augmented Generation systems which enable researchers to:

- Reduce Hallucinations the model produces only validated information which eliminates unsupported assertions.
- The system provides current answers which use recent facts despite the LLM model being trained on outdated information.
- The system enables correct results through domain-specific knowledge which applies to fields such as medicine and law and finance.
- User trust improves because users can check the sources of grounded responses which makes the system more reliable and trustworthy.

A RAG system will produce incorrect answers which sound plausible when it lacks grounding.

5.5.3 Mechanism of Knowledge Grounding

The mechanisms behind knowledge grounding establish multiple pathways which AI systems use for their grounding process.

Document-based Grounding

The first way to achieve grounding exists through document-based grounding which operates on the following principle:

- The system uses retrieved text passages and document materials which it finds in vector databases as its base source of actual information.
- The system uses these text passages as part of its response which it creates through LLM technology.

Structured Knowledge Bases

- The system operates through knowledge graphs which contain confirmed information storage.
- Structured entry records serve as the basis for verifying response accuracy through cross-checking.

Hybrid Grounding

- The system integrates unstructured document content with established structured knowledge material.
- The system achieves both text-based coverage together with precise data from its structured databases.

Confidence Scoring and Filtering

- The system uses a filtering process which assesses model results through examining how well retrieved knowledge matches the produced response.

- The system identifies low-confidence statements and unsupported statements to either flag them or remove them from the content.

EXAMPLE: The medical AI chatbot provides an answer to the user question about Drug X side effects.

- Query Processing: The system transforms the user query into a vector format.
- The system retrieves clinical documents and drug information from the vector database during this process.
- The LLM model uses retrieved documents as its main source of information instead of relying on its built-in knowledge.
- The system generates an answer which includes evidence from retrieved material about side effects documented in research studies.

The system produces a response which maintains complete accuracy and can be checked for correctness while using current information.

5.5.4 Important Factors to Examine

- **Source quality:** Grounded knowledge must come from reliable, authoritative sources.
- **Relevance filtering:** Only highly relevant context should be included to avoid noise.
- **Citation mechanism:** Responses should indicate sources whenever possible for traceability.
- **Real-time updates:** The grounding sources require frequent updates because they contain knowledge that evolves quickly in certain domains.

Knowledge grounding ensures that RAG systems generate responses which connect to actual world facts instead of using only statistical relationships found in their pre-trained datasets. The system operates as an essential element which drives accurate results together with trustworthy outcomes and relevant domain expertise in every AI system that is ready for production.

5.6 HYBRID RETRIEVAL CONCEPTS

5.6.1 Overview

Hybrid retrieval utilizes different retrieval methods to improve the precision and retrieval scope and operational performance of information retrieval systems. Traditional retrieval systems depend on two search methods which are lexical search that uses keywords and semantic search that employs embedding. Hybrid methods which combine dense and sparse retrieval techniques enable users to access the benefits of both approaches because each method has specific strengths yet contains particular weaknesses as shown in Figure 5.4.

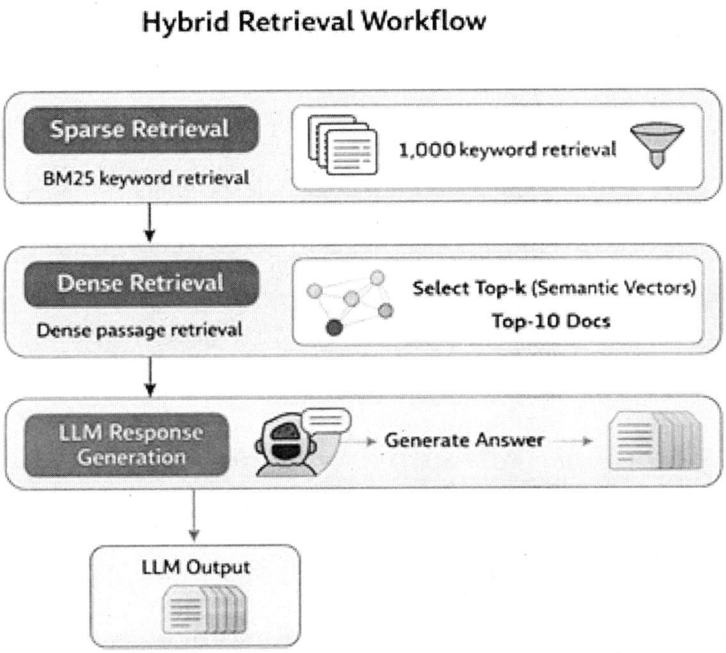

Figure 5.4: *Hybrid Retrieval Concept Workflow.*

Hybrid retrieval in RAG (Retrieval-Augmented Generation) enables the system to obtain both semantically relevant information and lexically precise content, which enhances response quality across various domains.

5.6.2 Main Hybrid Retrieval Methods

1. *Hybrid Hiera rchical Retrieval (HHR) System*

Hybrid Hierarchical Retrieval combines dense data retrieval through vector embeddings and sparse data retrieval using standard keyword search methods or BM25 search techniques.

- Dense Retrieval uses embeddings to locate documents which contain similar meanings to the original content.
- Sparse Retrieval matches documents through exact keyword and phrase matching.
- Hierarchical Integration uses sparse retrieval to create a candidate list which dense retrieval uses to identify the most relevant semantic content.

The HHR system enhances open-domain question answering because it establishes a system that retrieves all applicable documents while letting users choose the most relevant documents.

2. *Cascading Retrieval*

The method of Cascading Retrieval employs a sequential approach which uses multiple retrieval levels for its operation.

- **Initial Retrieval:** A broad search using lightweight models or keyword search.
- **Secondary Retrieval:** A more accurate semantic search applied to the initial candidate set.

The system works as a solution which decreases computational expenses but still delivers effective retrieval results.

The process begins by searching a vast knowledge base which first uses BM25 to filter documents and then applies vector similarity for document ranking.

3. *Multi-Modal or Cross-Source Retrieval*

Hybrid retrieval systems use multiple data sources which include different data types for their operations.

The system uses text embeddings which include documents and articles together with knowledge graphs that contain structured facts and relationships and image or video embeddings which support multi-modal applications.

RAG systems use multiple modalities to answer questions which need reasoning across different knowledge formats.

5.6.3 Advantages of Hybrid Retrieval

- The system achieves improved accuracy through its combination of semantic and lexical search capabilities.
- The system achieves higher recall through its ability to find documents which a single retrieval method would not discover.
- The system achieves efficiency through its use of sequential and hierarchical retrieval methods which eliminate the need for unnecessary calculations.
- The system provides domain flexibility because it can handle text-heavy and structured and multi-modal dataset types.

5.6.4 Example Workflow

The scenario requires open-domain question answering about AI ethics.

- The system employs BM25 for sparse retrieval which enables it to quickly filter 1,000 candidate documents from a million-document corpus.
- The system transforms filtered documents and the query into embeddings which it ranks according to cosine similarity.
- The system uses top-k retrieved documents as input for the LLM which generates a grounded and accurate response.

Pseudocode

```
# Step 1: Sparse Retrieval
candidates = bm25_search(query, corpus, top_n=1000)
# Step 2: Dense Retrieval
query_vector = embed_model.encode(query)
candidate_vectors = embed_model.encode(candidates)
similarities = cosine_similarity(query_vector, candidate_vectors)
# Step 3: Select top-k
top_docs = select_top_k(candidates, similarities, k=10)
# Step 4: Pass to LLM for response generation
response = llm.generate(query, context=top_docs)
```

5.7 APPLICATIONS OF RAG

RAG improves the performance of Large Language Models through its ability to use external information to generate accurate and relevant answers which match current context. Its applications span multiple domains:

- **Question-Answering Systems:** Provides precise answers by retrieving relevant documents from its database, which functions effectively for both open-domain and specialized queries (e.g., medical or legal).
- **Conversational Agents and Chatbots:** The system uses knowledge bases to decrease hallucinations while enabling multi-turn dialogues that maintain awareness of previous interactions.
- **Content Creation and Summarization:** The system creates accurate articles and reports and summaries through its ability to combine information from various sources.
- **Information Retrieval and Knowledge Management:** The system automatically retrieves documents and creates summaries which improve enterprise search capabilities and knowledge management systems.
- **Education and Tutoring:** The system provides personalized learning through interactive content which includes textbook materials and notes and research materials.

- **Emerging Domains:** Legal research, healthcare analytics, financial insights, and multi-modal AI applications.

RAG ensures relevance, accuracy, andefficiency in AI systems, making it a versatile solution across research, business, and educational application.

5.8 LIMITATIONS AND CHALLENGES OF RAG

While RAG significantly enhances LLM capabilities, it has several inherent limitations and practical challenges:

5.8.1 System Complexity

- RAG integrates retrieval and generation components, increasing architectural complexity.
- Requires careful tuning to ensure retrieval quality, prompt integration, and generation accuracy work seamlessly together.

5.8.2 Latency and Efficiency

- Retrieval steps can introduce delays, affecting real-time applications.
- Multi-stage retrieval (sparse → dense → LLM) demands computational resources and optimized vector search, especially with large knowledge bases.

5.8.3 Quality of Retrieved Data

- The overall system performance heavily depends on the relevance and accuracy of retrieved documents.
- Poor-quality or outdated knowledge sources can propagate errors into generated responses.

5.8.4 Model Hallucinations

Although RAG reduces hallucinations, LLMs may still generate incorrect or biased content if retrieval is incomplete or context is misaligned.

5.8.5 Maintenance and Scalability

- Knowledge bases require frequent updates to remain accurate and relevant.
- Scaling RAG systems for multi-domain or large-scale applications can be challenging due to storage and processing overhead.

5.8.6 Bias and Fairness

- External sources may contain biases or incomplete information, which can influence the generated outputs.
- Continuous monitoring and filtering are necessary to maintain fair and responsible AI outputs.

The RAG framework provides an effective tool for generating knowledge-based content. System developers need to assess multiple factors which include system design, data quality, latency issues and the presence of biases before they can use RAG effectively. The researchers and engineers need to understand these limitations because they will help them develop better RAG systems which can function in actual environments.

TEST YOUR KNOWLEDGE

1. Explain why a language model trained on static text cannot provide up-to-date or domain-specific information, and how external information access resolves this issue.
2. Two document vectors have cosine similarity 0.95, and another pair has 0.2. Which pair is more semantically related, and why is cosine similarity preferred over Euclidean distance?
3. Describe how storing high-dimensional vectors and their metadata allows large-scale information retrieval and why indexing is critical for performance.
4. Compare processing retrieved information in the encoder versus the decoder of a transformer model. Give one scenario where each method is preferable.
5. How can a system ensure outputs are factually accurate by checking retrieved documents, structured databases, and confidence scores?
6. Explain a method that combines semantic similarity and exact keyword matching for improved search results. Why is using both better than using one alone?
7. A two-step search retrieves 1,000 candidate documents from a million. Explain how refining these candidates improves precision and reduces computational load.
8. Design a system that gives domain-specific answers in a knowledge-heavy environment. Which retrieval and grounding methods ensure accuracy and relevance?
9. Discuss the trade-off between retrieval latency and answer correctness. How can approximate nearest neighbor search help balance this trade-off?
10. If retrieved data contains biased information, what strategies can reduce its effect on generated responses?

CHAPTER 6

Generative Adversarial Networks (GANs)

The organization of generative models works through an analysis of data patterns to create new authentic samples. Generative Adversarial Networks (GANs) represent a major advancement in this area by introducing an adversarial learning framework in which two neural networks are trained simultaneously through competition. The method produces modern AI systems that generate artificial data through its capacity to create authentic synthetic information.

The chapter introduces fundamental GAN concepts together with its system structure by providing intuitive explanations instead of using complex mathematical expressions. The text demonstrates how generator and discriminator systems work together with details about adversarial training methods and challenges that create difficulties in learning. The text addresses practical limitations through an examination of two main issues which include training instability and mode collapse.

The chapter explores essential GAN variants together with conditional architectures which provide the capability to produce domain-specific generated content. The practical value of GANs is shown through their use in real-world situations which include image synthesis data augmentation and creative AI applications in healthcare. The chapter concludes by establishing GANs as part of the broader generative AI ecosystem while explaining their advantages and disadvantages which maintain their importance in current AI technologies.

6.1 INTRODUCTION TO GENERATIVE ADVERSARIAL NETWORKS (GANS)

Generative Adversarial Networks (GANs) function as deep generative models which learn data distribution because they generate authentic samples that match real-world data. GANs which Ian Goodfellow and his team developed in 2014 introduced a new approach to generative modeling which uses adversarial learning for data generation instead of direct likelihood estimation methods as shown in Figure 6.1.

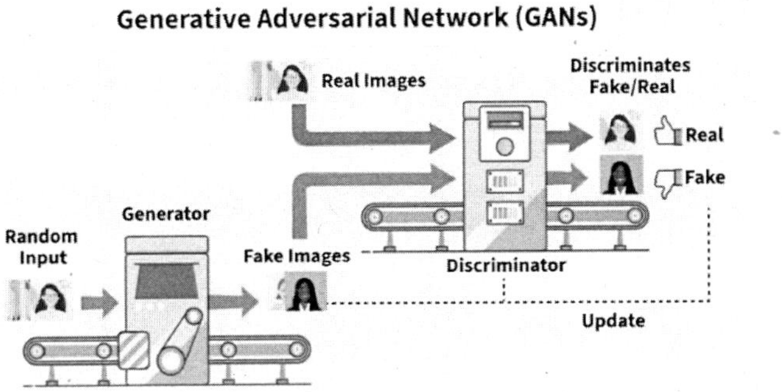

Figure 6.1: *Generative Adversarial Network.*

GANs create new data instances which can include images audio and text while traditional machine learning models concentrate on making predictions about specific classes. GANs became important in multiple fields because of their ability to generate new content which includes computer vision and healthcare and creative artificial intelligence and data augmentation.

The core idea of GANs operates through a competitive system which trains two neural networks at the same time as shown in Figure 6.2.

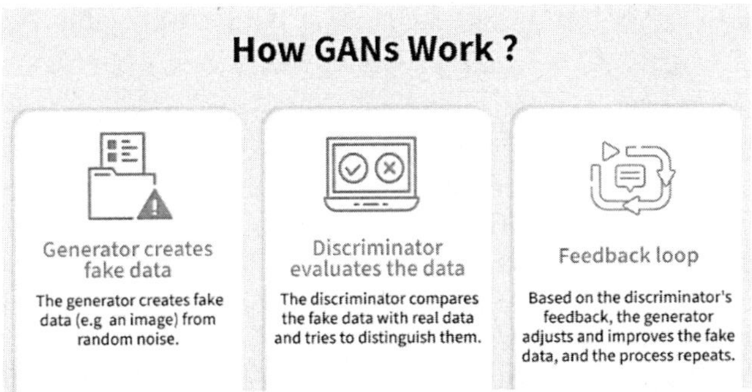

Figure 6.2: *How GAN's Work?*

- A Generator which works to produce realistic artificial data.
- A Discriminator which works to identify actual data from produced data.

The two networks engage in a minimax game which enables the generator to progress by learning how to deceive the discriminator while the discriminator advances through learning how to detect fake samples. The two networks develop their abilities through this process of adversarial learning which continues until better performance results are achieved.

6.1.1 Adversarial Learning Framework

Let the generator be denoted as $G(z)$, where, $z \sim p_z(z)$ is a random noise vector sampled from a simple distribution such as a normal or uniform distribution. The discriminator is denoted as $D(x)$, which outputs a probability indicating whether a given input x is real.

The training objective of GANs is defined as a minimax optimization problem:

$$\min_G \max_D V(G, D) = \mathbb{E}_{x \sim p_{\text{data}}(x)} [\log D(x)] + \mathbb{E}_{z \sim p_z(z)} [\log (1 - D(G(z)))]$$

- The discriminator maximizes this objective by correctly classifying real samples as real and generated samples as fake.
- The generator minimizes this objective by generating samples that maximize the discriminator's confusion.

At equilibrium, the generator learns the true data distribution $p_{\text{data}}(x)$, and the discriminator becomes unable to distinguish real data from generated data, outputting a probability close to 0.5.

6.1.2 Intuition behind GAN Training

The process of GAN training operates as a two-player game between two opponents.

- The generator starts its process by creating low-quality samples which it generates from random noise.
- The discriminator can easily identify these samples as fraudulent.
- The generator modifies its parameters according to the feedback which the discriminator provides.
- The generator generates more authentic samples through multiple iterations which he conducts.
- The discriminator develops itself to identify hidden defects in the system.
- The training process reaches its endpoint when both networks achieve equal performance without any network emerging as the more powerful system.

The adversarial approach allows GANs to create realistic data through their trained models which do not need to learn probability distributions, which makes them different from conventional generative methods that use Variational Autoencoders (VAEs) as their foundation.

6.1.3 Significance of GAN

GANs introduced new approaches to deep learning which created multiple fundamental transformations.

- The method enables scientists to model data distributions without needing to perform calculations for direct probability assessments.
- The method enables scientists to learn from data without needing to use any labeled records for training purposes.
- The method produces high-quality samples which directly benefit the process of synthesizing images.
- The method enables artists to develop innovative content through AI-based tools which create original works.

The same adversarial characteristics which grant GANs their strength present multiple obstacles which include training instability and mode collapse and hyperparameter sensitivity. The research work establishes need for better GAN models and training techniques which chapter shows in its subsequent sections.

6.1.4 Architecture of GAN

A Generative Adversarial Network (GAN) follows an adversarial architecture composed of two neural networks trained simultaneously: a generator and a discriminator. The generator takes random noise as input and transforms it into synthetic data samples, while the discriminator receives both real data and generated samples and predicts whether the input is real or fake as shown in Figure 6.3.

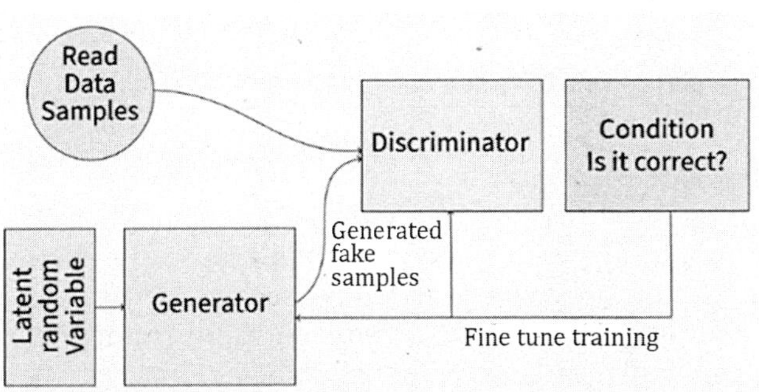

Figure 6.3: *Architecture of GAN.*

These two networks are connected through a feedback loop. The discriminator's output provides a learning signal that guides the generator to improve the realism of its outputs over time. Training is framed as a minimax optimization problem, where the generator attempts to fool the discriminator, and the discriminator attempts to correctly identify real versus generated data.

From a system perspective, GAN training follows a minimax optimization framework, where the generator and discriminator have opposing objectives:

$$\min_G \max_D V(G, D) = \mathbb{E}_{x\sim p_{\text{data}}(x)} [\log D(x)] + \mathbb{E}_{z\sim p_z(z)} [\log (1 - D(G(z)))]$$

Unlike traditional supervised models, GANs do not rely on explicit labels for generated samples. Instead, learning emerges from competition between the two networks. This architectural design enables GANs to model complex data distributions but also introduces challenges such as training instability and convergence sensitivity.

6.2 GENERATOR AND DISCRIMINATOR

A Generative Adversarial Network (GAN) consists of two neural networks which include the Generator (G) and the Discriminator (D). The networks the model uses for training create an adversarial dynamic which allows it to learn complex data distributions while producing realistic synthetic samples as shown in Figure 6.4.

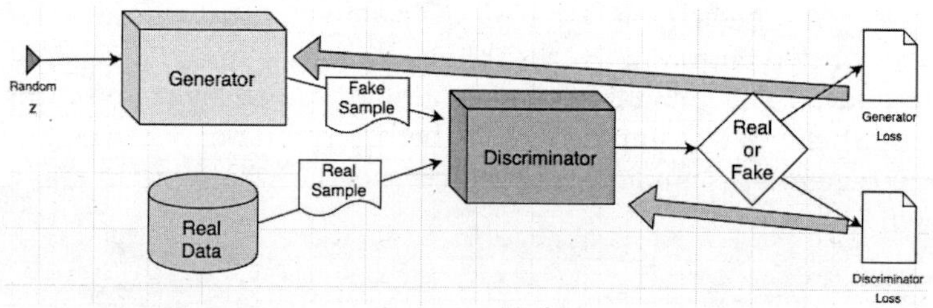

Figure 6.4: *Generator and Discriminator.*

6.2.1 Generator Model

The generator is a deep neural network that maps a random noise vector $z \sim p_z(z)$, drawn from a simple distribution such as Gaussian or uniform, to a synthetic data sample $G(z)$. The generated output is intended to resemble real data such as images, text, or signals.

The generator does not have direct access to real data. The generator learns through the feedback which it receives from the discriminator. The system updates its parameters through backpropagation during training to enhance the authenticity of its generated results.

The objective of the generator is to fool the discriminator into classifying generated samples as real. Its loss function is defined as:

$$J_G = -\frac{1}{m} \sum_{i=1}^{m} \log D(G(z_i))$$

where, m is the batch size and $D(G(z_i))$ denotes the discriminator's probability that the generated sample is real. Minimizing this loss encourages the generator to produce increasingly realistic outputs.

6.2.2 Discriminator Model

The discriminator is a binary classification neural network that distinguishes between real samples $x \sim p_{\text{data}}(x)$ and generated samples $G(z)$. It outputs a probability value in the range [0, 1], representing the likelihood that a given input is real.

For image-based tasks, the discriminator commonly employs convolutional layers to extract hierarchical features, allowing it to detect subtle differences between real and synthetic data.

The discriminator's objective is to correctly classify real samples as real and generated samples as fake. Its loss function is given by:

$$J_D = -\frac{1}{m}\sum_{i=1}^{m} \log D(x_i) - \frac{1}{m}\sum_{i=1}^{m} \log(1 - D(G(z_i)))$$

Minimizing this loss improves the discriminator's ability to separate real and fake data.

Adversarial Training Mechanism

Training proceeds in alternating steps:

1. The discriminator is updated using real samples and generated samples.
2. The generator is updated to produce samples that can fool the discriminator.

This process forms a minimax game:

$$\min_{G} \max_{D} \mathbb{E}_{x \sim p_{\text{data}}}[\log D(x)] + \mathbb{E}_{z \sim p_z(z)}[\log(1 - D(G(z)))]$$

As training progresses, the generator becomes increasingly capable of producing realistic data, while the discriminator's ability to differentiate real and fake samples diminishes. At equilibrium, generated samples closely approximate the real data distribution.

6.3 TRAINING DYNAMICS

The training of Generative Adversarial Networks (GANs) depends on the adversarial relationship between their generator G and discriminator D. The interaction between these two components creates complex training dynamics which result in three possible outcomes if not properly controlled as shown in Figure 6.5.

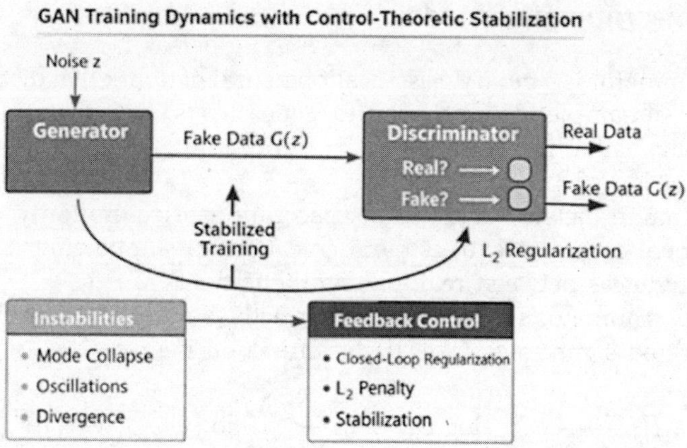

Figure 6.5: *Training Dynamics.*

6.3.1 Modeling GAN Training as a Dynamical System

GAN training can be represented as a nonlinear dynamical system:

$$\dot{\theta}_G = -\nabla_{\theta_G} V(G, D), \dot{\theta}_D = \nabla_{\theta_D} V(G, D)$$

where θ_G and θ_D and are the parameters of the generator and discriminator, respectively, and $V(G, D)$ is the minimax objective:

$$V(G, D) = \mathbb{E}_{x\sim p_{\text{data}}} [\log D(x)] + \mathbb{E}_{z\sim p_z} [\log (1 - D(G(z)))]$$

This formulation interprets training as a coupled differential game, explaining the oscillatory and non-convergent behavior often observed.

6.3.2 Analysis of Instability

The GAN training process experiences instability because the generator and discriminator both change their parameters in opposite directions.

- The generator tries to decrease the discriminator's capacity to tell real samples apart from fake ones.
- The discriminator works to achieve the highest possible accuracy in its classification tasks.

The updates can create two outcomes which include:

- **Divergence:** The loss function keeps fluctuating between different values without reaching a stable point.
- **Mode collapse:** The generator creates a narrow range of samples which shows no real variation.
- **Oscillatory behavior:** The parameters operate within a fixed cycle of movement.

The development of successful stabilization methods depends on our understanding of these patterns.

6.3.3 Stabilizing GAN Dynamics Using Control Theory

Control theory provides tools to analyze and stabilize these adversarial dynamics. One effective approach is the Closed-Loop Control (CLC), which introduces a feedback regularization term to the discriminator:

$$\mathcal{L}_D^{CLC} = \mathcal{L}_D + \lambda \| D(x) - D(G(z)) \|_2^2$$

This term acts as a negative feedback controller, damping oscillations and reducing mode collapse. From a control perspective, the discriminator and generator form a closed-loop system whose stability can be analyzed using Lyapunov functions or other dynamical systems tools.

6.3.4 GAN Training Algorithm with Stabilization

Input: Real data $\{x_i\}_{i=1}^m$, noise $p_z(z)$, learning rates η_G, η_D, regularization λ

Output: Trained generator and discriminator D

1. Initialize θ_G, θ_D randomly
2. Repeat until convergence:
   (a) Sample real data batch $\{x_i\}$
   (b) Sample noise batch $\{z_i\}$
   (c) Generate fake samples $G\{z_i\}$
   (d) Compute discriminator loss with CLC:

$$\mathcal{L}_D^{CLC} = -\frac{1}{m}\sum_i \log D(x_i) - \frac{1}{m}\sum_i \log(1 - D(G(z_i))) + \lambda \| D(x_i) - D(G(z_i)) \|_2^2$$

   (e) Update discriminator: $\theta_D \leftarrow \theta_D - \eta_D \nabla_{\theta_D} \mathcal{L}_D^{CLC}$

   (f) Compute generator loss: $\mathcal{L}_G = -\frac{1}{m}\sum_i \log D(G(z_i))$

   (g) Update generator: $\theta_G \leftarrow \theta_G - \eta_G \nabla_{\theta_G} \mathcal{L}_G$

The analysis of GANs as dynamical systems helps us understand the reasons behind training instability. The implementation of control-theoretic feedback mechanisms functions as a systematic method which stabilizes system behavior between two points while ensuring system evolution progresses toward its intended end state and prevents system failures while enhancing the quality of produced outcomes.

6.4 VARIANTS OF GAN

Generative Adversarial Networks (GANs) have evolved into multiple variants, which address specific training stability problems and data diversity issues and resolution challenges and application-specific constraints. The basic adversarial framework receives extension through these variants, which utilize different network architectures and loss function designs and conditioning mechanisms. A GAN system uses generator G and discriminator D to operate a minimax game system.

$$\min_{G} \max_{D} V(G, D) = \mathbb{E}_{x\sim p_{\text{data}}} [\log D(x)] + \mathbb{E}_{z\sim p_z(z)} [\log (1 - D(G(z)))]$$

Different variants adapt this framework to suit specific tasks or improve training dynamics as shown in Figure 6.6.

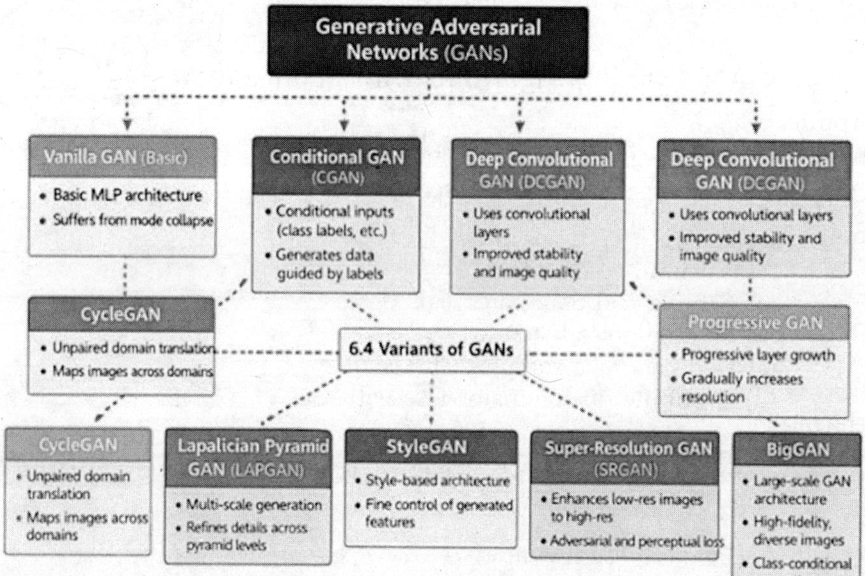

Figure 6.6: *Variants of GAN.*

6.4.1 Vanilla GAN

Vanilla GAN is the foundational GAN model introduced by Goodfellow et al. (2014). Both G and D are implemented as Multi-Layer Perceptrons (MLPs). The generator transforms noise $z \sim p_z(z)$ into synthetic samples $G(z)$, while the discriminator outputs $D(x)$, the probability that a sample is real.

Challenges:

- **Mode collapse:** G generates multiple outputs but restricts its output range to a fixed set of results.
- **Training instability:** The system experiences convergence problems because G and D training updates use alternating update methods.

6.4.2 Conditional GAN (CGAN)

Conditional GANs (CGANs) introduce additional information y (e.g., class labels) into both the generator and discriminator. This allows the generator to produce data conditioned on y:

$$G(z \mid y),\ D(x \mid y)$$

Loss functions:

$$\min_G \max_D V(G, D \mid y) = \mathbb{E}_{x \sim p_{\text{data}}} [\log D(x \mid y)] + \mathbb{E}_{z \sim p_z} [\log (1 - D(G(z \mid y) \mid y))]$$

Applications: Generating specific objects, text-to-image synthesis, or controlled image generation.

6.4.3 Deep Convolutional GAN (DCGAN)

DCGANs use convolutional layers to enhance their abilities to learn spatial patterns in images. The main improvements include the removal of fully connected layers which maintains the spatial arrangement of data and the use of strided convolutions as a replacement for pooling layers which enhances feature extraction capabilities.

The generator uses ReLU activations while the discriminator uses LeakyReLU activations to achieve stable gradient performance.

The system generates high-quality realistic images because of its enhanced ability to learn hierarchical features.

6.4.4 Laplacian Pyramid GAN (LAPGAN)

LAPGAN generates high-resolution images using a multi-scale approach:

- Uses a series of generator-discriminator pairs at different pyramid levels.
- Each level refines the image incrementally, reducing noise and improving detail.
- Effective for photorealistic, ultra-high-resolution outputs.

$$x_0 = G_0(z_0),\ x_1 = G_1(z_1, x_0),\ \ldots,\ x_L = G_L\ (z_L, x_{L-1})$$

6.4.5 Super-Resolution GAN (SRGAN)

SRGANs enhance low-resolution images I_{LR} to high-resolution I_{HR} using adversarial and perceptual losses:

$$\mathcal{L}_{\text{SR}} = \mathcal{L}_{\text{MSE}} + \lambda\mathcal{L}_{\text{adv}} + \gamma\mathcal{L}_{\text{perceptual}}$$

Applications: Image upscaling, medical imaging, satellite imagery.

6.4.6 CycleGAN

CycleGANs perform unpaired image-to-image translation:

Maps $X \rightarrow Y$ and $Y \rightarrow X$ using cycle consistency loss:

$$\mathcal{L}_{\text{cycle}} = \mathbb{E}_{x\sim p_X} [||F(G(x)) - x||_1] + \mathbb{E}_{y\sim p_Y} [||F(G(y) - y||_1]$$

Applications: Domain transfer (e.g., summer ↔ winter, horse ↔ zebra) without paired datasets.

6.4.7 Progressive GAN (PGGAN)

PGGANs expand their network through progressive development.

- The system begins with base visual data which it develops through additional components to achieve peak visual quality.
- The system decreases training problems which occur during high-resolution operations.
- The system creates more authentic results through its ability to develop detailed visual elements from basic to advanced stages.

6.4.8 StyleGAN

StyleGAN establishes a style-based generator system through its generator design.

- The latent vector z gets transformed into intermediate latent w which enables style control at multiple levels.
- The system enables precise management of specific elements which appear in the generated images.
- The system delivers outputs which maintain high-quality standards while offering multiple options for editing.

6.4.9 Wasserstein GAN (WGAN)

WGANs address GAN training instability using Earth-Mover (Wasserstein) distance instead of JS divergence:

$$\mathcal{L}_D = \mathbb{E}_{x\sim p_{\text{data}}} [D(x)] - \mathbb{E}_{z\sim p_z} [D(G(z))],\ \mathcal{L}_G = -\mathbb{E}_{z\sim p_z} [D(G(z))]$$

Advantages: Smooth gradients, reduced mode collapse, improved convergence.

6.4.10 BigGAN

BigGAN scales up GANs for high-fidelity images:

- Large batch sizes and channel widths.
- Class-conditional generation.
- Advanced normalization and regularization techniques to maintain stability at scale.

Applications: Large-scale image synthesis with high diversity and fidelity.

Each GAN variant extends the basic adversarial framework to address stability, diversity, control, or resolution challenges. The models developed through this research have expanded the usage of GAN technology to four different areas which include image synthesis and super-resolution and domain translation and style manipulation, making them essential tools for contemporary generative modeling.

6.5 CONDITIONAL GENERATIVE ADVERSARIAL NETWORKS (CGAN)

Standard GANs learn to generate samples from a data distribution $p_{\text{data}}(x)$ without any control over what kind of sample is produced. The generator system lacks the ability to create specific category or attribute-based samples. Conditional Generative Adversarial Networks cGANs solve this problem by using class labels attributes and semantic descriptions as additional information to guide their generation process.

cGANs use a conditioning variable y to create a model that generates conditional data through the distribution $p(x \mid y)$ which allows users to create specific output. This feature makes cGANs an ideal solution for both supervised and semi-supervised generative tasks.

6.5.1 Conditioning Mechanism

The key idea in cGANs is to provide the same conditioning information y to **both** the generator and the discriminator:

- y may represent class labels (e.g., *cat*, *dog*), attributes (e.g., *smiling*, *male*), or structured metadata.
- Conditioning is typically implemented by concatenation, embedding, or feature-wise modulation.

This shared conditioning enforces semantic consistency between generated samples and their intended categories.

6.5.2 Architecture and Functional Roles

In the given Figure 6.7:

- Noise vector z provides randomness and diversity.
- Condition vector y (labels, attributes, or context) is injected into:
    - ♦ the Generator, guiding what kind of data to generate,
    - ♦ the Discriminator, enforcing semantic consistency.
- The Generator $G(z, y)$ produces condition-aware synthetic samples.
- The Discriminator $D(x, y)$ evaluates both *realism* and *conditional correctness*.
- Adversarial feedback ensures the generator learns $p(x \mid y)$, not just $p(x)$.

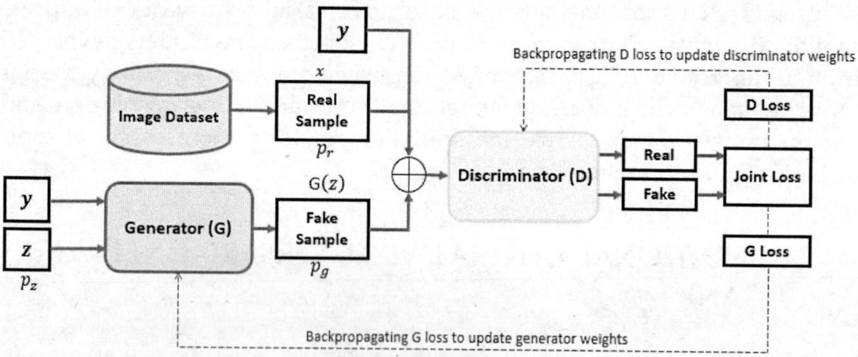

Figure 6.7: *Conditional Generative Adversarial Network.*

Generator $G(z, y)$

The generator receives two inputs:

- Noise vector $z \sim p_z(z)$, which introduces stochasticity and diversity.
- Condition vector y, which controls the semantic content of the output.

The generator learns a mapping:

$$G : (z, y) \rightarrow x_{\text{fake}}$$

such that the generated sample x_{fake} aligns with the condition y.

For example, when trained on CIFAR-10, specifying y = "airplane" forces the generator to synthesize images belonging to that class.

Discriminator $D(x, y)$

The discriminator acts as a conditional binary classifier. It receives:

- A data sample x (real or generated)
- The corresponding condition y

Its objective is to estimate:

$$D(x \mid y) = \Pr(\text{real} \mid x, y)$$

This forces the discriminator to jointly evaluate authenticity and conditional correctness, significantly tightening the adversarial game.

Adversarial Objective Function

The cGAN training objective extends the standard GAN minimax formulation to the conditional setting:

$$\min_G \max_D V(D, G) = \mathbb{E}_{x,\, y \sim p_{\text{data}}}(x,y) \, [\log D(x \mid y)] + \mathbb{E}_{z \sim p_z(z),\, y \sim p_{\text{data}}(y)} [\log (1 - D(G(z \mid y) \mid y))]$$

Interpretation

- The first term encourages the discriminator to correctly identify real samples given the condition.
- The second term pushes the generator to synthesize samples that appear real and condition-consistent.
- At equilibrium, the generator approximates $p_{\text{data}}(x \mid y)$, and the discriminator becomes maximally uncertain.

6.5.3 Training Dynamics

The training process uses an alternating optimization method which combines adversarial interaction with standard GANs. The generator must deceive the discriminator while meeting the established conditions of the evaluation. The discriminator needs to identify authentic and counterfeit samples which share identical testing conditions. The process of conditioning establishes structured sub-manifolds which divide the data distribution into separate segments that correspond to particular values of y.

PyTorch Illustration

```
# z: noise vector, y: class labels
z = torch.randn(batch_size, latent_dim)
y = torch.randint(0, num_classes, (batch_size,))
# Embed labels and concatenate
y_emb = label_embedding(y)
gen_input = torch.cat([z, y_emb], dim=1)
fake_images = generator(gen_input)
```

It highlights the core conditioning operation without diverting into implementation details.

6.5.4 Applications of cGAN

The cGANs framework has various applications in different fields.

Modern generative systems use conditional GANs as their core component for multiple applications which include:

- Image-to-image translation (e.g., Pix2Pix)
- Text-to-image synthesis
- Super-resolution and enhancement
- Class-aware data augmentation
- Style and attribute transfer

The capability of cGANs to enable users to control semantic aspects of their work makes them more useful for practical applications compared to traditional GANs.

6.6 APPLICATIONS OF GENERATIVE ADVERSARIAL NETWORKS

Generative Adversarial Networks have moved beyond theoretical interest and are now widely applied across multiple domains due to their ability to model complex data distributions and generate high-fidelity synthetic samples. Their strength lies in learning rich representations without explicit supervision, making them suitable for both creative and scientific applications.

1. *Image Generation and Synthesis*

One of the most prominent applications of GANs is realistic image generation. GANs learn the underlying distribution of image data and generate visually convincing samples that are often indistinguishable from real images.

Mathematically, the generator approximates:

$$p_g(x) \approx p_{\text{data}}(x)$$

where x represents high-dimensional image data.

Applications include:

- Face synthesis (e.g., StyleGAN)
- Artwork and design generation
- Synthetic image datasets for training vision models

This capability has significantly impacted fields such as digital art, gaming and media.

2. *Image-to-Image Translation*

GANs are widely used to transform images from one domain to another while preserving semantic structure. Conditional GAN variants model the conditional distribution:

$$p(x_{\text{target}} \mid x_{\text{source}})$$

EXAMPLES INCLUDE:

Sketch → photograph
Day → night scenes
Satellite images → maps

Models such as Pix2Pix and CycleGAN enable both paired and unpaired image translation, making GANs practical in scenarios where labeled data is limited.

3. *Super-Resolution and Image Enhancement*

GANs are applied to enhance low-resolution images by reconstructing high-frequency details. Super-Resolution GANs (SRGANs) combine pixel-wise loss with adversarial loss to generate sharper images.

Objective:

$$\mathcal{L} = \mathcal{L}_{\text{content}} + \lambda \mathcal{L}_{\text{adversarial}}$$

Applications include:

- Medical imaging enhancement
- Surveillance footage improvement
- Satellite and astronomical image analysis

4. *Data Augmentation for Machine Learning*

GANs are increasingly used to generate synthetic data to address data scarcity and class imbalance. By sampling from the learned distribution, GANs can create diverse training examples without manual data collection.

Common use cases:

- Medical datasets (e.g., rare diseases)
- Fraud detection
- Industrial fault diagnosis

Synthetic data improves model generalization while preserving privacy.

5. *Medical and Healthcare Applications*

GANs play a critical role in healthcare by generating realistic biomedical data while maintaining patient confidentiality.

Applications include:

- MRI and CT image synthesis
- Modality translation (MRI $\leftrightarrow$ CT)
- Disease progression simulation

GAN-generated medical images help improve diagnostic models where real data is limited or sensitive.

6.7 STRENGTHS AND WEAKNESSES OF GENERATIVE ADVERSARIAL NETWORKS

Generative Adversarial Networks (GANs) function as a superior generative modeling framework because they can learn to replicate complicated data distributions that exist in high-dimensional spaces. The adversarial optimization method that GANs use as their core design results in multiple basic restrictions that hinder their operational performance. The section provides a critical evaluation of both components.

6.7.1 Strengths of GANs

1. *High-Quality Sample Generation*

GANs are capable of generating highly realistic samples by implicitly learning the underlying data distribution $p_{\text{data}}(x)$. Unlike likelihood-based models, GANs do not rely on explicit probability density estimation, allowing them to avoid restrictive assumptions on data distributions.

Mathematically, the generator learns:

$$p_g(x) \approx p_{\text{data}}(x)$$

leading to sharp and visually convincing outputs, especially in image synthesis tasks.

2. *No Explicit Likelihood Modeling*

The explicit likelihood computation needs to be performed by GANs which creates difficulties when dealing with high-dimensional data that includes images and audio content. The computational efficiency of GANs exceeds that of Variational Autoencoders because GANs need no likelihood function approximations to operate.

3. *Flexibility across Modalities*

GANs can be adapted to various data types including Images which are processed through DCGAN and StyleGANText and speech which use SeqGAN Medical signals and time series data Graph data and 3D data. The system achieves this flexibility because its adversarial framework operates independently from any specific architectural design.

4. *Controlled and Conditional Generation*

Extensions such as Conditional GANs (cGANs) enable modeling of conditional distributions $p(x \mid y)$, allowing fine-grained control over generated outputs. This is particularly valuable for tasks like image-to-image translation and data augmentation.

5. *Strong Feature Learning*

The discriminator implicitly learns meaningful feature representations useful for downstream tasks such as classification, anomaly detection, and representation learning.

6.7.2 Weaknesses of GANs

1. *Training Instability*

GAN training is formulated as a non-convex min–max optimization problem:

$$\min_G \max_D V(G, D)$$

which often leads to oscillatory behavior, divergence, or failure to converge. Small imbalances between generator and discriminator learning rates can destabilize training.

2. *Mode Collapse*

Mode collapse arises due to insufficient gradient diversity, motivating Wasserstein-based and regularized GANs.

A major limitation where the generator maps multiple noise inputs to the same or limited outputs:

$$z_1, z_2, \cdots \rightarrow x_{\text{same}}$$

This reduces sample diversity and indicates poor coverage of the true data distribution.

3. *Difficult Evaluation Metrics*

GANs lack a straightforward quantitative evaluation metric. Metrics like Inception Score (IS) and Fréchet Inception Distance (FID) are proxy measures and may not fully capture sample diversity or semantic correctness.

GANs operate as distribution learning systems which generate samples with higher quality but present challenges in training their systems and understanding their internal workings. The system exhibits its strongest capabilities during artistic creation and visual recognition activities while its limitations drive researchers to create more stable versions of the system through WGAN and WGAN-GP and LSGAN and StyleGAN development.

6.8 GAN IN MODERN AI

Generative Adversarial Networks have evolved from experimental generative models into core building blocks of modern artificial intelligence systems. Today, AI systems use GANs in combination with deep learning architectures and multimodal systems and large-scale AI pipelines to create more realistic and robust and data-efficient outputs.

The data-centric AI field depends on GANs to create synthetic datasets which produce high-quality samples that solve data shortage problems and class imbalance issues and privacy protection needs. This is particularly important in domains such as healthcare, finance, and autonomous systems, where real data is expensive or sensitive. The synthetic data produced through GANs enables models to achieve better generalization capabilities while maintaining protection of secret data.

The computer vision field uses GANs as essential tools which support various applications such as image enhancement and restoration and simulation. Modern AI systems depend on GAN-based modules to perform super-resolution and image completion and domain adaptation which allows models to function correctly in new environments. GANs create realistic simulation environments which training self-driving cars and robotics systems use for their development.

The research focuses on transformers which achieve superior results in representation learning while diffusion models produce high-fidelity outputs, but GANs still maintain their usefulness because they enable quick sampling and controllable output generation and support adversarial learning systems. Hybrid systems increasingly combine GANs with VAEs, diffusion processes, and foundation models to balance speed, control, and quality.

GANs have shaped AI research by introducing adversarial optimization and game-theoretic learning and distribution matching principles which became essential components of modern AI research. The current applications of these concepts include adversarial robustness and representation learning and self-supervised learning.

TEST YOUR KNOWLEDGE

1. Why is GAN training fundamentally modeled as a minimax optimization problem, and how does this formulation contribute to instability during learning?

2. Explain how modeling GAN training as a nonlinear dynamical system helps in understanding oscillatory behavior and mode collapse.
3. Why does mode collapse indicate a failure in distribution learning even when generated samples appear visually realistic?
4. How does the introduction of a closed-loop control (CLC) term stabilize GAN training from a control-theoretic perspective?
5. Compare Vanilla GAN and WGAN in terms of their loss functions and explain why Wasserstein distance improves gradient behavior.
6. Why does conditioning in cGANs reduce mode collapse compared to standard GANs, and how does this relate to sub-manifold partitioning of the data distribution?
7. In CycleGAN, why is cycle consistency loss necessary when paired training data is unavailable?
8. Explain how StyleGAN's intermediate latent space enables fine-grained control over generated image attributes.
9. Why are evaluation metrics such as Inception Score and FID insufficient for fully assessing GAN performance?
10. In modern AI systems, why do GANs remain relevant despite the rise of diffusion models and transformer-based generators?

Generative AI | Large Language Models

CHAPTER 7

Diffusion Models and Modern Image Generation

More information about the current results shows that diffusion models have become the principal method used in contemporary generative artificial intelligence systems which create high-quality images. Diffusion models differ from previous generative methods because they use a probabilistic system which transforms random noise into valid output through a series of trained denoising stages. The system design produces stable training results while enabling diverse sample generation and high-quality visual output.

Diffusion-based techniques showed their capacity to produce text-to-image content and execute extensive creative tasks when they were applied in recent breakthroughs that included Latent Diffusion Models and Stable Diffusion and DALL·E. The existing models have made major contributions to various domains which include digital art and media as well as medical imaging and scientific visualization fields.

The chapter presents the theoretical basis and mathematical framework of diffusion models while it describes the forward and reverse diffusion methods and latent space methods which can be used for large-scale generation. The study compares diffusion models with GANs while it assesses their practical uses to show how diffusion models currently lead the field of image generation technology.

7.1 INTRODUCTION TO DIFFUSION MODELS

Diffusion models represent a group of probabilistic generative models which create new data through learning the process of reversing incremental noise addition. The generation process of diffusion models employs a series of specific noise-reduction steps which convert random noise into organized patterns found in images, audio, or video content. The implementation of this approach results in training stability, strong theoretical foundations, and the ability to produce high-quality samples as shown in Figure 7.1.

The essential structure of diffusion models includes two interdependent processes which operate through a forward diffusion process that progressively adds noise to data and a reverse diffusion process that

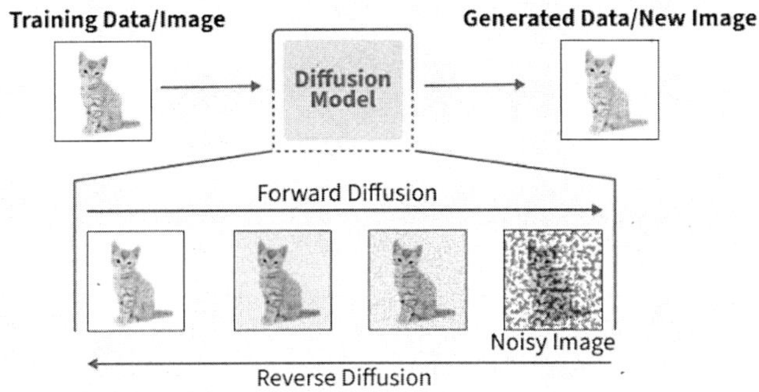

Figure 7.1: *Diffusion Model.*

acquires skills to eliminate that noise. Through training a neural network to understand the reverse process, diffusion models enable the creation of realistic samples which begin with random noise.

7.1.1 Why Diffusion Models Matter?

The significance of diffusion models derives from their ability to deliver a dependable generative modeling system which uses likelihood-based methods to prevent the problems that arise from mode collapse and training instability which occur in adversarial approaches. The system learns complex data patterns through its method of generating output which operates as a series of simple transformations that follow a denoising process.

The system becomes understandable through probability theory and score-based learning while its basic design allows users to perform text-based and label-based and other modal conditioning experiments. The properties of diffusion models function as the essential foundation which supports high-quality generative systems like Stable Diffusion and DALL·E because these systems want to deliver dependable results at a high level of output quality without worrying about how fast they can sample.

7.1.2 Architecture of Diffusion Models

The diffusion model's architecture generally involves two major components-forward diffusion and reverse diffusion.

A. Forward Diffusion Process

The forward diffusion process progressively corrupts a data sample by adding Gaussian noise over a sequence of time steps. The system operates through a Markov chain which transforms intricate data sets into a basic noise pattern as shown in Figure 7.2.

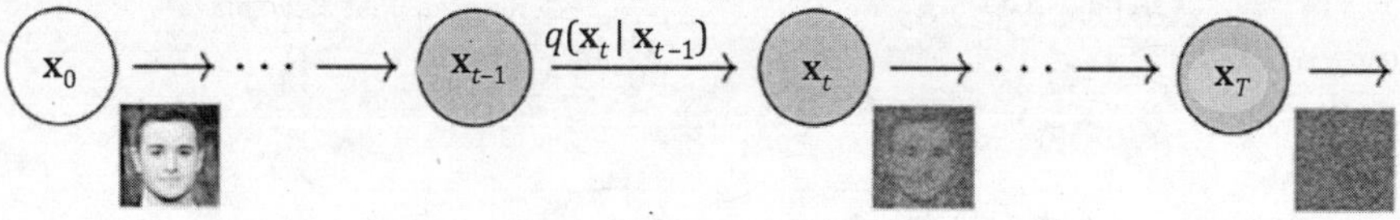

Figure 7.2: *Forward Diffusion Process.*

Formally, the forward process is expressed as:

$$q(x_t \mid x_{t-1}) = \mathcal{N}(x_t; \sqrt{\alpha_t} x_{t-1}, (1 - \alpha_t)I)$$

where,

x_t is the noisy data at time step t,
$\alpha_t \in (0, 1)$ controls the noise level,
I is the identity covariance matrix.

This formulation ensures that as increases, the data distribution converges to an isotropic Gaussian.

Intuition: Adding small amounts of noise step-by-step makes the learning of the reverse process tractable. A useful closed-form expression allows sampling at any time step directly from the original data:

$$x_t = \sqrt{\bar{\alpha}_t} x_0 + \sqrt{1 - \bar{\alpha}_t}\, \varepsilon, \ \varepsilon \sim \mathcal{N}(0, I)$$

where, $\bar{\alpha}_t = \prod_{i=1}^{t} \alpha_i$.

This avoids explicitly simulating all intermediate steps during training.

B. Reverse Diffusion Process

The reverse diffusion process reconstructs original data through its method of sequential noise elimination. The true reverse distribution cannot be computed directly which leads to the use of a neural network model that uses parameter θ for distribution approximation as shown in Figure 7.3.

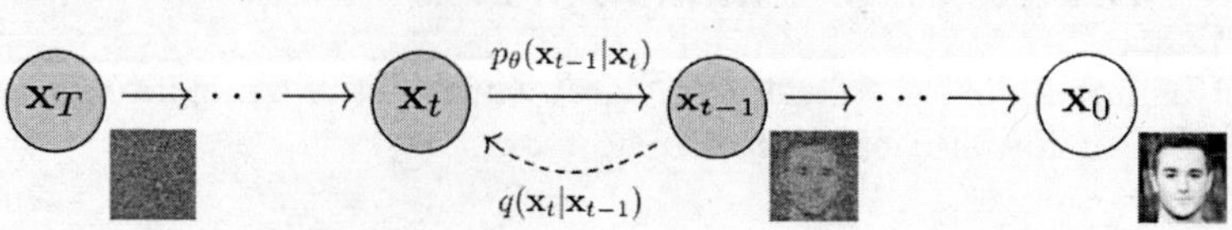

Figure 7.3: *Reverse Diffusion Process.*

The reverse transition is modeled as:

$$p_\theta (x_{t-1} \mid x_t) = \mathcal{N}(x_{t-1}; \mu_\theta (x_t, t), \sigma_\theta (x_t, t))$$

where, μ_θ and σ_θ are learned functions.

The network learns how to denoise data conditioned on the noise level. In practice, diffusion models predict the noise component instead of directly predicting x_{t-1}, which simplifies optimization and improves stability.

7.1.3 Training Objective

Training diffusion models reduces to a supervised learning problem where the model learns to predict the noise added during the forward process. The objective function is defined as:

$$\mathcal{L}(\theta) = \mathbb{E}_{x_0, \varepsilon, t)} [||\varepsilon - \varepsilon_\theta (x_t, t)||^2]$$

where,

ε is the true Gaussian noise,

ε_θ is the network's prediction.

Minimizing this mean squared error ensures accurate denoising at every time step, enabling high-quality generation. This objective is closely related to score matching, where the model learns the gradient of the data distribution with respect to noise, guiding the reverse diffusion trajectory.

7.1.4 Working Principle

The forward process gradually introduces noise to real data during training while the model develops its ability to forecast and eliminate this noise. The model begins with complete Gaussian noise and uses iterative denoising to create a realistic sample during the reverse process of generation. The modern diffusion-based generators achieve their robust performance and diverse output together with their accurate visual representation through this probabilistic framework.

7.1.5 Advantages of Diffusion Models

Diffusion Models provide two main advantages which help practitioners achieve better results because the models train without any competitive threats which make training processes more dependable and manageable.

- The system generates high-quality outputs which show precise details and varied content and authentic real-world appearance.
- The system builds its foundation on probabilistic modeling which uses likelihood estimation as its core element.
- The system provides flexible conditioning which enables users to work with text and labels and multiple types of multimodal guidance.

7.1.6 Disadvantage of Diffusion Model

The use of Diffusion Models presents two major drawbacks which lead to slow generation processes because the system needs multiple denoising steps to finish its work.

1. The system requires extensive resources to complete both training and sampling processes.
2. The system needs precise tuning of both noise schedules and architectural elements to achieve its intended performance.

7.2 MATHEMATICS OF DIFFUSION

Probabilistic generative modeling serves as the formal basis for diffusion models because their data generation process requires modeling a series of conditional probability distributions. The mathematical formulation provides both stable optimization and workable likelihood estimation methods.

7.2.1 Probabilistic Formulation

Let $x_0 \sim p_{\text{data}}(x)$ denote a data sample drawn from the true data distribution. Diffusion models define a latent variable sequence $\{x_1, x_2, \ldots, x_T\}$ such that:

$$x_0 \to x_1 \to \cdots \to x_T$$

where, x_T follows a known prior distribution, typically an isotropic Gaussian:

$$p(x_T) = \mathcal{N}(0, I)$$

This transforms an unknown complex distribution into a known simple distribution, enabling sampling via probabilistic inversion.

7.2.2 Forward Process as a Markov Chain

The forward diffusion process is defined as a fixed Markov chain that gradually perturbs data by injecting Gaussian noise:

$$q(x_t \mid x_{t-1}) = \mathcal{N}(x_t; \sqrt{\alpha_t x_{t-1}}, (1-\alpha_t)I)$$

where,

$\alpha_t = 1 - \beta_t$

β_t is a predefined variance schedule

This formulation guarantees that noise accumulation is controlled and analytically tractable.

A key mathematical property allows direct sampling at any time step:

$$x_t = \sqrt{\bar{\alpha}_t x_0} + \sqrt{1-\bar{\alpha}_t}\,\varepsilon, \ \varepsilon \sim \mathcal{N}(0, I)$$

with:

$$\bar{\alpha}_t = \prod_{i=1}^{t} \alpha_i$$

Why this matters:

It avoids simulating all intermediate steps during training, reducing computational cost.

7.2.3 Reverse Process Approximation

The reverse process attempts to estimate:

$$p(x_{t-1} \mid x_t)$$

which is intractable in closed form. Therefore, it is approximated using a parameterized model:

$$p_\theta(x_{t-1} | x_t) = \mathcal{N}(x_{t-1}; \mu_\theta(x_t, t), \sigma_t^2 I)$$

The parameters μ_θ are learned, while σ_t^2 is often fixed for stability.

Rather than predicting x_{t-1} directly, modern diffusion models reparameterize the mean in terms of noise prediction, improving convergence behavior.

7.2.4 Noise Prediction Parameterization

The model learns a function $\varepsilon_\theta(x_t, t)$ that estimates the noise added at time step t:

$$\varepsilon_\theta(x_t, t) \approx \varepsilon$$

Using this estimate, the reverse mean can be computed analytically:

$$\mu_\theta(x_t, t) = \frac{1}{\sqrt{\alpha_t}} \left(x_t - \frac{\beta_t}{\sqrt{1-\bar{\alpha}_t}} \varepsilon_\theta(x_t, t) \right)$$

Why predict noise?

Noise follows a simple distribution, making optimization easier and numerically stable.

7.2.5 Training Objective

Training reduces to minimizing the discrepancy between true and predicted noise:

$$\mathcal{L}(\theta) = \mathbb{E}_{x_0, \varepsilon, t}\ [\| \varepsilon - \varepsilon_\theta(x_t, t) \|^2]$$

This mean squared error (MSE) objective corresponds to denoising score matching, where the model implicitly learns:

$$\nabla x_t \log p(x_t)$$

These gradient guides the reverse diffusion trajectory toward high-probability regions of the data distribution.

7.3 FORWARD AND REVERSE PROCESS

The diffusion framework operates through two tightly coupled processes: a forward diffusion process, used only during training, and a reverse diffusion process, which enables data generation. The processes work together to create a framework which enables diffusion models to learn how to convert random noise into valuable data output as shown in Figure 7.4.

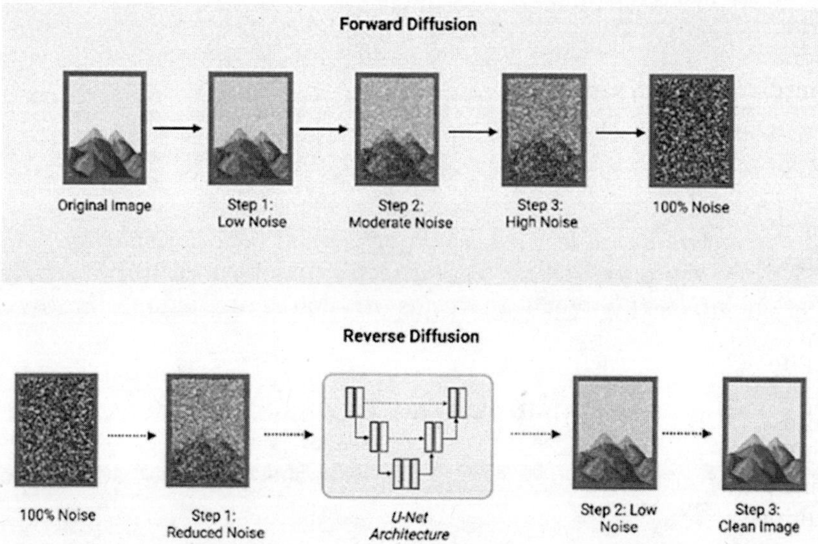

Figure 7.4: *Forward vs Reverse Diffusion Process.*

7.3.1 Forward Process: Controlled Noise Injection

The forward process uses controlled noise injection to create Gaussian noise from actual data through successive small disturbances which continue for predetermined time intervals. The process exists as a fixed system which maintains both analytical tractability and stability because it cannot be modified through learning.

The forward process exists to achieve two distinct functions which serve different purposes.

- The first function transforms complex data distributions into simple established prior distributions.

- The second function creates noisy intermediate states which serve as supervised training targets for the reverse model.

The forward process functions as a structured corruption method which the model uses to learn inversion although it has no application in generation.

7.3.2 Reverse Process: Learned Denoising Trajectory

The reverse process models the probabilistic inversion of noise addition. The model starts with pure Gaussian noise and uses its learned denoising steps to restore both structural elements and semantic information.

The model does not reconstruct clean data but instead determines which noise exists at every moment. The reparameterization process makes optimization easier to handle while maintaining continuous gradient flow during the training process. The process of generation involves multiple reverse steps which each refine the sample, creating a gradual improvement instead of producing a complete prediction.

7.3.3 Training vs Sampling Roles

The different processes used in diffusion models create their primary distinction. The training phase establishes its process through two steps. The forward process generates noisy samples, and the model learns to predict the injected noise at arbitrary time steps. The sampling phase starts its process through two steps. The forward process is discarded. Generation begins from random noise and relies exclusively on the learned reverse process.

The system maintains training control through supervised training while preserving stable operations, which enables sampling to run through multiple processes that operators can manage.

7.3.4 Temporal Conditioning and Consistency

The reverse process requires explicit time step index conditioning. This method enables the model to acquire separate denoising methods which operate according to different noise levels, while it maintains exact reconstruction throughout all phases of the process.

Time conditioning enables:

- Accurate handling of both high-noise and low-noise regimes
- Smooth transitions between intermediate latent states
- Robust convergence during long denoising chains.

The forward-reverse decomposition method establishes generative modeling through its development into multiple straightforward inference tasks for resolution. The model learns to incrementally restore structure instead of acquiring a direct mapping from noise to data, which results in strong stability and high fidelity for diffusion-based generators.

The stepwise formulation of diffusion models creates a distinction between their functionality and that of adversarial and autoregressive methods, which establishes the basic structure needed to create advanced systems like latent diffusion and text-conditioned generation.

7.4 LATENT DIFFUSION MODELS (LDM'S)

The researchers developed LDMs as a method to generate high-resolution images through diffusion-based generative modeling because they implemented their diffusion process in a compressed latent space instead of using pixel space. The design achieves a major decrease in computational expenses while maintaining all necessary capabilities to create authentic visual content as shown in Figure 7.5.

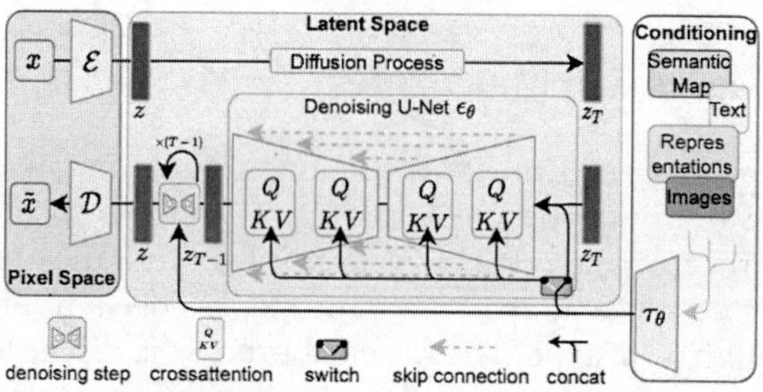

Figure 7.5: *Latent Diffusion Models.*

The key motivation behind LDMs is efficiency. High-resolution images need extensive memory and computation resources when using pixel-space diffusion models. LDMs first transform images into their lower-dimensional latent space through a pre-trained auto encoder before applying diffusion in that latent space. The system achieves improved scalability for both training and inference through its implementation of latent space diffusion.

7.4.1 Core Architecture

An LDM consists of two main components:

A. *Autoencoder (Encoder–Decoder)*

The encoder creates a compact latent representation from high-dimensional images. The decoder reconstructs images from this latent space. This stage preserves perceptually important features while discarding redundant details.

B. *Latent Diffusion Model*

A denoising diffusion probabilistic model operates on the latent representations of the data. The forward process adds noise in latent space and the reverse process learns to remove this noise step-by-step which gradually restores meaningful structure.

LDMs achieve efficient performance together with visually accurate results through their method of separating representation learning from generative modeling.

7.4.2 Conditioning and Control

Latent Diffusion Models provide support for conditioning mechanisms. The diffusion process can be controlled through additional inputs which include text embeddings and class labels and semantic layouts and reference images. The denoising network receives conditioning information which enables controlled generation without changing the main diffusion process. LDMs provide flexible functionality which allows them to operate as essential components in contemporary text-to-image systems and various multimodal generative systems.

7.4.3 Applications of LDMs

Latent Diffusion Models have been successfully applied to a wide range of generative tasks which include:

- Text-to-image generation
- Image inpainting and image completion
- Super-resolution of low-quality images
- Semantic and class-conditional image synthesis

The system generates high-resolution outputs which makes it suitable for use in real-world situations.

7.4.4 Pre-Trained Models and Inference

Pre-trained LDMs are available for various datasets, including CelebA-HQ, FFHQ, LSUN, and ImageNet. These models can be fine-tuned or used directly for inference. For example, text-to-image synthesis can be performed using the following command:

python scripts/txt2img.py --prompt "a sunset behind a mountain range, vector image" --ddim_eta 1.0 --n_samples 1 --n_iter 1 --H 384 --W 1024 --scale 5.0

This generates high-quality images with customizable parameters like resolution (H, W), sampling steps (ddim_steps), and diversity control (scale).

7.4.5 Advantages and Limitations

Advantages

- Significantly reduced computational and memory requirements.
- Scalable to high-resolution image generation.
- Flexible conditioning across multiple modalities.

Limitations

- Quality depends on the expressiveness of the latent autoencoder.
- Extremely fine-grained details may be lost during latent compression.
- Requires careful design of latent dimensionality and noise schedules.

Latent Diffusion Models show practical advancement as a new form of diffusion-based generative modeling. The framework allows diffusion models to operate at high-resolution production systems through its capacity to transfer processing tasks into a discovered latent space. The current image generation methods use this concept as their main foundation.

7.5 TEXT-TO-IMAGE GENERATION

Text-to-image generation through Large Language Models (LLMs) establishes a contemporary multimodal system which connects natural language comprehension with visual image creation systems. The framework requires LLMs to process and structure textual prompts which they use to control image creation systems that include diffusion models and GANs as less common options.

The separation between linguistic reasoning and visual generation allows users to produce interactive image synthesis which maintains semantic alignment and precise control as shown in Figure 7.6.

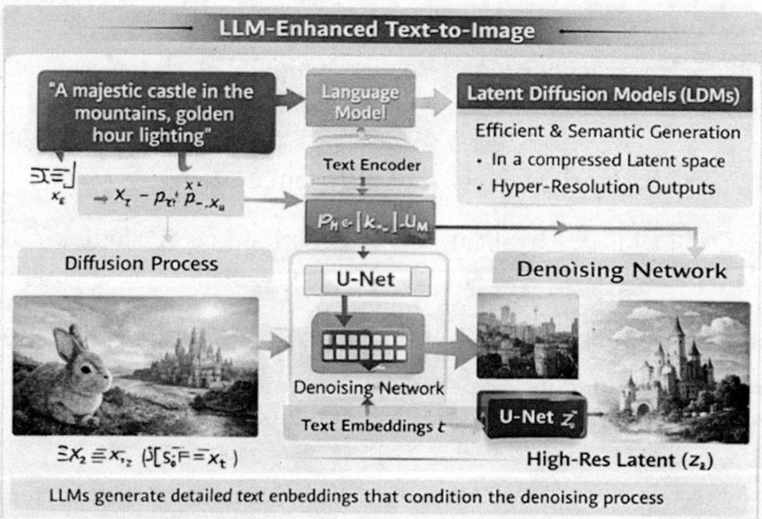

Figure 7.6: *LLM Text to Image Generation.*

7.5.1 Operational Pipeline

Modern text-to-image systems follow a structured pipeline that combines language modeling and probabilistic image generation:

- Prompt Understanding (LLM Layer)
- The LLM analyzes the user's natural language prompt to:

Identify objects, attributes, styles, and relationships

The user can choose to extend their prompt into a complete visual description from which they can create their desired content.

This step improves semantic grounding and reduces prompt under specification.

Text Encoding and Conditioning

The pretrained text encoder system transforms the processed prompt into a continuous embedding space through its implementation of CLIP and T5 systems.

The embeddings function as conditioning variables that direct the image generation sequence.

Text-to-image generation models acquire knowledge through mathematical lcarning that evaluates:

Mathematically, text-to-image generation models learn:

$$p(x \mid c)$$

where, x is the generated image and c is the text embedding.

Image Synthesis

Diffusion models perform their process by removing random Gaussian noise through multiple steps which receive guidance from text embeddings that use cross-attention mechanisms. The present-day use of GAN-based approaches has decreased because they developed important historical foundations but their users now experience problems with stability and controllability. Diffusion-based synthesis provides an accurate mechanism which enables precise matching of textual meaning to visual elements.

Post-Processing and Refinement

LLMs can further assist by generating:

- Image editing instructions (inpainting, outpainting)
- Style transformations

Users can refine their work through conversation-based feedback which enables them to make multiple iterations. The system enables users to direct the generation process through interactive controls which keep the process active without interruption.

7.5.2 Reference Implementation

The following implementation demonstrates the canonical design pattern used in modern systems such as Stable Diffusion.

The LLM improves semantic clarity, while the diffusion model converts structured noise into an image consistent with the textual condition as shown in Figure 7.7.

```
from transformers import pipeline
from diffusers import StableDiffusionPipeline
import torch

# Prompt enhancement using LLM
llm = pipeline("text2text-generation", model="google/flan-t5-large")
prompt = "A futuristic city at sunset"
enhanced_prompt = llm(
    f"Expand into a detailed image description: {prompt}"
)[0]["generated_text"]

# Image generation
pipe = StableDiffusionPipeline.from_pretrained(
    "runwayml/stable-diffusion-v1-5",
    torch_dtype=torch.float16
).to("cuda")

image = pipe(enhanced_prompt).images[0]
image.save("generated_image.png")
```

Figure 7.7: *Implementing Text to Image.*

7.5.3 Advantages of LLM–Diffusion Integration

- Enhanced semantic alignment for complex prompts.
- Automatic prompt optimization without manual engineering.
- Multimodal reasoning, enabling text–image–context fusion.
- Interactive refinement, allowing iterative user control.

7.5.4 Emerging Research Directions

- **DiffusionGPT:** Joint reasoning between LLMs and diffusion steps.
- **Composable generation:** Decomposing prompts into objects and layouts.
- **Agent-based systems:** LLMs acting as creative controllers for multi-step synthesis.

These developments form the conceptual basis of advanced systems such as DALL·E, Stable Diffusion XL, and Sora-like architectures.

7.6 STABLE DIFFUSION AND DALL·E

Stable Diffusion and DALL·E show two important implementations of contemporary text-to-image diffusion systems which transform theoretical diffusion modeling progress into operational large-scale creative generation systems. The two systems operate on the same foundation which consists of probabilistic denoising, text conditioning, and latent representations but they differ greatly in their architectural design, methods of deployment, and goals for system development.

7.6.1 Stable Diffusion

Stable Diffusion operates as an open-source system that scales its text-to-image capabilities through latent diffusion technology to produce high-resolution images. The denoising process of Stable Diffusion operates in compressed latent space which allows the system to maintain visual quality while using fewer computational resources than standard pixel-space diffusion models.

Core Architecture

Stable Diffusion consists of three tightly integrated components:

Variational Autoencoder (VAE)

It compresses images into a lower-dimensional latent space and reconstructs them back into pixel space after generation.

Text Encoder (CLIP-based)

The system converts natural language prompts into dense semantic embeddings which serve as conditioning elements.

Latent Diffusion Model (U-Net)

The system uses cross-attention mechanisms to align visual elements with text elements by performing denoising processes in latent space through multiple iterations.

Formally, Stable Diffusion learns:

$$p(x \mid c) = p(\text{Decoder}(\hat{z}) \mid c)$$

where, $\hat{z}$ is the denoised, latent representation conditioned on text embedding c.

Key Characteristics

- Operates entirely in latent space, enabling high-resolution generation ($\geq 1024 \times 1024$).

- Supports classifier-free guidance, allowing fine control over prompt adherence.
- Enables tasks such as inpainting, outpainting, super-resolution, and style transfer.

7.6.2 DALL·E

DALL·E functions as a closed text-to-image generation system which OpenAI developed to demonstrate its capacity for understanding meaning and solving complex problems while maintaining safe operational methods as shown in Figure 7.8.

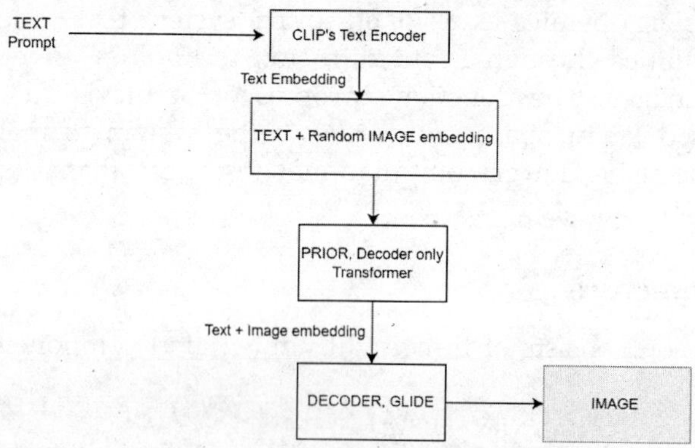

Figure 7.8: *DALL-E.*

The system functions as a closed system which delivers consistent results while maintaining optimal performance because DALL·E operates as a closed system but Stable Diffusion functions as an open system. DALL·E used autoregressive modeling for its first version, but later versions adopted diffusion-based generation which uses advanced language-vision alignment technology.

Design Focus

- Strong handling of abstract, compositional, and symbolic prompts.
- Robust prompt–image alignment even for rare or unusual concepts.
- Built-in content filtering and safety mechanisms.

Although architectural details are not fully disclosed, DALL·E follows the same core generative principle:

$$\text{Noise} \xrightarrow{\text{conditioned denoising}} \text{Image}$$

guided by powerful joint language–vision representations.

7.6.3 Comparison between Stable Diffusion and DALL-E

The research demonstrates that Stable Diffusion uses latent diffusion to create scalable generative modeling which operates as a public resource while DALL·E shows that semantic understanding and safety measures and system integration work together to create functional results as shown in Table 7.1. The two systems show two different pathways which modern generative AI operates through:

- The first pathway uses latent modeling to achieve both efficiency and openness.
- The second pathway establishes system reliability through controlled system deployment.

TABLE 7.1: Comparison between Stable Diffusion and DALL-E

Aspect	*Stable Diffusion*	*DALL·E*
Model Type	Latent Diffusion Model	Diffusion-based (proprietary)
Openness	Open-source	Closed-source
Execution	Local & cloud	Cloud-based
Customization	High (fine-tuning, plugins)	Limited
Prompt Control	Explicit guidance scaling	Implicit optimization
Target Users	Researchers, developers	General users

The systems represent the ultimate application of diffusion theory which this chapter presented earlier while they function as the core technological base for developing new multimodal generative systems.

7.7 DIFFUSION VS GANS

Diffusion models and Generative Adversarial Networks (GANs) exist as two distinct approaches to generative modeling. The two methods share a common goal of learning complex data distributions to produce authentic sample outputs, but they exhibit fundamental differences in their architectural design and training processes and their theoretical foundations and real-world performance as shown in Figure 7.9.

The Core Modeling Philosophy defines GANs as a two-player adversarial game that generates samples through generator attempts to deceive the discriminator which evaluates between authentic and counterfeit outputs. The system enables quick one-time sample generation yet leads to unpredictable system behavior. The Diffusion models through their probabilistic framework create structured data by reversing the process of incremental noise addition during generation. Their operations depend on likelihood measurements instead of using an adversarial framework.

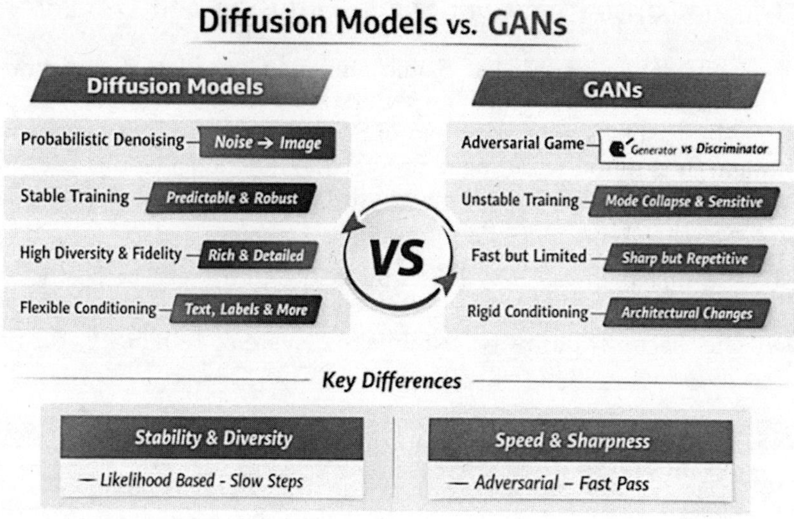

Figure 7.9: *Diffusion Models vs GAN's.*

Training Stability

GANs experience multiple stability issues because they face three problems which include mode collapse and oscillations and their dependence on specific architecture designs. The Diffusion models transform training processes into a supervised noise-prediction task which they solve through mean squared error optimization to achieve stable results and reliable output and reproducible outcomes.

Sample Quality and Diversity

The GAN system creates clear images through its image generation process but it cannot create diverse output because of its mode collapse problem. The Diffusion models create multiple samples from complete data distribution which produces samples that maintain global coherence while showing high-resolution details and fine-grained details.

Sampling Speed and Efficiency

The GAN system achieves quick inference results because it creates all outputs in one generation process. The Diffusion models need to complete multiple denoising steps which results in slower performance but latent diffusion and DDIM and optimized pipelines help to decrease this time difference.

Theoretical Foundations

The mathematical analysis of GANs becomes difficult because they do not provide direct likelihood measurements. The Diffusion models base their operations on three scientific concepts which include variational inference and score-based modeling and stochastic differential equations to deliver precise optimization targets and backend system understanding.

Conditioning and Control

The process of GAN conditioning requires users to make changes to the architecture through specific methods which include cGAN and StyleGAN. The system enables stable diffusion through text and label and image and mask and layout-based conditioning which Diffusion models support as their native functionality.

GANs prioritize speed and sharpness at the cost of stability and diversity. Diffusion models prioritize stability, diversity, and theoretical soundness at the cost of slower sampling, making them ideal for high-quality, controllable generative tasks.

7.8 REAL-WORLD APPLICATIONS OF DIFFUSION MODELS

The diffusion models establish themselves as fundamental technology which supports present-day generative artificial intelligence to create multiple high-quality outputs across different fields. Diffusion models achieve their best performance through their denoising process which operates in multiple steps together with their powerful statistical base because these features allow them to produce outputs that match real-world details.

1. *Image Synthesis and Editing*

- **High-Resolution Image Generation:** The diffusion models create photorealistic images from text prompts and sketches and low-resolution inputs. The tools Stable Diffusion and DALL·E demonstrate this particular capability.
- **Inpainting and Image Restoration:** It uses conditional noise removal to create missing or damaged parts of images complete.
- **Super-Resolution:** The process increases image quality by using multiple steps to clean up hidden image elements while keeping essential visual information.

2. *Text-to-Image Generation*

- It creates visual content for marketing purposes and gaming applications and virtual reality through its ability to create visual assets from natural language prompts.
- It uses LLM integration to improve prompt comprehension together with scene composition features which enable users to adjust object positioning and visual elements according to their needs.

3. *Video and Animation*

- It creates short videos or frame sequences through its ability to extend the denoising method into a time-based framework.
- It provides value for animation production together with synthetic video dataset creation and special effects development in movies and games.

4. *Medical and Scientific Imaging*

- It creates realistic medical image simulations which researchers and trainers can use without needing actual patient information.
- It helps improve MRI and CT and microscopy images by applying noise reduction techniques together with resolution enhancement methods.

5. *Multimodal AI Systems*

It creates multimodal content by integrating audio and text and 3D data. The system generates AI-based presentations which create augmented reality experiences and interactive 3D content.

TEST YOUR KNOWLEDGE

1. Explain the forward and reverse diffusion processes and how they enable noise-to-data transformation.
2. Derive the forward diffusion step equation $q(x_t \mid x_{t-1})$ and explain the role of α_t.
3. How does the training objective of a diffusion model relate to score matching and mean squared error optimization?
4. Compare GANs and diffusion models in terms of stability, diversity, and sampling speed.
5. Explain latent diffusion models (LDMs) and their computational advantages over pixel-space diffusion models.
6. Describe the role of LLMs in text-to-image generation and how they improve prompt understanding.
7. Using Stable Diffusion as an example, explain how time-step conditioning is applied in the reverse process.
8. Discuss the limitations of diffusion models and how latent-space methods and accelerated samplers mitigate them.
9. Provide a conceptual explanation of why diffusion models are likelihood-based and why this avoids mode collapse.
10. Enumerate real-world applications of diffusion models and justify why high-fidelity generation is critical in each domain.

CHAPTER 8

Multimodal AI and Vision-Language Models

Traditional AI systems operate by handling one type of data which includes either text or images as a single unit. The field of artificial intelligence developed multimodal systems to study various types of data together which allows machines to learn and reason about different data types that include visual data and linguistic data to achieve better understanding which resembles human comprehension.

The chapter investigates Vision–Language Models (VLMs) which develop common visual and textual representations to connect visual understanding with semantic comprehension. These models enable multiple functions which include generating image descriptions and answering questions based on visual content and conducting searches across different media and creating images based on text descriptions. VLM technology has become essential for contemporary AI systems because of recent developments in large-scale system training and contrastive learning methods.

The chapter presents basic concepts of multimodal learning together with methods for creating image and text representations while studying important system designs which include CLIP and BLIP. The study provides insights into cross-modal reasoning together with its industrial use cases and the critical obstacles which shape present multimodal AI research.

The chapter explains theoretical principles and practical applications of multimodal AI which demonstrate that vision–language models function as essential components for building more versatile artificial intelligence systems.

8.1 WHAT IS MULTIMODAL AI

The term multimodal AI describes artificial intelligence systems which possess the ability to process multiple data types simultaneously while maintaining alignment and conducting reasoning processes. Multimodal systems enable users to learn from two different data types because they develop cross-modal representations which explain how different data types interact with each other as shown in Figure 8.1.

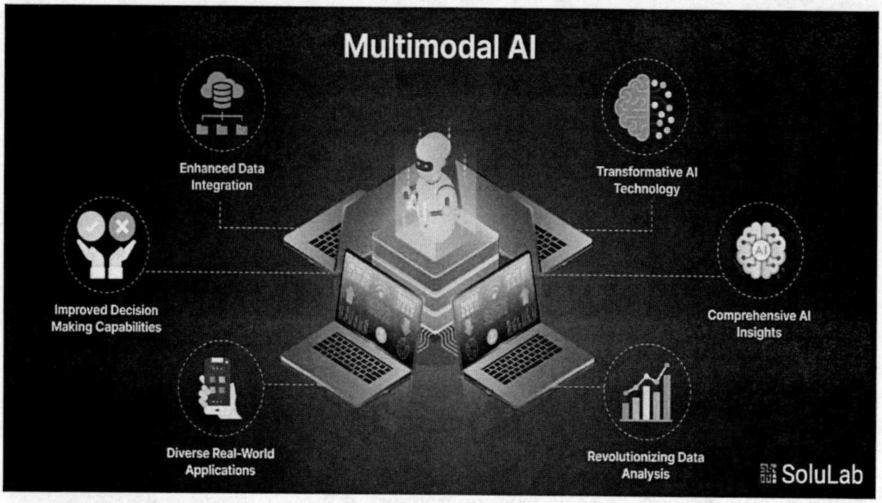

Figure 8.1: *Multimodal AI.*

Multimodal AI development stems from the fact that human intelligence needs to process multiple types of sensory information. Humans comprehend information through the combination of visual elements and spoken words and auditory sounds and the understanding of time-based sequences. Multimodal AI enables machines to understand complicated environments better than systems which rely on only one type of input.

The fundamental structure of a multimodal system includes three essential components as shown in Figure 8.2.

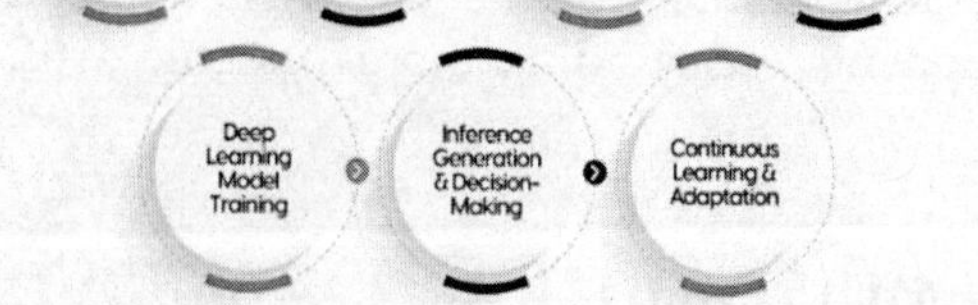

Figure 8.2: *Working of multimodal AI.*

A. Modality-Specific Encoding

It transforms each sensory input through dedicated encoders which use transformers to process text and convolutional or vision transformers to handle images and signal-based models to interpret audio signals. The encoders create shared embedding spaces which transform diverse inputs into matching formats.

B. Cross-Modal Fusion and Alignment

It uses alignment methods that it has learned to combine the encoded data. The system has three different methods for fusion:

1. Early fusion, which combines low-level features.
2. Late fusion, which merges high-level semantic outputs.
3. Hybrid fusion, which integrates both for complex reasoning tasks.

The aims to develop common meanings that various modalities can share while maintaining their unique characteristics.

C. Joint Reasoning or Generation

The unified representation supports various downstream tasks which include classification and retrieval and reasoning and generation. Multimodal models in generative settings create text which depends on images and images which depend on text and multimodal outputs which function together.

Formally, given multiple modalities $\{x^{(1)}, x^{(2)}, \ldots, x^{(M)}\}$, multimodal learning aims to model a joint distribution:

$$p(y \mid x^{(1)}, x^{(2)}, \ldots, x^{(M)})$$

or, in generative settings,

$$p(x^{(i)} \mid x^{(j)})$$

where semantic consistency across modalities is explicitly enforced during training.

Example in Python (Image + Text Fusion)

This PyTorch implementation demonstrates a simple multimodal learning architecture that fuses visual and textual information. A pre-trained ResNet-18 extracts high-level image features, while a linear layer encodes textual inputs into a compact representation. These modality-specific embeddings are concatenated and passed to a joint classifier, enabling unified reasoning across image and text modalities as shown in Figure 8.3.

The main advantage which multimodal AI systems present lies in their ability to handle uncertain situations and unclear data. The system achieves better prediction results because one modality can replace missing or faulty information from other modalities. Multimodal systems demonstrate their highest efficiency in actual applications used to build intelligent assistants, conduct medical assessments, operate autonomous technologies, and manage human–computer interactions.

```
import torch
import torch.nn as nn
from torchvision import models
class MultiModalNet(nn.Module):
    def __init__(self, text_dim, num_classes):
        super().__init__()
        self.image_model = models.resnet18(pretrained=True)
        self.image_model.fc = nn.Identity()
        self.text_model = nn.Linear(text_dim, 256)
        self.fc = nn.Linear(256 + 512, num_classes)
    def forward(self, image, text):
        img_feat = self.image_model(image)
        txt_feat = self.text_model(text)
        combined = torch.cat((img_feat, txt_feat), dim=1)
        return self.fc(combined)
# Example usage:
# image_input: tensor [batch, 3, 224, 224]
# text_input: tensor [batch, text_dim]
```

Figure 8.3: *Example usage.*

The basic structure of multimodal AI provides the essential foundation which supports the development of Vision–Language Models. This section establishes the fundamental concepts which govern multimodal learning, while the following sections will examine vision–language representation learning and model architectures and cross-modal reasoning mechanisms.

8.2 CONCEPT AND STRUCTURE OF VISION–LANGUAGE MODELS (VLMS)

Vision–Language Models (VLMs) use multimodal systems to process visual content and linguistic data through their development of matching semantic representations. VLMs create an all-inclusive system that enables users to work with images and text together because their components are merged into a single space that enables unified reasoning as shown in Figure 8.4.

VLMs operate to create a system that connects visual elements with language components including nouns and attributes and relations and actions. This enables machines to interpret images through language and ground language in visual perception.

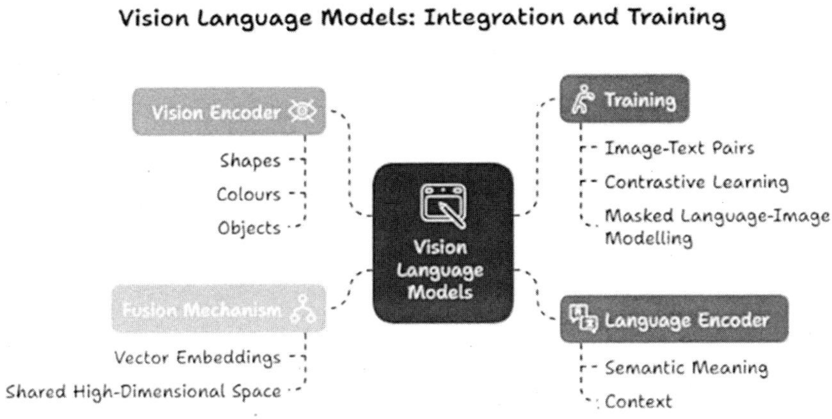

Figure 8.4: *Vision Language Model.*

8.2.1 Structural Components of Vision–Language Models

A standard VLM architecture consists of three fundamental components:

1. **Visual Encoder:** The visual encoder extracts high-level semantic features from an image I. It is typically implemented using convolutional neural networks (CNNs) or vision transformers (ViTs).

$$\mathbf{v} = f_v(I),\ \mathbf{v} \in \mathbb{R}^d$$

This representation captures objects, spatial layouts, textures, and global scene context.

2. **Language Encoder:** The language encoder processes textual input T using transformer-based models to produce contextualized word or sentence embeddings.

$$\mathbf{t} = f_t(T),\ \mathbf{t} \in \mathbb{R}^d$$

These embeddings encode semantic meaning, syntactic structure, and contextual relationships within language as shown in Figure 8.5.

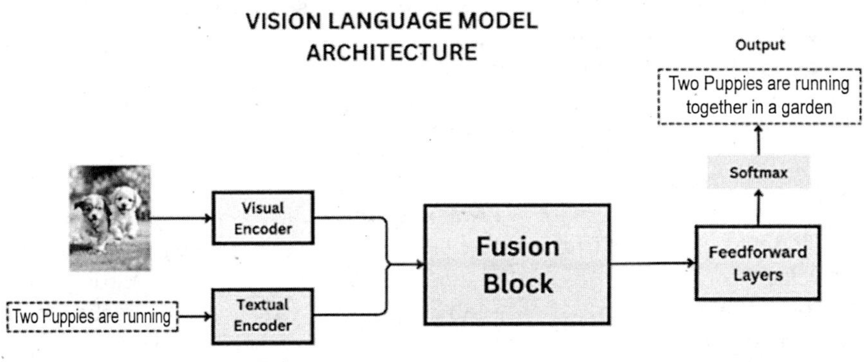

Figure 8.5: *VLM Architecture.*

3. **Multimodal Alignment/Fusion Module:** The alignment module brings visual and textual embeddings into a shared semantic space, enabling cross-modal interaction. Depending on the model design, this can be achieved via:
   - Contrastive alignment (e.g., CLIP-style)
   - Cross-attention mechanisms
   - Joint multimodal transformers

   Semantic consistency is enforced by maximizing similarity between matched image–text pairs:

$$\mathrm{sim}(\mathbf{v}, \mathbf{t}) = \frac{\mathbf{v} \cdot \mathbf{t}}{\| \mathbf{v} \| \| \mathbf{t} \|}$$

This alignment allows the model to learn visual concepts that are language-grounded, forming the conceptual backbone of VLMs.

8.2.2 Concept Learning and Generalization

Unlike task-specific vision or NLP models, VLMs learn concept-level abstractions rather than fixed labels. This enables:

- Zero-shot learning (recognizing unseen categories)
- Open-vocabulary recognition
- Instruction-driven reasoning

Because concepts are learned jointly from image–text pairs, VLMs generalize naturally to new tasks without retraining, making them suitable as foundation models for multimodal intelligence.

8.2.3 Role of VLMs in Advanced AI Systems

Vision–Language Models act as the semantic interface between perception and reasoning. They are central to:

- Text-to-image systems (e.g., Stable Diffusion guidance)
- Visual question answering
- Embodied AI and robotics
- Multimodal agents and assistants

In robotics, VLMs enable agents to interpret natural language instructions and map them to visual actions, bridging perception and control.

The main advantage of VLMs systems is their ability to transfer knowledge between different tasks. VLMs demonstrate the ability to apply learned concepts to new categories and instructions because they acquire knowledge through modality-agnostic learning. The technology is designed for robotics and embodied intelligence because those systems need to understand natural language commands within visually intricate surroundings.

The latest developments show that VLMs need to undergo pretraining on extensive image-text databases in order to develop into foundational systems for handling multiple types of visual and textual information. The current research investigates image-text representation learning because these models serve as essential components for contemporary systems which include CLIP and BLIP and multimodal assistants.

8.3 IMAGE–TEXT REPRESENTATION LEARNING USING CONTRASTIVE LOSS (InfoNCE)

The main goal of Image-Text Representation Learning is to create a unified semantic embedding space which connects images with their matching textual descriptions while keeping unrelated image-text pairs at a greater distance. The shared representation serves as the fundamental system which allows Vision-Language Models to execute tasks that include image retrieval and captioning and visual question answering and zero-shot classification as shown in Figure 8.6.

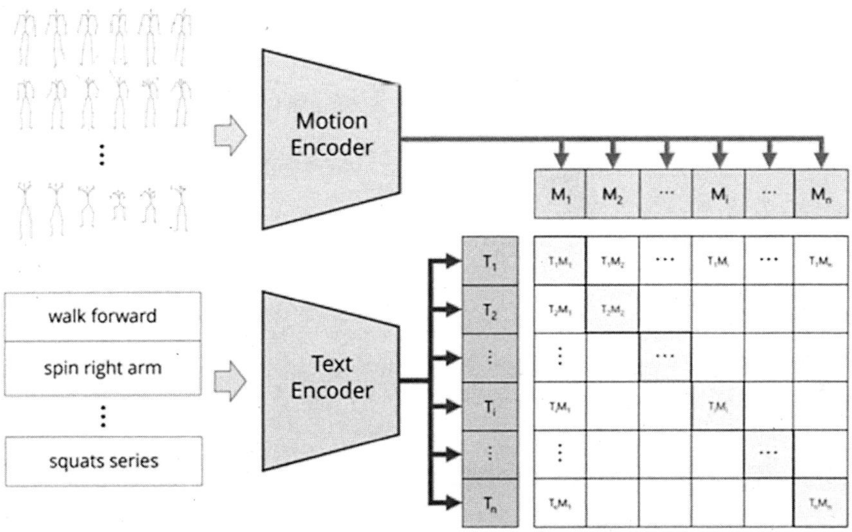

Figure 8.6: *Image—Text Representation Learning.*

Let an image I and a paired text description T be processed by two modality-specific encoders:

$$\mathbf{v} = f_{\text{img}}(I), \ \mathbf{t} = f_{\text{text}}(T)$$

where f_{img} is a vision encoder (e.g., CNN or Vision Transformer) and f_{text} is a language encoder (e.g., Transformer-based model). Both outputs are projected into a common latent space of equal dimensionality to allow direct comparison.

8.3.1 Contrastive Learning Principle

The training process uses contrastive learning to create a learning framework which enables the model to learn from both positive and negative instances that exist within each batch. A positive pair consists of a matched image and its correct caption, while negative pairs are formed by mismatched image–text combinations.

Similarity between image and text embeddings is typically computed using cosine similarity:

$$\text{sim}(\mathbf{v}, \mathbf{t}) = \frac{\mathbf{v} \cdot \mathbf{t}}{\| \mathbf{v} \| \| \mathbf{t} \|}$$

The objective is to maximize similarity for aligned pairs and minimize it for misaligned pairs.

8.3.2 InfoNCE Loss for Image–Text Alignment

The most widely used objective function is the InfoNCE (Information Noise-Contrastive Estimation) loss. For a batch of N image–text pairs $\{(I_i, T_i)\}_{i=1}^{N}$, the loss is defined as:

$$\mathcal{L}_{\text{InfoNCE}} = -\frac{1}{N} \sum_{i=1}^{N} \log \frac{\exp(\text{sim}(\mathbf{v}_i, \mathbf{t}_i)/\tau)}{\sum_{j=1}^{N} \exp(\text{sim}(\mathbf{v}_i, \mathbf{t}_j)/\tau)}$$

where, τ is a temperature parameter that controls how sharply the model distinguishes between correct and incorrect pairs.

The numerator rewards correct image–text alignment, while the denominator penalizes similarity with all non-matching text samples. This encourages the model to learn fine-grained semantic correspondences across modalities.

8.3.3 The Importance and Outcomes

Image–Text Representation Learning with contrastive loss permits:

- Zero-shot learning which enables recognition of new concepts through natural language prompts without the need for task-specific retraining.
- Cross-modal retrieval which enables users to search through both text-to-image and image-to-text platforms.
- The development of robust semantic grounding which provides essential support for advanced VLM systems including CLIP and BLIP.

This method redirects multimodal learning research toward a metric alignment challenge which delivers a scalable and theoretically sound method to achieve visual and linguistic comprehension integration.

8.4 ARCHITECTURES LIKE CLIP AND BLIP

8.4.1 Contrastive Language–Image Pretraining (CLIP)

CLIP (Contrastive Language–Image Pretraining) operates as a vision–language model which establishes direct semantic connections between visual content and spoken language descriptions. The core function of CLIP involves assessing the compatibility between textual descriptions and visual content which distinguishes it from conventional visual recognition systems.

CLIP operates by training its system to create combined image and text representations through the examination of extensive data that contains matched image and text pairs. The system uses existing label groups for its primary functions yet allows users to identify new visual categories through textual descriptions in its zero-shot learning capability.

What Makes CLIP Different?

CLIP learns to connect images with text through semantic understanding instead of using traditional image classification methods. CLIP differs from standard vision models because it neither creates captions nor produces set identification results. The system evaluates text description accuracy by measuring its compatibility with particular image content.

Previous image classification systems operated within fixed boundaries because they recognized only the categories which they had been trained to identify. The system required new labeled data and processing time to create new classification categories. CLIP enables image classification of new categories without system training by using its zero-shot learning capability. CLIP establishes a unified system for open-vocabulary visual understanding by learning from extensive image-text datasets which it connects through shared embedding space.

Architectural Design

CLIP consists of three main components as shown in Figure 8.7.

1. **Image Encoder:** An image I is encoded using a Vision Transformer (ViT) or ResNet-based encoder:

$$\mathbf{v} = f_{\text{img}}(I)$$

These embedding captures high-level semantic visual information.

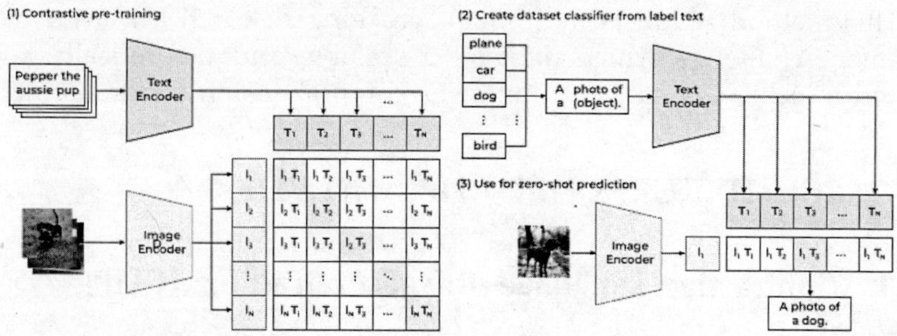

Figure 8.7: *CLIP Architecture.*

2. **Text Encoder:** A Transformer-based language model encodes a text prompt T:

$$\mathbf{t} = f_{\text{text}}(T)$$

The text embedding represents semantic meaning rather than syntactic structure.

3. **Shared Embedding Space:** Both embeddings are projected into a common latent space of equal dimensionality and normalized:

$$\hat{\mathbf{v}} = \frac{\mathbf{v}}{\|\mathbf{v}\|}, \hat{\mathbf{t}} = \frac{\mathbf{t}}{\|\mathbf{t}\|}$$

Contrastive Training Objective

CLIP is trained using contrastive learning, where matching image–text pairs are pulled closer, and mismatched pairs are pushed apart. For a batch of N pairs, cosine similarity is maximized using a contrastive loss:

$$\mathcal{L} = -\frac{1}{N}\sum_{i=1}^{N} \log \frac{\exp(\mathbf{v}_i^{\mathrm{T}}\mathbf{t}_i/\tau)}{\sum_{j=1}^{N} \exp(\mathbf{v}_i^{\mathrm{T}}\mathbf{t}_j/\tau)}$$

Here,

- τ controls similarity sharpness
- The loss enforces cross-modal alignment, not classification.

This objective directly implements the contrastive learning principle discussed in Section 8.3, making CLIP a practical realization of image–text representation learning.

Zero-Shot Learning Capability

Unlike conventional classifiers, CLIP does not require retraining for new classes.

At inference time,

1. Converting class labels into text prompts (e.g., *"a photo of a cat"*)
2. Computing similarity between an image embedding and all text embeddings
3. Selecting the label with maximum similarity

$$\text{label}^* = \arg\max_k \hat{\mathbf{v}} \cdot \hat{\mathbf{t}}_k$$

This removes the need for retraining classifiers and explains CLIP's scala.

Key Strengths

- Zero-shot generalization across unseen categories.
- Strong semantic grounding between vision and language.
- Task-agnostic representations, reusable across retrieval, classification, and generation.

Limitations

- Lacks fine-grained spatial reasoning (no explicit localization).
- Performance depends on prompt design.
- Inherits biases from large-scale web data.

CLIP operationalizes image–text representation learning and forms the core backbone of modern Vision–Language Models. It sets the stage for BLIP, which extends CLIP by incorporating generative and bidirectional reasoning capabilities, discussed next.

8.4.2 BLIP: Bootstrapping Language–Image Pre-training

BLIP (Bootstrapping Language–Image Pre-training) operates as a dual-learning system that enables its vision-language model to process both visual images and textual data. BLIP establishes a complete multimodal system that combines understanding with production capabilities because it handles both comprehension and creation tasks at once with its system. The large-scale image-text pair pre-training process that BLIP uses allows the system to identify semantic connections between visual elements and human language which supports various multimodal applications.

Given an image I and a text sequence T, BLIP learns a shared representation space in which semantic alignment, matching, and generation can be performed efficiently.

Formally, BLIP learns functions:

$$f_I : I \rightarrow \mathbf{v}_I \in \mathbb{R}^d,\ f_T : T \rightarrow \mathbf{v}_T \in \mathbb{R}^d$$

where, $\mathbf{v}_I$ and $\mathbf{v}_T$ represent image and text embeddings in a common latent space.

The importance of BLIP lies in its ability to solve problems that previous vision-language systems faced because it combines three approaches into one system. It enables users to perform tasks that include image captioning and visual question answering and cross-modal retrieval and multimodal reasoning.

Architecture of BLIP

BLIP follows a multimodal encoder–decoder architecture that supports both representation learning and text generation:

- **Unimodal Encoders**: Images and text are first encoded separately using transformer-based encoders, producing high-level visual and linguistic representations. Image encoder E_I and text encoder E_T independently produce feature representations:

$$\mathbf{h}_I = E_I(I),\ \mathbf{h}_T = E_T(T)$$

- **Image-Grounded Text Encoder**: This component integrates visual information into text representations using cross-attention, allowing the model to understand text in the context of image content. Cross-attention integrates visual features into text representations:

$$\mathbf{h}_{T|I} = \text{CrossAttn}(\mathbf{h}_T, \mathbf{h}_I)$$

- **Image-Grounded Text Decoder**: The decoder generates text conditioned on image features using causal self-attention, enabling tasks such as image captioning and answer generation. An autoregressive decoder generates text tokens conditioned on image features:

$$P(T|I) = \prod_{t=1}^{N} P(t_i \mid t_{<i}, \mathbf{h}_I)$$

- This flexible design allows BLIP to switch seamlessly between understanding-oriented tasks and generation-oriented tasks as shown in Figure 8.8.

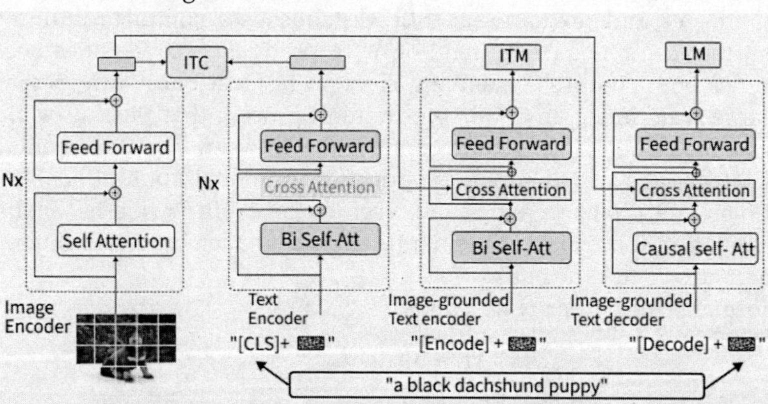

Figure 8.8: *BLIP Architecture.*

Pre-Training Objectives of BLIP

The BLIP system uses three distinct training methods which together create a complete multimodal learning system.

A. Image–Text Contrastive Loss (ITC)

This method matches image and text embeddings into one common semantic space while pulling matching image-text pairs together and pushing apart mismatched pairs. The system creates effective cross-modal retrieval together with matching representation development.

Given a batch of N image–text pairs, cosine similarity is computed as:

$$s(I, T) = \frac{\mathbf{v}_I \cdot \mathbf{v}_T}{\| \mathbf{v}_I \| \, \| \mathbf{v}_T \|}$$

The InfoNCE loss is then defined as:

$$\mathcal{L}_{\text{ITC}} = -\frac{1}{N} \sum_{i=1}^{N} \log \frac{\exp(s(I_i, T_i)/\tau)}{\sum_{j=1}^{N} \exp(s(I_i, T_j)/\tau)}$$

where τ is a temperature parameter.

B. Image-Text Matching Loss (ITM)

The ITM test establishes whether a picture and its corresponding text match through a binary classification process. The system needs multiple different paths to develop its understanding of multimodal content because it requires more than basic similarity assessment.

ITM performs binary classification to determine whether a given image–text pair is semantically matched:

$$P(y = 1 \mid I, T) = \sigma(W^{\mathrm{T}} \mathbf{h}_{T \mid I})$$

The loss is computed using binary cross-entropy:

$$\mathcal{L}_{\text{ITM}} = -\,[y \log P + (1 - y) \log (1 - P)]$$

C. Language ModelingLoss (LM)

The system uses visual input data to produce accurate text which maintains logical structure and relevant content. The system needs this autoregressive function to support both caption generation and open-ended question answering.

BLIP learns to generate text conditioned on image features using an autoregressive likelihood:

$$\mathcal{L}_{\text{LM}} = -\sum_{i=1}^{N} \log P(t_i \mid t_{<i}, I)$$

The combination of these three objectives enables BLIP to develop skills which allow it to identify and create multimedia content.

Unified Training Objective

The total pre-training loss is a weighted combination:

$$\mathcal{L}_{BLIP} = \lambda_1 \mathcal{L}_{ITC} + \lambda_2 \mathcal{L}_{ITM} + \lambda_3 \mathcal{L}_{LM}$$

where λ_1, λ_2, λ_3 balance alignment, matching, and generation.

Comparison with Other Vision–Language Models

BLIP differs from existing models in its unified design:

- **CLIP** focuses on image–text matching and zero-shot classification but does not generate text.
- **DALL·E** specializes in text-to-image generation rather than image understanding.
- **Vision Transformers (ViT)** process images effectively but lack native language integration.

BLIP bridges this gap by supporting matching, reasoning, and generation within a single framework.

Advantages and Limitations

Advantages

- Strong multimodal reasoning and generation
- Unified framework for diverse tasks
- Open-source availability encourages research and customization

Limitations

- Performance depends heavily on data quality
- Computationally expensive to train
- May struggle with highly complex or ambiguous visual scenes

8.5 CROSS-MODAL REASONING

A model needs to use cross-modal reasoning because it must understand and process information from different sensory modalities which include vision and language. Cross-modal reasoning goes beyond basic alignment or matching because it enables users to understand the relationships between two elements through their actual contextual usage and their associated meanings as shown in Figure 8.9.

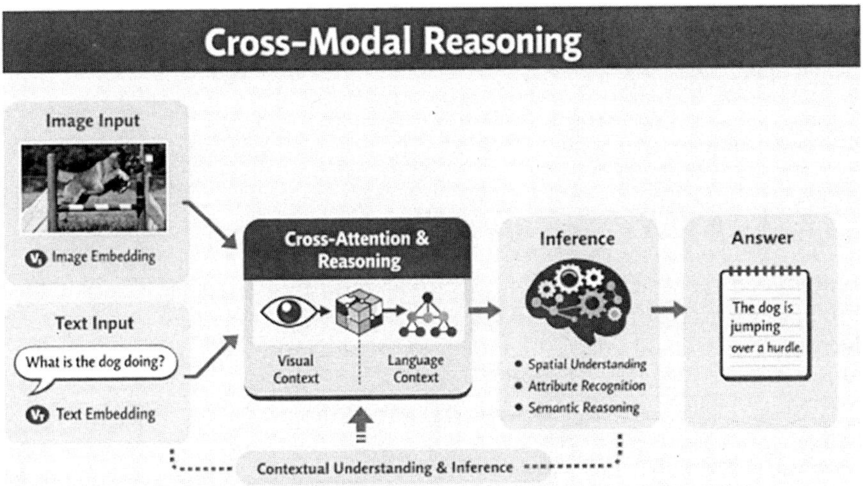

Figure 8.9: *Cross-Modal Reasoning*

Given an image I and a text input T, earlier stages in Vision-Language Models (VLMs) learn embeddings $\mathbf{v}_I$ and $\mathbf{v}_T$ in a shared latent space. Cross-modal reasoning operates on top of these representations to perform inference:

$$\mathcal{R}(I, T) \to Y$$

where, $\mathcal{R}$ denotes a reasoning function and Y represents a task-specific output such as an answer, decision, or explanation.

8.5.1 Mechanism of Cross-Modal Reasoning

Modern VLMs implement cross-modal reasoning using cross-attention mechanisms, where textual tokens attend to visual features and vice versa. For a text query token q_t and image feature set $\{k_i, v_i\}$, cross-attention is computed as:

$$\text{Attn}(q_t, K_I, V_I) = \sum_i \text{softmax}\left(\frac{q_t \cdot k_i)}{\sqrt{d}}\right) v_i$$

This allows the model to selectively focus on relevant image regions when processing language instructions, enabling grounded understanding.

While contrastive learning (Section 8.3) ensures that semantically related image-text pairs are close in embedding space, cross-modal reasoning enables logical inference, such as:

- Spatial reasoning (e.g., object relationships)
- Attribute reasoning (e.g., color, size, action)
- Compositional reasoning (e.g., combining multiple visual cues)

Formally, reasoning can be viewed as a transformation over multimodal features:

$$\mathbf{h}_{\text{reasoned}} = f(\mathbf{h}_I, \mathbf{h}_T)$$

where $f(\cdot)$ is a learned function realized via stacked transformer layers.

8.5.2 Role in Vision-Language Models

In architectures such as BLIP and similar multimodal transformers, cross-modal reasoning bridges the gap between representation learning and decision making. It enables models to move from "what is present" to "what does it mean in context".

This capability is essential for tasks including:

- Visual Question Answering (VQA)
- Instruction-guided image understanding
- Multimodal decision support systems

8.5.3 Importance and Limitations

Multimodal systems gain better generalization and interpretability through the implementation of cross-modal reasoning. The approach only succeeds when the system has high-quality learned representations and diverse training data. The system will produce incorrect reasoning results because of misaligned data and biased representation.

Cross-modal reasoning transforms aligned image-text representations into context-aware, inferential understanding, making it a core capability of advanced Vision-Language Models. The platform enables intelligent systems to reason, explain, and perform tasks across both visual and linguistic domains.

8.6 APPLICATION IN INDUSTRY

Multimodal AI has transitioned from research laboratories to real-world deployment by enabling systems to jointly reason over visual and textual information. Vision-Language Models (VLMs), trained using contrastive and generative objectives, form the backbone of these industrial applications.

8.6.1 Healthcare and Medical Diagnostics

Multimodal models in healthcare assess medical images and clinical text to support diagnostic and reporting processes. It creates automated reports and visual answers to questions and retrieves previous cases by converting radiology images I and doctor notes T into a common framework. It enables faster diagnosis and maintains uniform diagnostic results as shown in Figure 8.10.

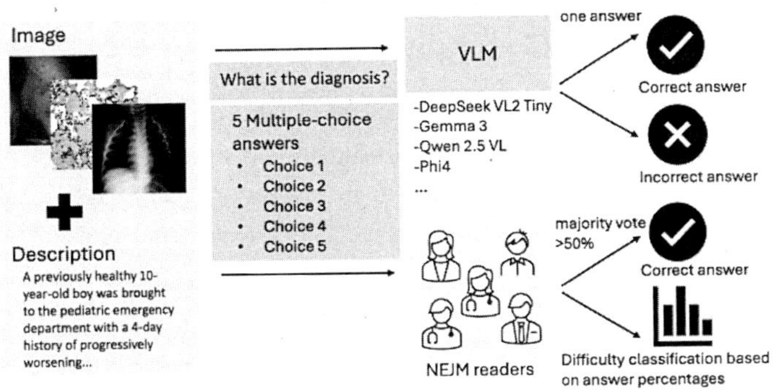

Figure 8.10: *Health Care Diagnosis.*

8.6.2 E-Commerce and Retail Intelligence

E-commerce platforms use multimodal AI for visual search, product tagging, and recommendation systems. Image embeddings of products are aligned with textual descriptions and user queries, allowing customers to search using images or natural language. The product visuals and metadata achieve semantic alignment through contrastive learning.

8.6.3 Autonomous Systems and Robotics

Robotics systems use multimodal models to enable robots to perceive their environment and execute tasks based on user instructions. The robot executes object manipulation and navigation operations after it processes a language command T and links it to the visual scene I. Cross-modal reasoning links visual spatial information with language instructions to assist in decision-making processes.

8.6.4 Media Analysis and Content Moderation

Social media platforms deploy multimodal AI to detect harmful or misleading content by jointly analyzing images, videos, and associated text. Vision-language alignment helps identify context that would be missed by unimodal systems, improving moderation accuracy.

8.6.5 Education and Assistive Technologies

Multimodal AI supports image captioning, diagram explanation, and visual question answering, enhancing accessibility for visually impaired users and improving learning tools. These systems rely on learned image-text representations to convert visual content into meaningful language.

8.6.6 Creative and Generative Industries

Text-to-image and image-to-text systems in design, advertising, and entertainment use multimodal representations to generate or edit content. Language prompts guide visual generation, while vision feedback refines semantic accuracy.

8.6.7 Industrial Impact

By integrating perception and language, multimodal AI systems deliver:

- Improved decision-making through complementary modalities.
- Zero-shot adaptability using aligned embeddings.
- Natural human–AI interaction across domains.

As industries increasingly rely on unstructured visual and textual data, multimodal AI has become a core enabling technology rather than a supplementary feature.

8.7 CHALLENGES IN MULTIMODAL AI

Despite rapid progress, Multimodal AI systems face several fundamental challenges that limit their robustness, scalability, and real-world reliability.

One major challenge is modality alignment. Visual data and language data follow very different distributions, and learning a shared embedding space that preserves semantic meaning across modalities is non-trivial. Even with contrastive objectives such as InfoNCE, imperfect alignment can lead to shallow correlations instead of true semantic understanding.

Another critical issue is data bias and imbalance. Large-scale image–text datasets collected from the web often contain noisy captions, cultural bias, and underrepresented concepts. Since multimodal models learn associations directly from data, these biases propagate into downstream tasks, affecting fairness and generalization.

Computational cost and scalability also pose significant challenges. Training Vision-Language Models requires massive datasets, large transformers, and high memory bandwidth. Let $f_I(I)$ and $f_T(T)$ be image and text encoders; jointly optimizing both encoders with contrastive and generative losses significantly increases training complexity compared to unimodal models.

Multimodal systems also struggle with compositional and fine-grained reasoning. While models like CLIP excel at global semantic matching, they often fail to reason about precise spatial relationships, counting, or causal interactions within a scene.

Another open challenge is evaluation. Unlike traditional classification tasks, multimodal reasoning lacks standardized benchmarks that fully capture grounding, alignment, and reasoning quality. High similarity scores do not always imply correct understanding.

Finally, robustness and interpretability remain unresolved. Multimodal models can be sensitive to prompt phrasing, adversarial inputs, or irrelevant visual features, making their decisions difficult to explain—especially in high-stakes domains like healthcare and autonomous systems.

These challenges highlight that while multimodal AI is powerful, it is still an evolving field requiring careful design, better data curation, and stronger theoretical foundations.

TEST YOUR KNOWLEDGE

1. Explain why contrastive learning is more suitable than classification loss for image-text representation learning in VLMs.
2. Derive the role of cosine similarity in aligning image and text embeddings in CLIP-style models.
3. Compare CLIP and BLIP in terms of architectural design and supported tasks.
4. Why does zero-shot learning naturally emerge in Vision-Language Models?
5. Discuss how cross-modal reasoning differs from simple multimodal fusion.
6. Analyze the limitations of contrastive objectives in capturing fine-grained visual relationships.
7. Explain how BLIP integrates discriminative and generative objectives during pretraining.
8. Why is evaluation of multimodal models fundamentally harder than unimodal models?
9. Describe the trade-off between model scalability and interpretability in multimodal AI systems.
10. Propose one architectural or training improvement to address current challenges in multimodal reasoning.

CHAPTER 9

Synthetic Data and Data Generation

Modern machine learning systems need large diverse datasets to function properly while generative AI models require these same datasets for their operations. The process of gathering actual data from the world faces multiple obstacles which include privacy issues and expensive operations and uneven distribution of data and legal and ethical limitations. The growing demand for synthetic data solutions exists because these solutions offer an effective method to create training materials which help researchers evaluate their data-driven systems.

Synthetic data consists of computer-generated information which imitates the statistical characteristics and structural elements of actual data while safeguarding delicate details. The development of realistic synthetic data through generative modeling techniques has reached new heights because of Generative Adversarial Networks and Variational Autoencoders and Diffusion Models. These models discover the fundamental data pattern which enables them to produce fresh outputs that maintain important traits of the initial dataset.

This chapter establishes the definition of synthetic data while it shows how to create artificial text and image and video content through different generation techniques which include generative models that perform data augmentation. The study presents synthetic data quality assessment methods which include ethical and legal aspects related to synthetic data creation.

9.1 CONCEPT OF SYNTHETIC DATA

Synthetic data refers to artificially created data which simulates actual data through its statistical properties and structural relationships and distributional patterns without using actual observations. Synthetic data serves as a data representation system which modern data-driven systems use when they cannot access actual data because of limited availability or sensitive nature or difficulties in data collection. The defining characteristic of synthetic data is that it is generated through algorithmic modeling of data behavior rather than direct replication of real records as shown in Figure 9.1.

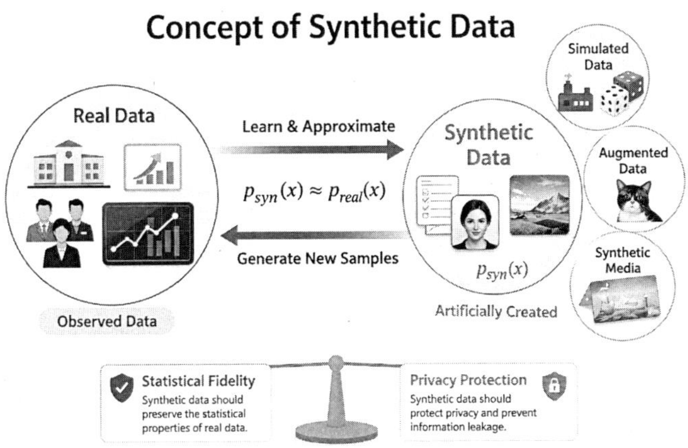

Figure 9.1: *Concept of Synthetic Data.*

From a theoretical standpoint, synthetic data aims to approximate the underlying data-generating process of real datasets. Let a real dataset be represented by samples

$$X = \{x_1, x_2, \ldots, x_n\},\ x_i \in \mathcal{X}$$

drawn from an unknown probability distribution $p_{\text{real}}(x)$. The objective of synthetic data is to construct an alternative distribution $p_{\text{syn}}(x)$ such that:

$$p_{\text{syn}}(x) \approx p_{\text{real}}(x),$$

allowing new samples $\tilde{x} \sim p_{\text{syn}}(x)$ to preserve important data characteristics such as feature dependencies, variance, and correlation structures.

9.1.1 Definition and Characteristics of Synthetic Data

The definition of synthetic data exists through its ability to keep statistical properties while creating separate datasets from actual individual data. The synthetic dataset establishes its statistical fidelity by demonstrating how accurately it replicates real data distributions and relationships and its data independence feature which prevents any original data from being reconstructed through the synthetic dataset.

The main attributes that define synthetic data include:

- **Distributional similarity:** The system must preserve both the marginal and joint distributions.
- **Structural consistency:** The system has to sustain its feature relationships and patterns.
- **Non-identifiability:** The system does not contain any elements that can identify actual data records.
- **Task utility:** The system enables users to conduct important learning and analysis activities.

The synthetic data concept exists as a point between actual data verification and total data protection. Excessive similarity to real data increases privacy risk, whereas excessive randomness reduces usefulness. The establishment of this equilibrium functions as the main principle that governs how machine learning systems employ synthetic data.

9.1.2 Synthetic Data vs Related Data Types

Synthetic data should not be mistaken for other types of created artificial data because it possesses distinct conceptual elements which separate it from those other types. Real data exists as actual data which researchers gather through direct observation of genuine processes and their corresponding entities and events. Simulated data uses predefined mathematical or physical models to create outputs which depend on custom-made rules that fail to replicate actual world conditions. Data augmentation uses existing real samples which undergo transformations that include scaling and noise addition and geometric changes to create new data points.

Synthetic data formation occurs through the complete data distribution modeling process which generates new samples that maintain statistical properties yet do not result from actual data transformations. The important distinction between synthetic data and actual data exists because synthetic data enables users to create generalizations which remain independent from the specific dataset and its individual data points.

9.2 NEED FOR ARTIFICIAL DATA

Real-world data is fundamental to machine learning systems; however, in many practical scenarios, relying solely on real data is neither feasible nor sufficient. This limitation creates the need for artificial (synthetic) data as a complementary data source.

9.2.1 Limitations of Real-World Data

In multiple fields, researchers face challenges because they cannot access complete and accurate real data which exists in limited amounts. The process of learning becomes biased because the training data fails to include rare events and minority classes and edge cases which are not common situations. The real datasets include missing values and noise and inconsistencies which result in decreased performance of the model.

Privacy and legal restrictions prevent researchers from accessing and using actual data for their research work. Researchers cannot share or reuse sensitive data from healthcare and finance and social systems for their experiments and model development.

9.2.2 Role of Artificial Data in Learning

Artificial data helps overcome these limitations by expanding the effective training distribution. The models create approximations of an unknown function which they develop using a limited dataset. The dataset restriction leads to empirical distribution different from actual data distribution which results in increased generalization error. Artificial data reduces this gap by enriching the sample space and improving distributional coverage.

Artificial data assists with two tasks because it allows researchers to manage class imbalance while they need to introduce rare classes and create extreme situations for complete model testing.

Artificial data supports better approximation of the underlying data distribution. Let a learning model attempt to estimate a function $f(x)$ based on empirical risk minimization over a dataset D. When D is limited or biased, the empirical distribution deviates from the true data distribution, increasing generalization error. Artificial data helps reduce this deviation by enriching the sample space and improving distributional coverage.

Beyond training, artificial data supports scalable experimentation, reproducibility, and safe data sharing. Since artificial datasets can be generated and modified systematically, they enable consistent testing and rapid iteration without dependence on repeated real data collection.

9.3 TEXT DATA GENERATION

The term text data generation describes how generative models create human-readable text, while synthetic text data refers to generated text that researchers design and organize through artificial means to serve as machine learning training materials. The chapter presents text generation as a technique that researchers use to create artificial datasets which they employ in all stages of Natural Language Processing (NLP) model development. The study focuses on three research areas which include data utility and control and statistical relevance instead of allowing unrestricted language generation.

9.3.1 Conceptual Foundation

At its core, text generation is a sequence modeling problem. Language can be represented as an ordered sequence of tokens:

$$(w_1, w_2, w_3, \ldots, w_n)$$

The objective of a text generation model is to learn the probability of the next token given previous tokens:

$$P(w_t \mid w_1, w_2, \ldots, w_{t-1})$$

By repeatedly predicting the next token, the model generates complete sentences and documents that resemble real text.

9.3.2 Synthetic Text Generation Process

In synthetic data settings, text generation is often conditional. The model generates text based on predefined attributes such as topic, class label, or intent.

This can be expressed as:

$$P(x \mid c)$$

where,

x is the generated text

c represents conditioning information (e.g., category or domain)

This approach enables the creation of labeled synthetic datasets, which are essential for supervised NLP tasks.

9.3.3 Different Approaches to Text Generation

Text generation models use different strategies to produce meaningful text as shown in Figure 9.2.

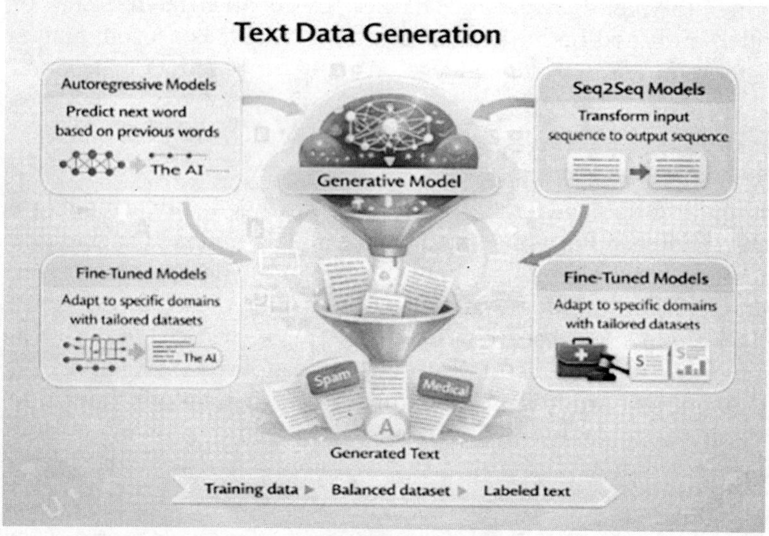

Figure 9.2: *Approaches for Text Data Generation.*

- **Autoregressive models**, such as GPT-4, generate text by predicting the next word based on previously generated words, ensuring coherence and contextual flow.
- **Sequence-to-Sequence (Seq2Seq) models** convert an input text sequence into an output sequence and are commonly used in applications like machine translation and summarization.
- **Fine-tuned models** are pre-trained language models adapted using domain-specific data to generate specialized content such as medical, legal, or financial text.

Popular text generation models include GPT, PaLM 2, Claude, and LLaMA.

Implementation of Text Generation in Python

This code sends a user prompt to the GPT-4 model using the OpenAI API and receives AI-generated text as a response. It demonstrates a simple way to perform text generation by passing an input prompt and printing the generated output as shown in Figure 9.3.

```
import openai

def generate_text(prompt, model="gpt-4"):
    response = openai.ChatCompletion.create(
        model=model,
        messages=[{"role": "user", "content": prompt}]
    )
    return response["choices"][0]["message"]["content"]


prompt = "Write a short paragraph about the benefits of AI in healthcare."
print(generate_text(prompt))
```

Figure 9.3: *Implementing text data generation.*

Output

Text generation is a fascinating field within artificial intelligence, focusing on creating human-like text through algorithms. Leveraging models such as GPT (Generative Pre-trained Transformer), these systems learn from vast datasets to produce coherent and contextually relevant content. Applications range from chatbots to creative writing, offering novel ways to interact with technology. However, challenges like ensuring accuracy, managing biases, and maintaining ethical use remain crucial. As models evolve, they promise enhanced realism and utility, transforming how we generate written content and engage with digital platforms, and pushing the boundaries of machine creativity and communication.

9.3.4 Applications in Machine Learning

Synthetic text data is widely used to:

- Address class imbalance in text classification problems.
- Increase dataset size when real data is limited.
- Support training while reducing exposure to sensitive text.

By augmenting real datasets with generated text, models achieve better generalization and robustness.

9.3.5 Key Characteristics of Generated Text

For synthetic text to be useful, it must satisfy the following properties:

- Grammatical correctness
- Semantic coherence
- Statistical similarity to real data
- Task relevance

Failure to meet these criteria reduces the effectiveness of synthetic text in downstream learning tasks.

9.3.6 Limitations

Despite its benefits, synthetic text generation may introduce:

- Repetitive patterns
- Semantic drift
- Bias inherited from training data

Therefore, generated text must be carefully validated before use.

9.4 IMAGE AND VIDEO SYNTHESIS

Image and video synthesis is a key component of synthetic data generation in Generative AI, where artificial visual data is created to train, validate, and test computer vision models. Unlike creative image generation, the focus here is on data realism, diversity, and task relevance.

9.4.1 Synthetic Image Generation

The purpose of synthetic image generation exists to create artificial images which replicate the statistical distribution found in actual images. The generative models acquire knowledge about this distribution during their training process and they use latent variables to create fresh samples in the image space.

Mathematically, image generation can be expressed as:

$$z \sim \mathcal{N}(0, I), \; x = G(z)$$

where,

z is a latent noise vector
G is a generative model
x is the generated image

Synthetic images are widely used in applications such as object detection, facial recognition, medical imaging, and defect detection, especially when real annotated images are scarce or sensitive as shown in Figure 9.4.

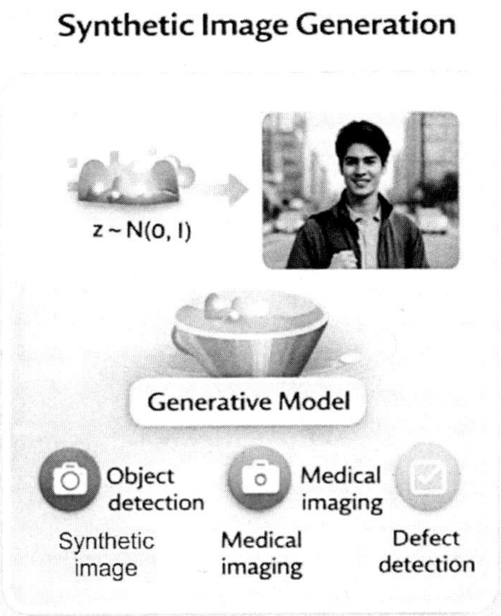

Figure 9.4: *Synthetic Image Generation.*

Implementation: Synthetic Image Generation using GAN

```
import torch
import torch.nn as nn

# Generator model
class Generator(nn.Module):
    def __init__(self, noise_dim=100):
        super().__init__()
        self.model = nn.Sequential(
            nn.Linear(noise_dim, 256),
            nn.ReLU(),
            nn.Linear(256, 512),
            nn.ReLU(),
            nn.Linear(512, 784),
            nn.Tanh()
        )

    def forward(self, z):
        return self.model(z)

# Generate a synthetic image
noise = torch.randn(1, 100)
generator = Generator()
synthetic_image = generator(noise)

print(synthetic_image.shape)
```

```
torch.Size([1, 784])
```

Figure 9.5: *Implementation using GAN.*

The generator learns to map random noise vectors to image space. Once trained, it can produce realistic synthetic images that resemble real data and can be used for model training or augmentation as shown in Figure 9.5.

9.4.2 Synthetic Video Generation

Video synthesis extends image generation by modeling temporal consistency across frames. Instead of generating independent images, video models learn both spatial features and time-dependent motion patterns.

A video sequence can be represented as:

$$V = \{x_1, x_2, \ldots, x_T\}$$

where each frame x_t is generated while preserving temporal relationships:

$$x_t = G(z_t, h_{t-1})$$

Here, h_{t-1} represents information from previous frames, ensuring smooth transitions and realistic motion.

Synthetic videos are particularly useful in autonomous driving, human activity recognition, and surveillance systems as shown in Figure 9.6.

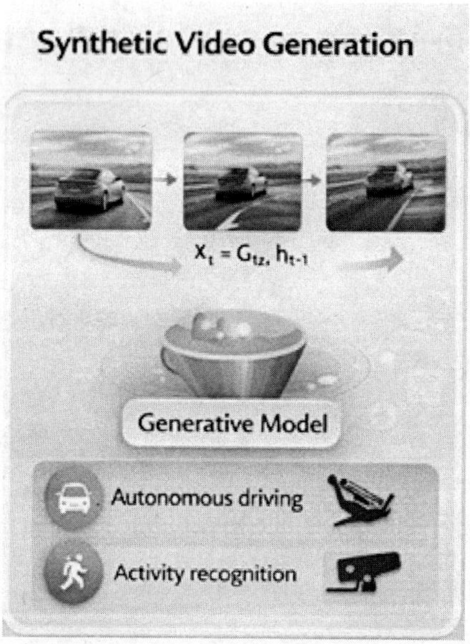

Figure 9.6: *Synthetic video Generation.*

Implementation:

This implementation generates synthetic video frames using a diffusion model and combines them into a video file. Each frame is generated independently and then temporally stitched to form a synthetic video sequence as shown in Figure 9.7.

```
import torch
from diffusers import StableDiffusionPipeline
import cv2
import numpy as np

# Load pretrained text-to-image diffusion model
pipe = StableDiffusionPipeline.from_pretrained(
    "runwayml/stable-diffusion-v1-5"
).to("cuda")

prompt = "A car moving on a highway at sunset"

frames = []

# Generate multiple frames
for i in range(16):
    image = pipe(prompt).images[0]
    frame = np.array(image)
    frames.append(frame)

# Save frames as video
height, width, _ = frames[0].shape
video = cv2.VideoWriter(
    "synthetic_video.mp4",
    cv2.VideoWriter_fourcc(*'mp4v'),
    8,
    (width, height)
)

for frame in frames:
    video.write(frame)

video.release()
```

Figure 9.7: *Implementing Video Generation.*

Video generation is performed by generating consecutive frames using generative models and maintaining visual consistency across time. Modern systems extend this idea using temporal diffusion and 3D latentrepresentations.

9.4.3 Role in Synthetic Data Pipelines

In a synthetic data pipeline, image and video synthesis is used to:

- Increase dataset size
- Balance underrepresented classes
- Reduce data collection and annotation cost

These generated datasets are then combined with real data or used independently for training machine learning models.

9.5 ROLE OF GANS AND DIFFUSION MODELS IN SYNTHETIC DATA GENERATION

The two main generative frameworks used to create high-quality synthetic data are Generative Adversarial Networks (GANs) and Diffusion Models. The two methods aim to model actual data distribution but exhibit distinct differences in their training processes and system stability and generated results which make them appropriate for specific synthetic data production needs.

9.5.1 Role of GANs in Synthetic Data Generation

GANs consist of two neural networks: a Generator (G) and a Discriminator (D), trained in an adversarial manner. The generator produces synthetic samples, while the discriminator attempts to distinguish real data from generated data.

The GAN objective function is defined as:

$$\min_G \max_D \mathbb{E}_{x \sim p_{\text{data}}}[\log D(x)] + \mathbb{E}_{z \sim p(z)}[\log(1 - D(G(z)))]$$

Role in synthetic data generation

- Rapid generation of synthetic samples after training.
- Effective for structured data such as images and tabular data.
- Suitable when large volumes of synthetic data are required quickly.

Limitations:

- Training instability
- Mode collapse (limited diversity)
- Sensitive to hyperparameters

Implementation: GAN for synthetic image data

The generator transforms random noise into synthetic data resembling real samples. Once trained, it can rapidly produce large volumes of artificial data as shown in Figure 9.8.

9.5.2 Role of Diffusion Models in Synthetic Data Generation

Diffusion models generate data by learning to reverse a gradual noise corruption process. Instead of adversarial training, they rely on probabilistic denoising, which leads to more stable training.

```
import torch
import torch.nn as nn

# Generator Model
class Generator(nn.Module):
    def __init__(self):
        super().__init__()
        self.model = nn.Sequential(
            nn.Linear(100, 256),
            nn.ReLU(),
            nn.Linear(256, 784),
            nn.Tanh()
        )

    def forward(self, z):
        return self.model(z)

# Generate synthetic sample
G = Generator()
noise = torch.randn(1, 100)
synthetic_data = G(noise)

print("Synthetic data shape:", synthetic_data.shape)
```

```
Synthetic data shape: torch.Size([1, 784])
```

Figure 9.8: *GAN for Synthetic Image Data.*

The forward diffusion process is defined as:

$$x_t = \sqrt{1 - \beta_t}\, x_{t-1} + \sqrt{\beta_t}\, \varepsilon$$

where, $\varepsilon \sim \mathcal{N}(0, I)$

The model learns to reverse this process to recover clean data from noise.

Role in synthetic data generation

- High-fidelity and diverse synthetic samples
- Stable and predictable training
- Strong performance in image and video synthesis

Limitations:

- Computationally expensive
- Slower sample generation

Implementation: Diffusion-based Synthetic Data Generation

Diffusion models generate synthetic data by gradually adding noise and learning to reverse this process. This produces stable and diverse synthetic samples with high realism as shown in Figure 9.9.

```
import torch

# Forward diffusion (add noise)
def forward_diffusion(x, beta=0.1):
    beta = torch.tensor(beta)  # convert float to tensor
    noise = torch.randn_like(x)
    return torch.sqrt(1 - beta) * x + torch.sqrt(beta) * noise

# Reverse diffusion (simple denoising step)
def reverse_diffusion(x_noisy, beta=0.1):
    beta = torch.tensor(beta)
    return x_noisy / torch.sqrt(1 - beta)

# Original data
x = torch.randn(1, 784)

# Apply diffusion
x_noisy = forward_diffusion(x)
x_synthetic = reverse_diffusion(x_noisy)

print("Original shape:", x.shape)
print("Noisy shape:", x_noisy.shape)
print("Recovered shape:", x_synthetic.shape)
```

```
Original shape: torch.Size([1, 784])
Noisy shape: torch.Size([1, 784])
Recovered shape: torch.Size([1, 784])
```

Figure 9.9: *Diffusion Based Synthetic Data.*

9.5.3 GANs vs Diffusion: Synthetic Data Perspective

GANs enable organizations to create extensive synthetic data sets through their low-cost data processing capabilities. Diffusion models offer better sample variety and system reliability but require additional processing resources for their operation. Modern synthetic data pipelines use diffusion models to create images and videos because they need automated data generation, while GANs serve as a viable solution for organizations that require rapid data creation and data sets that can expand without limits as shown in Table 9.1.

TABLE 9.1 GAN vs Diffusion Synthetic Data Perspective

Aspect	*GANs*	*Diffusion Models*
Training	Adversarial	Probabilistic
Stability	Moderate	High
Sample quality	Sharp but limited diversity	High diversity and realism
Speed	Fast inference	Slower generation
Best Use	Large-scale synthetic datasets	High-quality synthetic images/videos

9.6 DATA AUGMENTATION WITH GENAI

Data augmentation works to enhance model performance through expansion of training datasets with new samples that maintain original data distribution. Generative AI provides distribution-aware augmentation which differs from traditional augmentation methods by creating new samples through understanding data joint probability patterns instead of using basic surface transformations as shown in Figure 9.10.

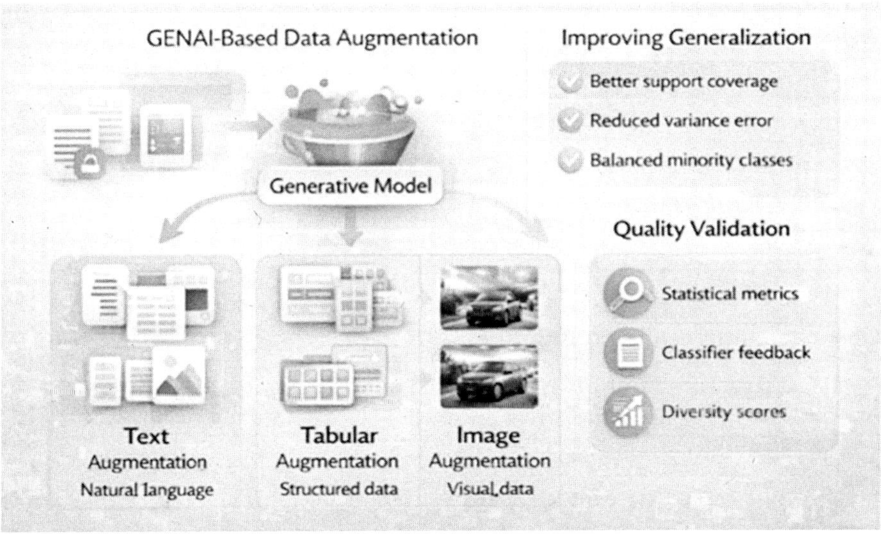

Figure 9.10: *Data Augmentation with GenAI.*

9.6.1 Why Traditional Augmentation is Limited

Classical augmentation techniques use deterministic transformations which include rotation and scaling and cropping and synonym replacement. The methods succeed in vision and NLP tasks but they have two main limitations because:

- The methods do not create additional semantic content.
- The methods cannot identify intricate relationships between features.
- The methods provide minimal benefits for situations which have insufficient data.

The result shows that models which training used only standard augmentation methods become overfit because they learn to recognize slight sample differences.

9.6.2 Generative Perspective of Data Augmentation

Let the real data distribution be denoted as:

$$p_{\text{data}}(x)$$

Generative models aim to learn a parameterized approximation:

$$p_\theta(x) \approx p_{\text{data}}(x)$$

Synthetic samples drawn from $p_\theta(x)$ act as valid extensions of the original dataset, enabling the model to observe previously unseen but plausible examples during training.

The augmented dataset is:

$$\mathcal{D}_{\text{aug}} = \mathcal{D}_{\text{real}} \cup \{x \sim p_\theta(x)\}$$

This formulation ensures augmentation at the distribution level, not merely at the feature level.

9.6.3 How GenAI Improves Generalization

Generative augmentation improves learning by:

- Increasing **support coverage** of the data manifold.
- Reducing **variance error** in model estimation.
- Providing balanced samples for underrepresented classes.

From a learning theory perspective, this reduces empirical risk minimization bias when real data is sparse.

9.6.4 Model-wise Augmentation Strategies

GAN-based Augmentation

GANs generate samples that closely resemble real data, making them suitable for:

- Image augmentation
- Tabular data synthesis
- Class balancing

Diffusion-based Augmentation

Diffusion models produce highly diverse samples by progressively denoising noise, making them effective for:

- High-fidelity image augmentation
- Medical and scientific datasets
- Video and spatiotemporal data

9.6.5 Implementation: Distribution-level Augmentation

The generator learns the real data distribution and produces new samples from it. These samples expand the dataset beyond simple transformations and improve generalization as shown in Figure 9.11.

```
import torch
import torch.nn as nn

class Generator(nn.Module):
    def __init__(self):
        super().__init__()
        self.model = nn.Sequential(
            nn.Linear(100, 256),
            nn.ReLU(),
            nn.Linear(256, 784),
            nn.Tanh()
        )

    def forward(self, z):
        return self.model(z)

G = Generator()
z = torch.randn(50, 100)
synthetic_samples = G(z)

print("Synthetic samples added:", synthetic_samples.shape)
```

```
Synthetic samples added: torch.Size([50, 784])
```

Figure 9.11: *Distribution Level Augmentation.*

9.6.6 Risks and Validation in Generative Augmentation

While powerful, generative augmentation introduces risks:

- Distribution drift if the generator is poorly trained.
- Mode collapse leading to redundant samples.
- Bias amplification from skewed training data.

Therefore, generative augmentation must be combined with quality validation techniques such as classifier-based filtering or diversity metrics.

9.7 QUALITY AND VALIDATION OF SYNTHETIC DATA

The process of synthetic data generation requires trustworthy generated samples which can be used for learning activities. The validation process establishes quality requirements which need to be fulfilled through statistical testing and structural analysis and operational validation of synthetic data compared to actual data.

Synthetic data of low quality can create misleading information which leads to model errors and introduces bias and decreases the ability to generalize.

9.7.1 Dimensions of Synthetic Data Quality

Synthetic data quality is evaluated across three core dimensions:

1. *Statistical Similarity*

The synthetic dataset should follow the same probability distribution as the real data.

$$P_{\text{synthetic}}(x) \approx P_{\text{real}}(x)$$

This includes matching:

- Mean and variance
- Feature correlations
- Marginal and joint distributions

2. *Structural and Semantic Consistency*

Generated samples must respect real-world constraints and logical relationships.

Examples:

- Age ≥ 0
- Valid sentence grammar
- Anatomically correct images

This is especially critical in text, medical, and financial data.

3. *Task Utility*

Synthetic data should improve or maintain model performance when used for training.

If a model trained on synthetic data performs well on real test data, the synthetic data is considered task-valid.

9.7.2 Validation Techniques

1. *Statistical Tests*

- Kolmogorov–Smirnov (KS) test
- Chi-square test
- Pearson correlation comparison

These tests measure how close synthetic data is to real data numerically.

2. *Model-based Validation*

Train a downstream model using synthetic data and evaluate it on real validation data.

$$\text{Utility Score} = \text{Accuracy}_{\text{real test}}$$

Higher scores indicate better synthetic data quality.

3. *Discriminator-based Validation*

If a classifier cannot distinguish real data from synthetic data better than random guessing, the synthetic data is considered high quality.

$$\text{Accuracy} \approx 50\%$$

9.7.3 Trade-off between Privacy and Quality

Improving realism often reduces privacy. Highly realistic synthetic data may unintentionally memorize real samples.

Hence, validation must balance:

- Data utility
- Privacy preservation
- Generalization ability

9.8 ETHICAL AND LEGAL ISSUES IN SYNTHETIC DATA

While synthetic data offers powerful solutions to data scarcity, privacy, and bias, its use introduces important ethical and legal challenges. Since synthetic data is generated by learning patterns from real data, improper design or misuse can still lead to privacy leakage, bias amplification, and misuse of generated content. Understanding these issues is essential for responsible deployment of Generative AI systems as shown in Figure 9.12.

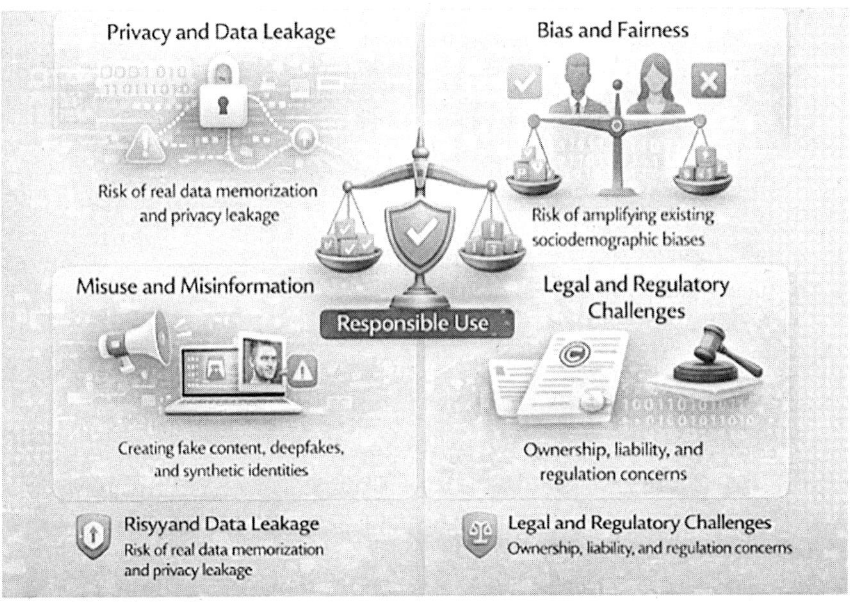

Figure 9.12: *Ethical and Legal Issue.*

9.8.1 Privacy and Data Leakage

Synthetic data is often promoted as privacy-preserving, but this is not automatically guaranteed.

- If a model overfits, it may unintentionally reproduce samples close to real individuals.
- This risk is known as memorization or data leakage.

Conceptually, a safe synthetic generator should satisfy:

$$P(x_{\text{synthetic}} = x_{\text{real}}) \approx 0$$

In practice, techniques such as differential privacy, noise injection, and strict validation checks are used to reduce this risk.

9.8.2 Bias and Fairness Concerns

Synthetic data models learn from historical data, which may already contain social, gender, or demographic biases.

- If biased data is used for training, synthetic data can amplify existing bias.
- This can lead to unfair outcomes in sensitive applications like hiring, lending, or healthcare.

Hence, ethical synthetic data generation requires:

- Balanced training data
- Bias evaluation before deployment
- Regular auditing of generated samples

9.8.3 Misuse and Misinformation

Generative models can be misused to create:

- Fake text (spam, misinformation)
- Deepfake images or videos
- Synthetic identities

Such misuse raises concerns around trust, authenticity, and social harm, making regulation and responsible usage critical.

9.8.4 Legal and Regulatory Challenges

From a legal perspective, key concerns include:

- **Data ownership:** Who owns synthetic data derived from real data?
- **Copyright issues:** Generated content may resemble protected material.

- **Accountability:** Determining responsibility when synthetic data causes harm.

Many countries are actively developing AI regulations to govern these issues, emphasizing transparency, consent, and accountability.

9.8.5 Responsible Use of Synthetic Data

Ethical use of synthetic data requires:

- Clear documentation of data sources and generation methods
- Transparent disclosure when synthetic data is used
- Continuous monitoring for unintended consequences

Responsible design ensures that synthetic data remains a tool for innovation, not a source of harm.

TEST YOUR KNOWLEDGE

1. Explain why synthetic data generation must operate at the distribution level rather than the feature level, with reference to generative models.
2. Compare text data generation and synthetic text data generation in the context of dataset augmentation. Why are they not interchangeable?
3. Derive and explain the objective function of a GAN and discuss how it affects diversity in synthetic data.
4. Why are diffusion models considered more stable than GANs for synthetic data generation? Explain using the forward and reverse diffusion processes.
5. Discuss how generative data augmentation reduces generalization error in low-resource learning scenarios.
6. Explain the trade-off between data utility and privacy in synthetic data generation. Why can higher realism increase privacy risks?
7. How can discriminator-based validation be used to evaluate synthetic data quality? What does a 50% accuracy imply?
8. Compare the suitability of GANs and diffusion models for synthetic video generation, focusing on temporal consistency.
9. Explain how bias present in real-world datasets can be amplified through synthetic data generation and how this can be mitigated.
10. Justify why synthetic data cannot be considered automatically ethical or legally safe, even if no real records are directly copied.

CHAPTER 10

Evaluation, Ethics and Future of Generative AI

The evaluation of Generative AI systems which gain power and become more common requires assessment of their performance together with their responsible implementation as two main challenges. Generative models must undergo tests which evaluate their performance through accuracy assessment and quality evaluation and fairness assessment and safety evaluation and assessment of their effects on society. The chapter examines the processes which we use to assess generative models and the methods which we use to regulate their development into responsible and sustainable applications.

The chapter begins by examining evaluation strategies and metrics for text and image generation, highlighting the limitations of conventional performance measures. The text explains how bias and fairness and privacy and security issues develop when generative models create interactive systems which use actual data and users. The concept of Responsible AI is introduced to address ethical deployment and accountability.

The chapter investigates Generative AI development in research together with rising autonomous AI agents and upcoming advancements which will create intelligent systems of the future. The research examines three main areas which show how scientists should assess Generative AI systems and control their development and develop their future.

10.1 EVALUATING GENERATIVE MODELS

The evaluation process for generative models differs from the evaluation method which applies to discriminative and predictive models. The assessment of traditional machine learning models proceeds through accuracy-based measures which compare their performance against established labels. The evaluation process needs to assess their distributional quality and realistic appearance and diverse content creation and their ability to meet requirements and complete tasks.

Formally, if a real dataset follows an unknown distribution $P_{\text{data}}(x)$ and a generative model learns a distribution $P_{\text{model}}(x)$, the goal of evaluation is to measure how closely:

$$P_{\text{model}}(x) \approx P_{\text{data}}(x)$$

This comparison cannot be performed directly and requires proxy metrics and structured evaluation strategies.

10.1.1 Evaluation Objectives in Generative AI

The evaluation of generative models exists to fulfill four primary goals which serve as its main evaluation focus.

A. *Quality (Realism)*

The generated samples must demonstrate realistic appearance that makes them impossible to distinguish from actual data.

B. *Diversity (Coverage)*

The model needs to show all existing data patterns because it must prevent itself from reaching a single operational state.

C. *Faithfulness and Alignment*

It should produce outputs which maintain consistency with the input prompt and conditioning signal and retrieved context particularly in RAG-based systems.

D. *Safety and Reliability*

It should produce outputs which do not contain any harmful content or biased information or factually incorrect material.

The measurement of these objectives differs according to the specific modality yet they exist as common standards across all text, image, audio, and video generation processes.

10.1.2 Model-specific Evaluation Perspectives

Different generative paradigms require different evaluation viewpoints.

GAN-based Models

GANs are evaluated by comparing statistical properties of real and generated samples. Since GANs lack an explicit likelihood function, evaluation relies on distribution similarity and sample realism, often detecting issues such as mode collapse as shown in Figure 10.1.

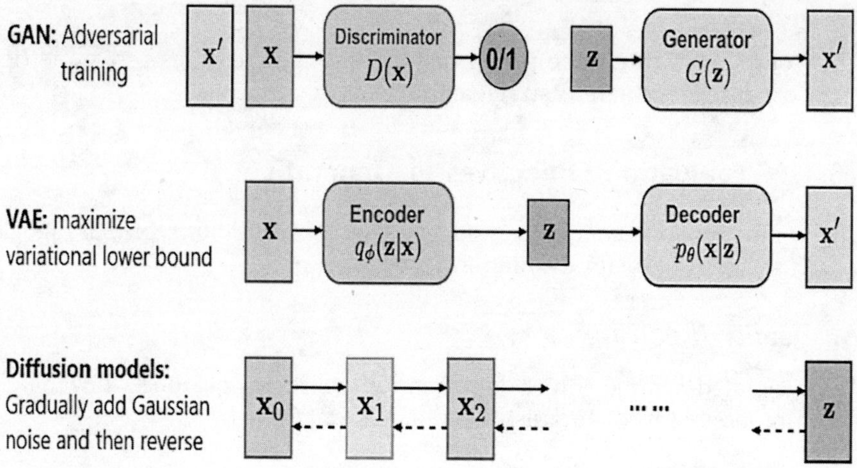

Figure 10.1: *Evaluating Generative Models.*

Diffusion Models

Diffusion models define a probabilistic forward and reverse process. Their evaluation focuses on:

- Sample fidelity after denoising
- Stability across timesteps
- Consistency of generated samples

The reverse process aims to estimate:

$$p_\theta\,(x_0 \mid x_T)$$

where evaluation checks how accurately the model reconstructs realistic samples from noise.

RAG and LLM-based Generators

For retrieval-augmented generation, evaluation extends beyond generation quality to include:

- Correctness of retrieved context
- Faithful grounding of outputs in retrieved evidence
- Reduction of hallucination

Thus, evaluation becomes system-level, not just model-level.

10.1.3 Why Accuracy-based Metrics Fails?

The method of measuring accuracy depends on a model which produces only one correct answer. The generative tasks enable multiple correct answers when processing identical inputs. The following example shows this:

- Multiple correct summaries
- Many valid images for one prompt
- Different correct answers grounded in different retrieved documents

Evaluation needs to assess three levels which include distribution semantic and perceptual differences instead of relying on exact label matching.

10.1.4 Evaluation Paradigms

The evaluation of generative models typically uses three different but complementary assessment methods:

A. *Automatic Statistical Evaluation*

This method uses mathematical distances to determine how similar generated content matches actual content.

B. *Human-centered Evaluation*

The assessment measures fluency and coherence and creativity while also evaluating usefulness.

C. *Task-oriented Evaluation*

The method evaluates whether the generated outputs lead to better performance in subsequent tasks which includes synthetic data classification accuracy assessment.

The three evaluation methods require combination because no single method can provide complete evaluation results.

10.1.5 Role of Evaluation in Responsible Deployment

Evaluation is not only a performance check but also a governance mechanism. Poorly evaluated generative systems can amplify bias, leak private information, or produce unsafe outputs. Therefore, evaluation directly connects to:

- Ethics (bias and fairness)
- Privacy (memorization and leakage)
- Trustworthiness (hallucination control)

These aspects are expanded in later sections of this chapter.

The next section (10.2) introduces concrete evaluation metrics for text and imagegeneration, grounded in the principles discussed here.

10.2 METRICS FOR TEXT AND IMAGE

The assessment of generative models needs additional metrics beyond common accuracy measures because generated outputs lack one correct solution. The evaluation process examines four different aspects of generated text and images which include their quality, similarity, diversity, and semantic consistency.

The diagram illustrates the evaluation pipeline for generative models, separating text and image generation outputs and mapping them to appropriate automatic and human-centric metrics as shown in Figure 10.2.

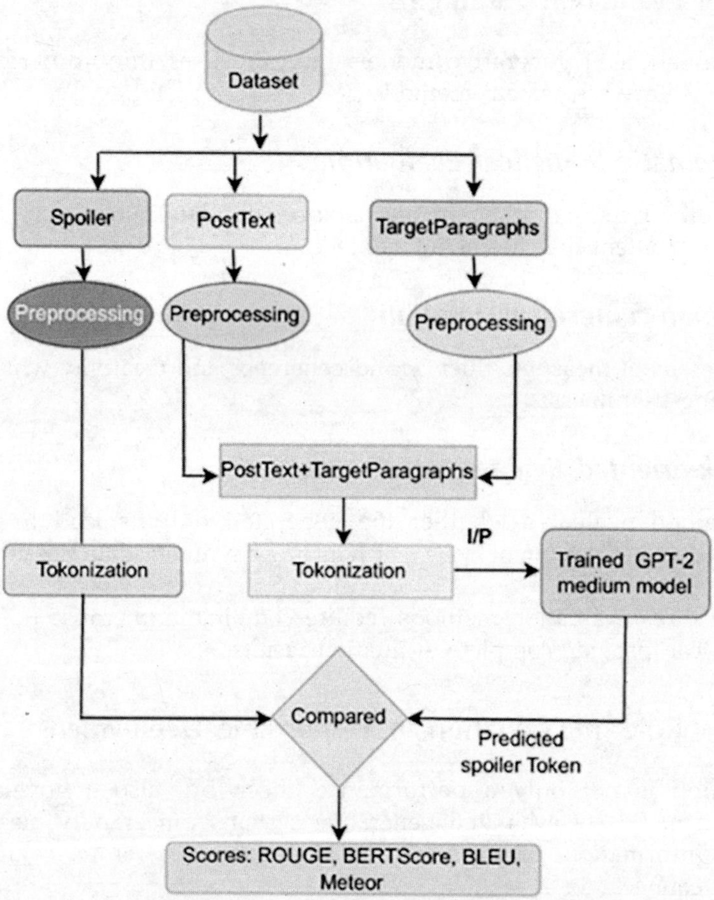

Figure 10.2: *Pipeline for Evaluating generative models.*

The system employs separate metrics to evaluate text generation and image generation because each metric assesses different performance elements of the model.

10.2.1 Metrics for Text Generation

Text generation evaluation aims to assess whether generated content is fluent, meaningful, relevant, and semantically aligned with human-written text.

A. BLEU (Bilingual Evaluation Understudy)

BLEU was designed to automatically evaluate machine translation by measuring exact word and phrase overlap with reference text. It provides a fast and reproducible way to compare generated text across models.BLEU measures n-gram overlap between generated text and reference text R.

$$\text{BLEU} = \text{BP} \cdot \exp\left(\sum_{n=1}^{N} w_n \log p_n \right)$$

where p_n is n-gram precision and BP is the brevity penalty.

B. ROUGE (Recall-oriented Understudy for Gisting Evaluation)

ROUGE focuses on content coverage, making it suitable for summarization where capturing key information is more important than exact phrasing. ROUGE emphasizes recall, commonly used in summarization tasks to check how much important content is preserved.

C. BERTScore

Traditional n-gram metrics fail when models generate correct meaning using different words. BERTScore solves this by measuring semantic similarity using contextual embeddings.

Instead of surface word matching, BERTScore computes semantic similarity using contextual embeddings:

$$\text{BERTScore} = \cos\left(\mathbf{e}_{\text{gen}}, \mathbf{e}_{\text{ref}}\right)$$

This makes it more suitable for LLM-based text generation.

D. Human Evaluation

Human judgment remains the gold standard because it can evaluate aspects that metrics cannot quantify. Human judges evaluate fluency, coherence, and factual correctness, which automated metrics often fail to capture fully.

10.2.2 Metrics for Image Generation

Image generation evaluation focuses on visual realism, diversity, and distributional similarity between real and generated images.

A. Inception Score (IS)

IS evaluates whether generated images are clear and classifiable, assuming that a good image should strongly activate a pretrained classifier. IS evaluates image quality and diversity using a pretrained classifier:

$$IS = \exp(\mathbb{E}_x [KL(p(y|x) \parallel p(y))])$$

High IS indicates clear and diverse images but does not compare with real data.

B. Fréchet Inception Distance (FID)

FID directly compares the distribution of generated images with real images, making it the most reliable metric for GANs and diffusion models as shown in Figure 10.3.

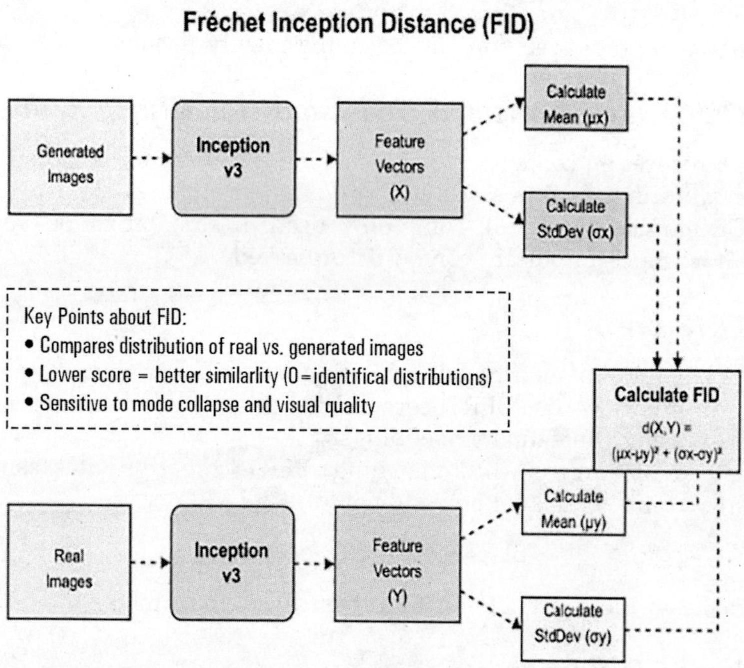

Figure 10.3: *Fréchet Inception Distance (FID).*

FID compares real and generated image distributions:

$$FID = \| \mu_r - \mu_g \|^2 + Tr(\Sigma_r + \Sigma_g - 2(\Sigma_r \Sigma_g)^{1/2})$$

Lower FID values indicate better quality and realism.

C. Precision and Recall for Generative Models

Precision measures image realism, while recall measures diversity and coverage of the real data distribution.

What they capture well:

- Precision → image realism
- Recall → coverage of real data modes

A model may generate sharp images (high precision) but lack diversity (low recall), or vice versa.

10.2.3 Key Insight

No single metric can fully evaluate generative models. Effective evaluation requires:

- Multiple complementary metrics
- Task-specific selection
- Human validation for critical applications

This is especially important for GANs, diffusion models, and LLM-based systems, where perceptual quality and semantic meaning matter more than exact correctness.

10.3 BIAS AND FAIRNESS IN GENERATIVE AI

Generative AI systems produce original content through their ability to forecast results. The existence of bias in generative models enables unfair representations to spread and become more severe until the system generates entirely new unfair representations which need to be addressed as vital issue in contemporary Generative AI systems.

The three main sources of bias in Generative AI systems include the training data and model architecture together with the deployment context which directly impacts the ethical trustworthiness of all generated results.

10.3.1 Bias in Generative AI

In Generative AI, bias refers to systematic distortion in generated content that favors or disadvantages certain groups, attributes, or viewpoints.

Unlike discriminative models, generative models can:

- Reproduce historical stereotypes
- Over-represent dominant groups
- Under-represent minority concepts
- Generate harmful or exclusionary content

This issue is especially prominent in LLMs, diffusion models, GANs, and RAG-based systems.

10.3.2 Major Sources of Bias

(a) Data Bias

Generative models learn directly from large-scale datasets. The generated outputs will have the same bias as the training data when the data becomes unbalanced.

EXAMPLES:

- Text models trained mainly on Western literature → cultural bias
- Image generators trained on limited demographics → representation bias

Synthetic data generated from biased models can reinforce bias recursively.

(b) Model-induced Bias

Architectural choices can amplify bias:

- GANs may suffer from mode collapse, generating limited representation.
- Diffusion models may converge toward dominant visual or semantic patterns.
- Autoregressive LLMs may reinforce frequent token sequences linked to stereotypes.

(c) Prompt and Interaction Bias

In instruction-following systems:

- Prompt phrasing influences output bias.
- Retrieval bias in RAG systems depends on document selection.
- User feedback loops can unintentionally reinforce biased generations.

10.3.3 Fairness in Generative AI

Fairness in Generative AI aims to ensure that generated content does not systematically disadvantage individuals or groups, while maintaining utility and creativity.

Fairness is context-dependent and must be defined according to the application domain.

10.3.4 Fairness Definitions Relevant to Generative Models

(a) Group Fairness

Ensures equitable representation across demographic groups in generated outputs.

Mathematically:

$$P(\text{Generated Attribute} \mid A = a) \approx P(\text{Generated Attribute} \mid A = b)$$

Used in:

- Image generation
- Text profiling
- Content recommendation

(b) Individual Fairness

Similar inputs should yield similar outputs, regardless of protected attributes.

Used in:

- Personalized text generation
- AI assistants
- Resume or profile generation

(c) Counterfactual Fairness

A generated output should remain unchanged if sensitive attributes are altered in a hypothetical scenario.

EXAMPLE: Changing gender or ethnicity in a prompt should not change job competence descriptions.

10.3.5 Bias Mitigation Strategies

Bias mitigation in Generative AI must be applied across the lifecycle:

- **Pre-training:** Curated, balanced datasets
- **Training:** Fairness-aware objectives, adversarial debiasing
- **Generation-time:** Prompt constraints, safety filters
- **Post-generation:** Output auditing, human review
- **Evaluation:** Fairness-aware metrics alongside quality metrics

While fairness focuses on equitable outcomes, generative systems also raise critical concerns regarding data privacy, model security, and misuse, which are discussed in the next section.

10.4 PRIVACY AND SECURITY IN GENERATIVE AI

Generative AI systems learn from massive datasets and create new content by modeling complex data distributions rather than retrieving stored records. The ability to generate authentic text and images and multimedia content through this technology creates new privacy and security risks because it operates differently from standard predictive AI systems.

Domains like healthcare and finance and law and scientific research face severe ethical and legal and social repercussions from even minor security breaches or privacy breaches.

10.4.1 Privacy Risks in Generative AI

Unlike classical machine learning models that map inputs to fixed outputs, generative models learn internal representations of entire data distributions. This makes them powerful, but also increases the risk that sensitive information from the training data becomes implicitly embedded within the model.

(a) Data Memorization and Leakage

When generative models are trained on real-world datasets, especially those containing sensitive or repetitive information, they may memorize specific data patterns rather than learning generalizable representations. As a result, the model may unintentionally reproduce personal identifiers, confidential text fragments, or proprietary content during generation. This issue is more pronounced when datasets are small, lack diversity, or when the model capacity is very large relative to the data size.

Conceptually, this problem arises because the model minimizes training loss without understanding the ethical boundaries of the data it learns from. If memorization leads to lower loss, the model has no intrinsic incentive to avoid it unless explicitly constrained.

(b) Membership Inference Attack

Membership inference attacks use model behavior differences between training data and untrained data to launch their attacks. An attacker can analyze model outputs to infer whether a particular data record was part of the training set.

Conceptually, this can be expressed as a difference in output probability distributions:

$$P(\text{Model Output} \mid x \in D_{\text{train}}) \neq P(\text{Model Output} \mid x \notin D_{\text{train}})$$

If such differences exist, they can be exploited to infer private information about individuals or organizations. This threat is particularly severe in medical datasets, user-generated platforms, and confidential enterprise data, where mere inclusion in a dataset can itself be sensitive information.

(c) Reconstruction Attacks

The attackers in reconstruction attacks use multiple queries to a generative model until they succeed in recreating the original training data. The design of generative models enables their users to obtain complete insights into the underlying data through multiple interactions with the system. Publicly accessible APIs and synthetic data pipelines together with federated learning environments create a critical security risk because attackers can deduce information from model behavior even when they lack direct data access.

10.4.2 Security Threats in Generative AI

It examines all security risks which exist within generative artificial intelligence systems. The security threats emerge from two sources because attackers use adversarial techniques to create attacks and they use generative models for their malicious purposes. The threats which exist in these systems, create risks both to their operational functions and to public security.

(a) Prompt Injection Attacks

The attackers who carry out prompt injection attacks, use the instruction-following capabilities of generative models to create their attacks. The attackers use their advanced input techniques to disable all safety features of the system, which enables them to access protected information and direct the model to create dangerous or deceptive results. This particular weakness presents a serious threat because it exists within large language models which function as chatbots and autonomous agents and retrieval-augmented generation systems, which allow their model outputs to affect decision-making processes and operational results.

(b) Data Poisoning

Data poisoning attacks occur when malicious or biased data is intentionally introduced during training or fine-tuning. Because generative models learn patterns holistically, poisoned data can subtly alter behavior, introduce hidden biases, or activate malicious responses under specific conditions. These effects may remain undetected during standard evaluation, making them particularly dangerous.

(c) Model Misuse and Abuse

Even when models are technically secure, their generative power can be misused to create deepfakes, disinformation, phishing attacks, or malicious code. This shifts the security challenge beyond model correctness to include governance, access control, and responsible usage policies.

10.4.3 Privacy-preserving Techniques

To mitigate privacy risks, generative AI systems increasingly incorporate privacy-preserving mechanisms during training and deployment.

Differential privacy introduces controlled randomness during training, ensuring that the presence or absence of a single data record has minimal impact on the model's output. Conceptually, this guarantees that:

$$M(D_1) \approx M(D_2)$$

where datasets D_1 and D_2 differ by only one record. This limits the model's ability to memorize specific individuals.

Privacy-aware synthetic data generation produces samples which show only statistical characteristics of the original dataset without disclosing actual personal information. The federated training method together with secure training techniques prevents direct data access by storing data on local systems while only permitting the sharing of combined model updates.

10.4.4 Why Privacy and Security are Central to Generative AI

The essential elements of privacy and security function as fundamental requirements which underpin generative AI technology. User trust disappears when these requirements get violated while organizations face difficulties maintaining compliance and synthetic data loses its trustworthiness and autonomous systems turn dangerous. The growing use of generative AI for making decisions and producing content at large scale requires organizations to integrate privacy and security standards into their system design process to achieve ethical and legal and sustainable results.

10.5 RESPONSIBLE AI

The rising presence of Generative AI systems in human decision-making and communication and knowledge production has made it necessary to evaluate AI systems based on their responsible operation instead of their actual functionality. Responsible AI refers to the systematic design, development, deployment, and governance of AI systems in a manner that is ethical, trustworthy, and aligned with human values. The primary goal of this system exists to achieve maximum social advantages while reducing all potential negative effects and unintentional results as shown in Figure 10.4.

The need for responsibility becomes essential in Generative AI systems because these systems develop new content and they create new content and they create new content which creates new content which creates new content which develops new content and develops new content which creates new content that leads to widespread opinion formation and behavioral influence. Datasets which contain large volumes of data, yet imperfect data, create a situation where trained models develop biases and produce false information and exhibit untraceable operational patterns. Responsible AI provides a structured framework to address these risks proactively rather than reactively.

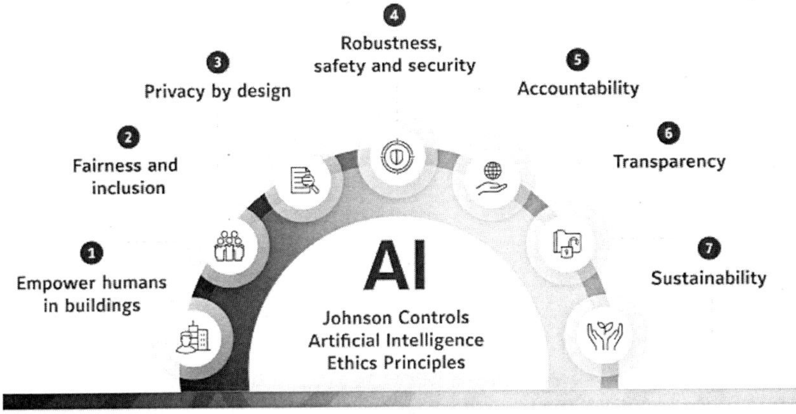

Figure 10.4: *Responsible AI.*

At a conceptual level, Responsible AI consists of multiple components which collectively create its framework. The system operates through a series of guiding principles that help users make decisions from data collection until they reach their final operational stage which includes ongoing improvements throughout their AI operational period.

10.5.1 Core Principles of Responsible AI

(a) Fairness

Generative AI systems must operate without creating advantages or disadvantages for specific individuals or groups who share protected characteristics like gender and race and ethnicity. Fairness requires careful dataset design because it needs both bias-aware training and ongoing evaluation to stop historical and societal inequalities from getting worse.

(b) Transparency

Responsible AI systems must provide clarity about how they are trained, what data influences them, and the limitations of their outputs. The process of transparency enables users and stakeholders to understand and question AI-generated content while building their capacity to trust it.

(c) Accountability

All AI-driven systems require human responsibility to be the main guiding principle. The developers and organizations must take responsibility for all choices made by their Generative AI models from the moment of creation until they finish their operational phase and post-deployment evaluation.

(d) Privacy and Security

Generative AI systems must safeguard confidential information against unauthorized access and protect against internal and external threats. The responsible systems protect personal information from being stored permanently or disclosed or exploited while they implement strong protections against both internal and external security breaches.

(e) Reliability

A responsible Generative AI system should maintain the same output results throughout all input variations and environmental changes. The process of reliability guarantees that all generated outputs will remain constant while delivering correct information which decision-makers can use in actual situations.

10.5.2 Implementing Responsible AI in Practice

Implementing Responsible AI requires embedding ethical considerations directly into technical and organizational workflows. This includes designing interpretable systems, maintaining clear documentation of model decisions, and continuously monitoring system behavior after deployment. Diverse development teams play a crucial role by bringing multiple perspectives that help identify blind spots and reduce bias.

Explainable AI techniques further support responsibility by enabling insight into model reasoning, especially in high-stakes domains. Regular audits, feedback loops, and post-deployment evaluations ensure that Generative AI systems evolve responsibly as data distributions, societal norms, and regulatory expectations change.

10.5.3 Challenges in Responsible AI

Difficulties emerge in Responsible AI because AI development needs to follow ethical standards. The speed of Generative AI development exceeds the ability of existing policy and governance systems to create effective regulations. The use of principle-based frameworks permits organizations to operate with flexibility while maintaining their ethical standards.

The process of evaluating theoretical concepts such as fairness or transparency presents a second obstacle. Responsible AI requires organizations to assess their operations through qualitative methods and through quantitative assessment methods which require technical assessment and human judgment. Organizations with restricted resources face challenges when trying to implement new processes, yet they can achieve important results through small actions like conducting bias assessments and providing ethical training.

10.5.4 The Importance of Responsible AI for Generative Systems

Responsible AI requirements exist to prevent Generative AI systems from damaging public trust through their tendency to reinforce negative stereotypes while they infringe upon user privacy and produce false information. The systems will continue to function through responsible implementation which connects their operations to societal standards and legal requirements according to the leadership of the organization. Responsible AI transforms Generative AI into a reliable technology which delivers advantages to humanity through its innovative capabilities.

10.6 GENERATIVE AI IN RESEARCH

The research ecosystem experiences rapid transformation through Generative AI which functions as an intelligent assistant throughout the research process. The technology enhances researchers' abilities in various tasks which include generating ideas and conducting experiments and performing analysis and sharing information.

The early research stage benefits from Generative AI which helps researchers explore existing literature through its ability to summarize numerous research papers and discover research gaps and provide relevant citation recommendations. Researchers can use Large Language Models (LLMs) to analyze thousands of publications which helps them progress from problem identification to hypothesis development.

The methodology and experimentation stage receives support from Generative AI which helps researchers create synthetic data and conduct simulations and develop model prototypes. Researchers can use synthetic datasets that GANs and diffusion models generate for controlled experiments because they do not involve actual data which becomes inaccessible due to high costs or privacy concerns that exist in medical research and climate research and social science research. The automated design of experiments and the automated search for parameters benefit from the capabilities of Generative models.

The analysis and interpretation process receives help from Generative AI because it enables researchers to understand how complex models function through its ability to create visual displays and transform unprocessed data into organized findings. The system helps users translate numerical data into understandable text which enables researchers from different fields to work together more effectively.

Human researchers must maintain control over the research process because it requires human researchers to work together with Generative AI technology. Critical thinking and model validation and originality and ethical responsibility require human intervention. The system functions as a research accelerator instead of establishing itself as a research authority.

10.7 AI AGENTS AND AUTONOMOUS AI

AI Agents represent a fundamental shift in how intelligent systems are designed and deployed. AI agents differ from traditional rule-based programs because they can perceive their surroundings and use their observations to make independent decisions that help them reach their established goals. The agent independently chooses the steps needed to achieve goals which humans have set.

Autonomous agents in this concept operate their functions with little to no need for human help. These agents continuously observe changing environments, adapt their strategies and improve their behavior through learning mechanisms. Autonomous agents operate best in actual dynamic situations because established rules cannot handle those conditions.

10.7.1 Core Characteristics of AI Agents

AI agents exhibit several defining characteristics that distinguish them from conventional software systems:

- **Autonomy:** Agents can operate independently without continuous human supervision.
- **Goal Orientation:** Actions are selected to optimize predefined objectives.
- **Perception:** Agents collect information from sensors, user inputs, databases or APIs.
- **Adaptability:** Behavior evolves based on feedback and experience.
- **Collaboration:** Agents may interact with humans or other agents to achieve shared goals.

These properties enable AI agents to function effectively in complex and uncertain environments.

10.7.2 Internal Working of AI Agents

The behavior of an AI agent is governed by four tightly integrated components:

1. **Profiling Module:** Defines the agent's role, personality, responsibilities and constraints. This ensures consistent behavior aligned with its purpose.
2. **Memory Module:** Stores contextual and historical information. This includes short-term interaction memory, long-term knowledge storage and episodic memory for recalling specific experiences.
3. **Planning Module:** Responsible for reasoning and decision-making. It evaluates alternative actions, predicts outcomes and selects the most effective strategy to achieve goals.
4. **Action Module:** Executes decisions in the environment, such as responding to users, controlling devices or triggering workflows.

10.7.3 Classification of AI Agents

AI agents are classified based on how they perceive the environment, reason about decisions, and adapt over time. Each category represents a different level of intelligence and autonomy.

A. Simple Reflex Agent

These agents operate their systems by using their current sensory input to follow established condition–action patterns as shown in Figure 10.5. Their system performs well in speed and efficiency but loses functionality when the environment presents complex or hidden elements.

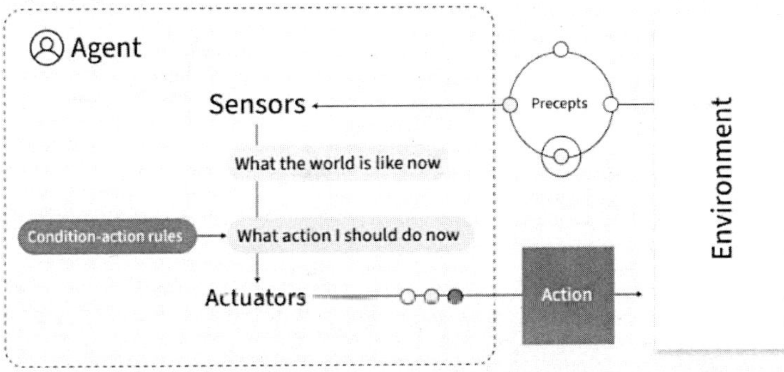

Figure 10.5: *Simple Reflex Agent.*

B. Model-based Reflex Agents

These agents build internal models which represent their knowledge of physical world changes that exceed their immediate perceptual abilities. The agents use environmental hidden elements to create models which allow them to switch between pure reactivity and cognitive reasoning as shown in Figure 10.6.

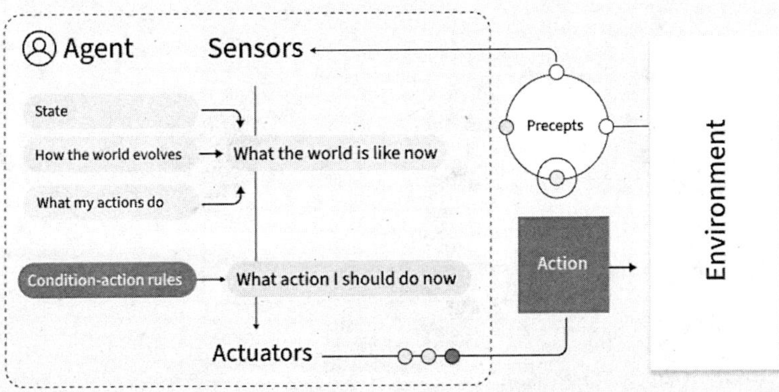

Figure 10.6: *Model Reflex Agent.*

C. Goal-based Agents

Agents select actions according to their assessment of which option brings them closer to their targeted objective. The system establishes forward-looking planning capabilities which enable agents to assess future results instead of concentrating on short-term advantages as shown in Figure 10.7.

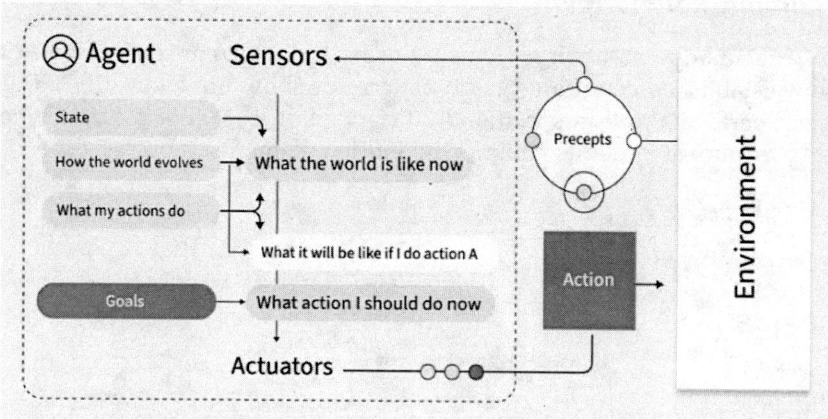

Figure 10.7: *Goal-based Agent.*

D. Utility-based Agents

The agents use their utility function to evaluate different results and make decisions when they face uncertain situations. They perform better than other solutions in situations which require people to make decisions between different options while knowing that their choice will not reach perfection as shown in Figure 10.8.

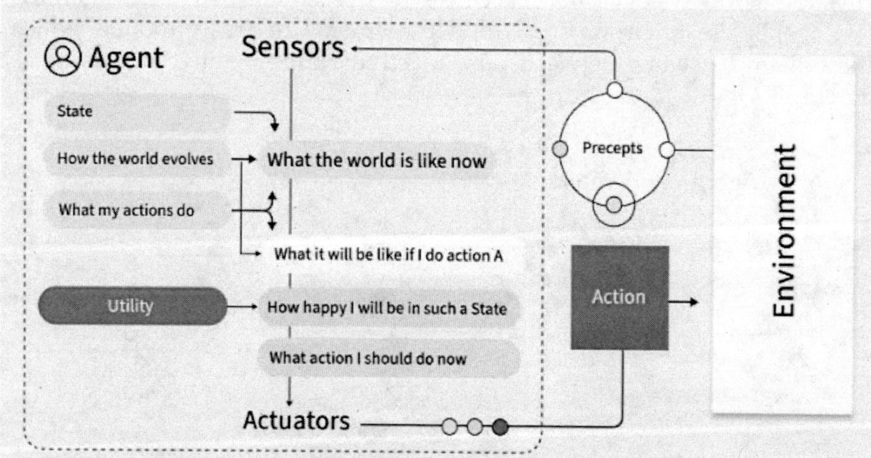

Figure 10.8: *Utility-based Agent.*

E. Learning Agents

Learning agents improve their skills through knowledge acquisition from their feedback and their experiential learning process. The systems develop into adaptive intelligent systems which can adjust to new circumstances because of their ability to learn from experience as shown in Figure 10.9.

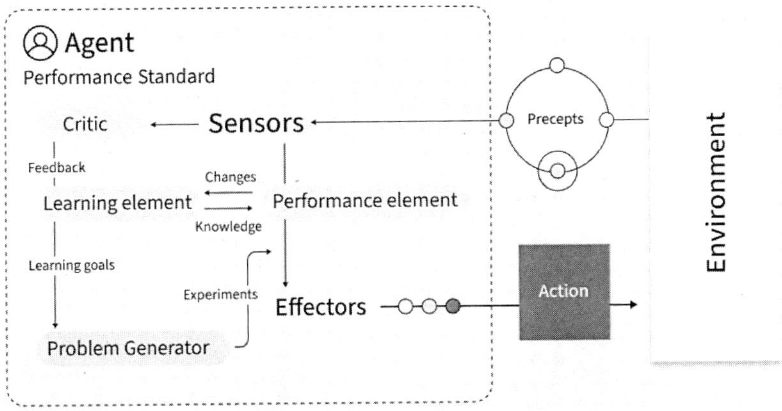

Figure 10.9: *Learning Agents.*

F. Multi-Agent Systems (MAS)

Multiple agents interact within a shared environment, either cooperatively or competitively. The system develops collective intelligence through agent interaction which enables it to handle problems at a larger scale while maintaining system strength and solving problems with multiple agents as shown in Figure 10.10.

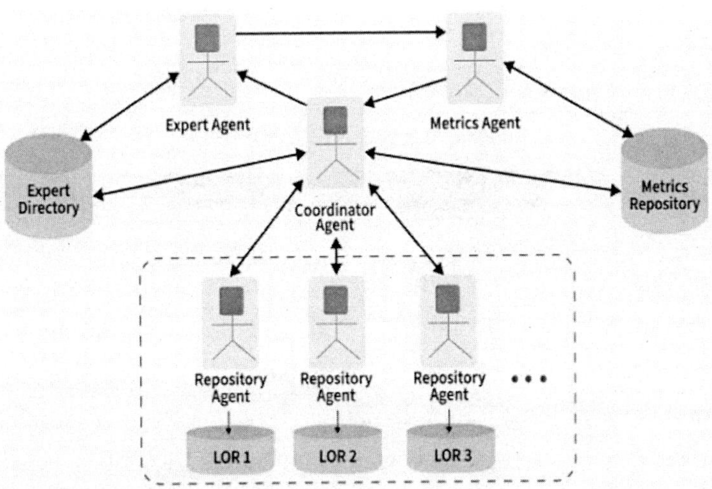

Figure 10.10: *Multi-Agent System.*

10.7.4 Autonomous Agents in Practice

Autonomous agents represent the most advanced form of AI agents. They continuously learn, self-optimize and make independent decisions in real time.

Unlike conventional AI agents that often require supervision, autonomous agents operate with higher degrees of freedom and adaptability as shown in Figure 10.11.

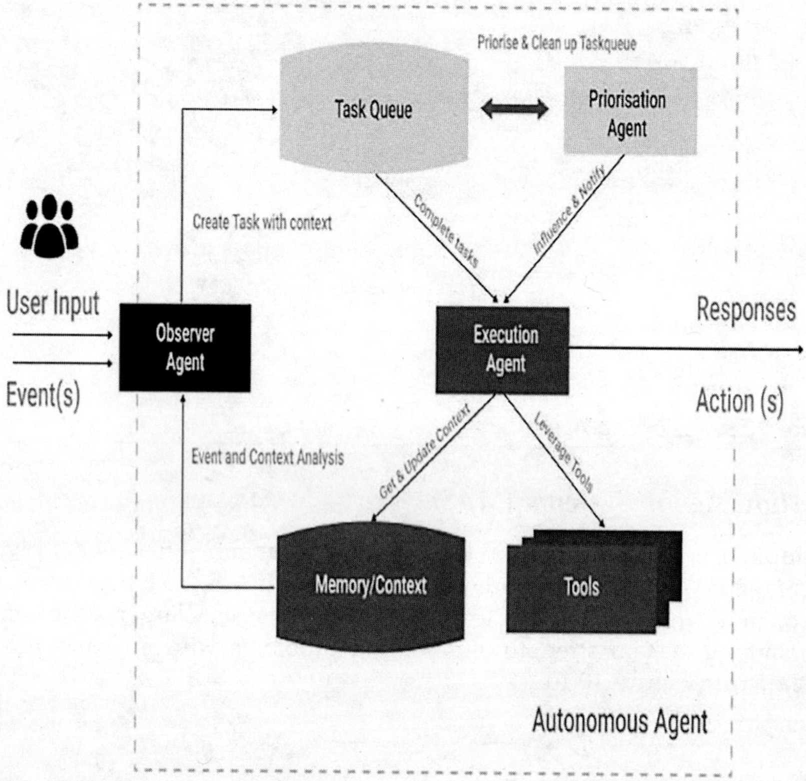

Figure 10.11: *Autonomous Agent.*

TABLE 10.1: AI Agents vs Autonomous Agent

Aspect	*AI Agents*	*Autonomous Agents*
Human Intervention	Moderate	Minimal or none
Adaptability	Limited	Continuous learning
Decision Making	Rule or model-based	Self-optimizing
Environment Handling	Semi-dynamic	Highly dynamic
Examples	Chatbots, recommenders	Robotics, cyber-security agents

10.7.5 Mathematical Perspective of AI and Autonomous Agents

From a formal viewpoint, an AI agent can be modeled as a system that selects actions based on its perception of the environment to optimize a performance measure.

An agent's behavior can be represented as a policy:

$$\pi : S \rightarrow A$$

where, S represents the set of environment states, and A represents the set of possible actions.

The policy π defines the action an agent should take in a given state.

10.7.6 Applications of Autonomous Agents

Autonomous agents are increasingly used across industries:

- **IT Operations:** Automated incident resolution and system monitoring.
- **Healthcare:** Patient monitoring and personalized care coordination.
- **Finance:** Fraud detection, automated auditing and trading systems.
- **Customer Support:** Intelligent self-service and issue resolution.

10.7.7 Benefits and Challenges

Autonomous agents provide significant advantages, including improved efficiency, reduced human error, real-time decision-making and scalable automation. However, they also introduce challenges such as security risks, governance issues, ethical concerns and potential bias in decision-making. Ensuring transparency, accountability and human oversight remain critical when deploying autonomous agents in sensitive domains.

10.8 FUTURE TRENDS AND DIRECTIONS IN GENERATIVE AI

Generative AI has evolved from its initial function as a strong content creation system to its current role as a basic element that powers intelligent systems which possess reasoning capabilities and adaptive abilities and work independently. The upcoming research will create new ways for artificial intelligence systems to interact with people and process information and understand their surroundings which will go beyond simply increasing systems' size and precision.

10.8.1 From Single Models to Agentic AI Systems

The future of Generative AI lies in agent-based architectures, where models are no longer passive responders but active decision-makers. The systems will integrate perception and memory and planning and action capabilities to enable AI systems to execute extended activities which include research automation and software development and scientific discovery and enterprise operations.

10.8.2 Multimodal and World-aware Intelligence

Next-generation models will natively integrate text, image, audio, video, sensor data, and structured knowledge into a single reasoning framework. The new approach enables artificial intelligence systems to develop better real-world understanding which improves their capacity to replicate human thinking.

Future Generative AI will not only produce content but also comprehend how physical elements and time and cause-and-effect relationships interact which allows its use in robotics and healthcare diagnostics and climate modeling and digital twin technology.

10.8.3 Trust-centric and Regulation-aware AI

The adoption of Generative AI into essential system infrastructure will create a need for trust and governance systems which will protect against compliance risks. Future systems will be designed with privacy-by-design, built-in auditability, and alignment mechanisms that ensure ethical and lawful behavior across jurisdictions. Responsible AI will evolve from a guideline to a core engineering requirement, which will impact all aspects of model training and deployment and evaluation.

10.8.4 Towards Artificial General Capabilities (AGC)

In distant future research scientists will create Generative AI systems that demonstrate domain-independent reasoning abilities through their capability to learn from small data sets and their ability to establish changing objectives which will enable machines to approach human intelligence across specific tasks.

The future of Generative AI develops through its study of intelligence which combines responsible use with autonomous operations and creative work that maintains accountability. The development of models into agents and ecosystems requires researchers to maintain their focus on matching technological advancements with essential human values and their social requirements and upcoming environmental needs.

TEST YOUR KNOWLEDGE

1. Why are likelihood-based metrics insufficient for evaluating Generative AI models in real-world applications?
2. Compare BLEU, ROUGE, and BERTScore in terms of what aspect of text generation quality each capture.
3. Why does high perceptual quality not always imply high semantic correctness in image generation metrics?
4. How does bias propagate differently in generative models compared to discriminative models?
5. Explain how privacy leakage can occur even when training data is anonymized.
6. Why is differential privacy particularly challenging to apply to large-scale generative models?
7. How does prompt injection differ from traditional adversarial attacks in machine learning systems?
8. In what ways do Responsible AI principles influence model architecture and deployment decisions?
9. Why are autonomous AI agents considered higher risk than standalone generative models?
10. Explain why efficiency and sustainability are becoming central research goals in future Generative AI systems.

CONCLUDING REMARKS

The final section of this document investigates the effects of Generative Artificial Intelligence on various fields of study. The book begins with essential mathematical concepts that establish foundational principles before progressing to advanced systems which include generative models and multimodal platforms and synthetic data systems and intelligent agent frameworks. The study combined theoretical concepts with real world examples to create educational materials that undergraduate and postgraduate students could comprehend.

The increasing impact of Generative AI systems on actual decision-making processes and creative work and automated systems makes it essential to establish evaluation methods and ethical standards and guidelines for responsible system implementation. The future development of Generative AI requires scientists to work on two main objectives which involve developing better models and establishing trustworthiness and fairness and human compatibility. The author of this book present Generative AI as a dual force which represents a major technological achievement that also requires responsible development through strategic planning and social accountability.

Index